A HISTORY OF THE
FIRST WORLD WAR

JOHN BUCHAN

A HISTORY OF THE FIRST WORLD WAR

Abridged and introduced by
VICTOR NEUBURG

LOCHAR PUBLISHING
MOFFAT · SCOTLAND

For Caroline
V.N.

Nelson's History of the War first published 1915-19 in twenty-four volumes
by Thomas Nelson and Sons Ltd
This abridged edition first published 1991 by Lochar Publishing Ltd,
High Street, Moffat, Scotland, DG10 9ED

An Albion Book

Conceived, designed and produced by The Albion Press Ltd,
P.O. Box 52, Princes Risborough, Aylesbury, Bucks HP17 9PR

British Library Cataloguing in Publication Data
Buchan, John *1875-1940*
A history of the First World War.
1. World War 1
I. Title II. Neuburg, Victor E. (Victor Edward) *1924-*
940.3

ISBN 0-948403-53-5

Designer: Emma Bradford
Copy-editor: Elizabeth Wilkes

The title page illustration is a detail from The Mule Track *by Paul Nash.*

Typesetting and origination by York House, London
Printed and bound in Hong Kong by South China Printing Co.

CONTENTS

SIR WILLIAM ORPEN *"Good-bye-ee": Cassel*

INTRODUCTION

John Buchan's history of the Great War was the only comprehensive account of the conflict to be published while the fighting was going on and the outcome, without the benefit of hindsight, was not entirely predictable. It was issued serially, in twenty-four undated volumes bound in red cloth, by the firm of Thomas Nelson. Buchan had been friendly at Oxford with T.A. Nelson, who was to become Managing Director of this old-established Edinburgh publishing house, and Buchan himself joined the board in 1906.

Buchan was ill and bedridden during the first months of the war. During this time he wrote his most famous novel, *The Thirty-Nine Steps*, and also began *Nelson's History of the War*. He had originally suggested Hilaire Belloc as the writer for this project, but in the end all 1,200,000 words were written by Buchan himself. He did have a research assistant, Hilliard Atteridge, to verify references, analyse data and prepare the maps, but even so it is an astonishing achievement for a sick man with many other duties. One thing which kept him going was the knowledge that all profits from the work, including his own royalties, were going to the families of enlisted Nelson employees, and to war charities. He describes the origins of the history in his autobiography, *Memory Hold-the-Door*:

> . . . during the autumn months of 1914 I had begun a popular history of the War in monthly volumes, designed to keep my work-people in employment, and its wide circulation induced the authorities to advise its continuance.

Buchan was in fact in a unique position from which to write such a history. Not himself a combatant, he was nevertheless closely involved in many aspects of the conflict. As he wrote in his preface to the revised four-volume *History of the Great War* published in 1921-22:

> My duties, first as a War Correspondent and then as an Intelligence officer, gave me some knowledge of the Western Front; and later, in my work as Director of Information, I was compelled to follow closely events in every theatre of war, and for the purposes of propaganda to make a study of political reactions and popular opinions in many countries.

He had striven, he wrote, to tell the truth, "free from bias or petulance or passion". It was this cool, considered approach which most impressed his contemporaries: a calm voice at the centre of the storm.

It is worth recalling that when B. H. Liddell Hart published *The Real War* in 1930 (and under a subsequently different title this was to remain a standard work for many years), the only general history cited in the bibliography was that written by Buchan. Clearly Liddell Hart thought highly of Buchan; but this is by no means the only reason why *Nelson's History of the War* deserves our attention in the final decade of the twentieth century, some seventy-five years after the events that are described in its pages.

Because it was written while the war was being fought, and because Buchan possessed a consummate mastery of narrative, his book has an immediacy and a freshness that is inevitably absent from works written long after the events of which they tell. As Buchan himself wrote, again in the preface to the revised edition, "I believe that the main features of the war can be more accurately seen and more truly judged by those who lived through it than by a scholar writing after the lapse of half a century." In terms of censorship there is a price to be paid for immediacy, and Buchan was well aware of this. In a prefatory note to Volume XVI he wrote:

> It has been decided by British General Headquarters in France that for the present it is undesirable to mention specifically the Divisions, Brigades, and Battalions engaged in the Battle of the Somme. These details must therefore be deferred until the publication of a revised edition of this work after the close of the war.

Notwithstanding such omissions in detail which occur throughout, it seems to me worth abridging the first edition of Buchan's work rather than the second, revised edition, because the earlier one conveys most vividly the way the campaigns were presented at the time to a readership whose daily lives at many levels were being radically changed by the progress of the war. This seems to me one major justification for revisiting Buchan and offering a shortened version of his book to modern readers: another must be its sheer readability and a mastery of detail which is never allowed to impede a brisk narrative.

Buchan, I suspect, was too shrewd an observer to have many illusions about the book he was writing. "We are", he wrote (Vol. XVI p. 163), "still too close to events to attempt an estimate of the Battle of the Somme as a whole. It will be the task of later historians to present it in its true perspective." More than seventy years later, despite a continuing flood of books, articles and theses concerned with men and events, no "true perspective" has emerged – and there seems no reason to suppose that it ever will. Within recent years, for example, the *Official History* has been the object of telling criticism by a Canadian historian, Tim Travers, in his book *The Killing Ground*, 1987. The fact that discussion is still lively, and contentious issues still unresolved, tells us why Buchan's history is neither out of date nor superseded.

The son of a minister in the Free Church of Scotland, Buchan was born in 1875 in relatively humble circumstances. After a grammar school education he went to Glasgow University and then to Oxford, where he gained a first class degree. While still an undergraduate he began to establish himself as a writer, and in his autobiography mentions receiving at this period "considerable emoluments from books and articles". After graduating, his success as an author continued while he brought highly individual intellectual and personal gifts to varied careers as publisher, soldier, barrister and Member of Parliament. Five years before his death in 1940 he was created Baron Tweedsmuir and became Governor-General of Canada.

In spite of this success in public life, Buchan seems never to have embraced wholeheartedly the patrician culture which characterized it. He always remained something of an "outsider". As a Scot he had sprung from a society in which success through personal endeavour was both more common and more acceptable than it ever was in England, where a rigid class system and the persistence of inherited privilege made such transformations very much more difficult. Thus his values and his outlook were rather more complex than one might expect. One of his novels in particular demonstrated this: *Mr Standfast*, first published in 1919, set during the Great War. The range of characters is wide, and the ease with which Richard Hannay, the hero, slips from the comfortable world of a senior army officer into that of the working class, whose denizens are described by Buchan without condescension, indicates the writer's sensitivity to the complexities of a society dominated by entrenched notions of class. *Mr Standfast* even shows a sympathy, remarkable for its time, with the position of conscientious objectors. At the end of the war, Buchan appealed to the Prime Minister for the immediate release of the 1,500 conscientious objectors still in prison, on the grounds that they "acted under the demands of their conscience and in accordance with deep moral or religious convictions". He was probably the only Lieutenant-Colonel to be much exercised by the injustice of their treatment.

When he came to assess the progress of the war he was quite specific about his priorities, arguing that victory had been dependent upon the fighting vigour and endurance of the ordinary soldiers rather than upon any peculiar brilliance and subtlety in the leadership (Vol. XXIV p. 119). "The hero of the war", he wrote, "was the ordinary man" (ibid p. 123). On the basis of such a comment it would not be accurate to suggest that Buchan was in any sense a proponent of what has come to be known as "history from below". He was too much a patrician for that; but he did, unlike so many of his contemporaries, believe that the ordinary soldier was the most important element in the army and that the story of the war from his point of view was worth the telling.

Buchan had an especial – even instinctive – feeling for the army and the way it worked. Not only was he deeply aware of its inner life but he also had a shrewd eye for all aspects of the conflict. In his account of the Second Battle of Ypres in 1915 – to cover which he had been appointed Special Correspondent of *The Times* – when the casualties incurred by the British army were high, he wrote: "The Royal Army Medical Corps have never done more brilliant work in all their brilliant history . . . cases were brought from the cellars and dug-outs,

and silently and swiftly carried along the dark road beyond the fire zone . . . ''
(Vol. VII pp. 35-36). Buchan was always ready to praise the army services
which backed up the men who fought with rifle, bayonet and grenade in the
front line.

Again, when he writes about the landscape of war, he reveals a degree of
sensitivity that is unusual in so many accounts of armed conflict and human
slaughter. He visited the scarred city of Ypres towards the close of the second
battle for its possession, and was struck by the ruin and desolation that he found
(Vol. VII pp. 50-51):

> Houses . . . were skeletons, and through the gaps there were glimpses
> of greenery. A broken door admitted to a garden, for the grass had once
> been trimly kept, and the owner must have had a pretty taste in spring
> flowers. A little fountain still plashed in a stone basin. But in one corner
> an incendiary shell had fallen on the house, and in the heaps of charred
> debris there were human remains.

About a year later he described conditions in the Ypres Salient battlefield as
"Waterlogged soil now churned into glutinous mire by the shelling and the
mine explosions" (Vol. XIV p. 114). But it was nearly always to humanity that
he returned, and he wrote about one Scotsman who, during a gas attack in the
battle of Loos in 1915, literally rose to the occasion (Vol. X p. 177):

> The gas caused this brigade [the 46th] to hesitate for a moment,
> whereupon Piper Daniel Laidlaw of the 7th K.O.S.B. [King's Own
> Scottish Borderers], mounted the parapet and marched up and down,
> piping the company out of the trenches. The tune he played was "Blue
> Bonnets over the Border", and then he continued with "The Standard on
> the Braes of Mar", till he fell wounded. For this fine deed he received the
> Victoria Cross.

It was inevitable that he would write at length about the execution of Nurse
Edith Cavell in 1915. He was conscious that the German military authorities
had created a martyr. "It was", he wrote, "the death of one Englishwoman in
Brussels which did more than any other incident of the war — more than the
sinking of the *Lusitania* or the tragedy of Belgium — to keep the temper of
Britain to that point where resolution acquires the impetus of passion" (Vol. XI
p. 62).

Buchan allowed the facts of the Cavell case to speak for themselves, but he
was always ready to place events within an historical perspective, and the
facility and effectiveness with which he does this lends an increased depth and
intensity to his writing. The evacuation of Gallipoli Peninsula at the beginning
of 1916 is a case in point. Before describing in some detail how the expeditionary force was successfully withdrawn from a military position which had grown
increasingly untenable, he refers to an obscure episode in 1758 during the
Seven Years War when heavy losses were incurred in a withdrawal from the

JOHN SINGER SARGENT *The Gates of a Château, Ransart*

French coast. When the Army was re-embarked from Gallipoli, only one man was wounded and the rearguard, consisting of the Highland Mounted Brigade, left without firing a shot in anger . . . This kind of detail adds vividness to a brisk narrative.

2

The problems of abridging a long work are manifold and it is, perhaps, arguable that even to attempt such an undertaking is an impertinence. Purists will undoubtedly think so, and to some extent I agree with them. But, good as it is, Buchan's history of the war is – in the original twenty-four volumes or the revised four – too long for any but the specialist reader. It has been abridged once before into a single volume, by Adrian Alington as *Episodes of the Great War*, 1936, but this has been long out of print.

Any reader of a shortened version of a much longer original is entitled to query the principles on which the abridgement has been made. Such a reader may also wonder about the text used. In this case, unlike Alington, I have gone back to the first edition. The critic David Daniell, in his study of Buchan, *The Interpreter's House*, 1975, remarks on the way in which the revision loses the "original sharpness", and it is as much for this greater crispness and immediacy as for its historical importance that I have returned to the earlier text. There is a minor price to pay in terms of accuracy – Buchan may, for instance, place an action in the morning of a particular day in the first edition, and correct this to the afternoon in the second – but there are no serious errors. Therefore, except for minor adjustments, I have left Buchan's text untouched, in order to preserve the sense of history in the making. This is the Great War as it appeared at the time.

What to include or, more crucially, what to leave out? The process of selection becomes an exceedingly complex one, for in fact most of what Buchan wrote about the war will have to be omitted. He attempted to cover the conflict pretty comprehensively, and indeed he triumphantly succeeded, for the reader is conducted over all the battlefields on land, sea and air in every theatre of war. In addition, we are allowed to see something of the political discussion and decision-making that lay behind the fighting.

Yet, going through the narrative volume by volume, it is impossible to escape the feeling that some of it is extraordinarily remote from the experience of the contemporary reader of English who is not a specialist in the Great War. The Russian and German armies wheeling and clashing on the plains and in the forests of Eastern Europe are a case in point: places like Kutno, Lowicz or Strykov can, despite their importance at the time, have few resonances for the reader who is not familiar with the background of the engagements which took place in or near them.

In saying this I am not, I hope, guilty in any sense of a narrow chauvinism, nor infected by the virus of "Little Englandism". Some sort of selection has to be made, and to present a series of brief extracts which mirror the totality of Buchan's work would be seriously misleading and, I suspect, tedious. Far better to attempt to convey something of the vigour and pace of his clearly written prose . . . and so I have concentrated upon the British role in the war, and more specifically upon the Western Front. This was the crucial area of conflict and decision, the theatre in which the German army – despite the myth that was later put about of a "stab in the back" – was finally and decisively defeated; and the defeat came about largely as the result of a long series of bloody infantry engagements. To say this is not in any sense to denigrate the significance of other areas of battle or the important role played by the allied forces and, in the war's closing phases, by the Americans. The American army arrived in Europe fresh from the United States. They had not been worn down by lengthening casualty lists over the years or by long periods of bitter internecine trench warfare, and their intervention on the Western Front tipped the balance in favour of the Allies.

I am conscious that this emphasis on the Western Front is at the expense of material bearing upon the many secondary theatres of war in which British and Empire troops (as they were then called) were engaged. It is interesting to compare, for instance, Buchan's account of the fall of Erzerum in Volume XIII of the *History* with that in his novel, *Greenmantle*, 1916. Equally, Buchan's chapters on the vitally important role played by the navy throughout the world are full of interest, but as they have twice been collected in single-volume form (by H. C. O'Neill as *A History of the British Navy during the War*, 1918, and by Stanley Williams as *Naval Episodes of the Great War*, 1938), I have neglected this aspect of his coverage in favour of substantial extracts from various chapters covering the war in the air. They comprise the earliest history of aerial warfare in English known to me and as such, dealing as they do with the Royal Flying Corps and the early days of the Royal Air Force, are of quite extraordinary and compelling interest.

While this abridgement of Buchan's history of the war, then, does not reflect the balance of the work from which it is derived, I hope it conveys something of the sweep and vigour of Buchan's original.

3

Finally, some suggestions for further reading. Two of the earlier standard histories have stood the test of time well. B. H. Liddell Hart, *The Real War*, 1930, was reissued in 1934, enlarged and with a new title, *A History of the World War 1914-1918*. This is now known, in paperback, as *History of the First World War*. The second book is C.R.M.F. Cruttwell, *A History of the Great War 1914-1918*, 1934. It has been reissued as a paperback.

Both of the foregoing books are long. A much shorter and more recent study is Keith Robbins, *The First World War*, 1984. This too is now in paperback, and is probably the best introduction to the whole subject. The economic background to the conflict is discussed in Gerd Hardach, *The First World War 1914-1918* published in 1977 and available ten years later as a paperback.

Arthur Banks, *A Military Atlas of the First World War*, 1975, and Anthony Bruce, *An Illustrated Companion to the First World War*, 1989, provide a wealth of important background material and a great deal of detail. Until it was reprinted with some additional entries in 1989, Cyril Falls, *War Books*, 1930, had been long out of print and was extremely scarce. The new edition underlines its enduring value.

Ian F. W. Beckett and Keith Simpson, *A Nation in Arms*, 1985, is the nearest thing we yet have to a social history of the British 1914-1918 army, and is excellent. In 1944 a limited edition of *The Occupation of the Rhineland 1918-1929* by Sir J. E. Edwards, official War Historian, was published. A reissue in 1987 was extremely welcome and throws much light on what happened to the armed forces when the fighting stopped. In *The Countryside at War 1914-1918*, 1987, Caroline Dakers describes the impact of the war in rural areas of Britain that Buchan loved so well.

It should be emphasized that these books represent a tiny fraction of those which deal with the war. Although memoirs by veterans still come out – Bernard Martin, *Poor Bloody Infantry*, 1987, for example – there are in the nature of things fewer and fewer of them. For this reason a collection of soldiers' memories entitled *Great War Memories*, compiled by D. A. Clarke and published as a pamphlet by THCL Books in Blackburn, Lancashire, in 1987, is especially evocative. A 92-year-old veteran, B. A. Steward, contributed a piece to *The Guardian* (23 December 1989) on Christmas on the Western Front in 1915 with the London Rifles . . . Buchan would have loved this moving and deeply felt article.

For details of John Buchan's war service, see Janet Adam Smith, *John Buchan: A Biography*, 1965, and for information on his relations with the official War Artists, see Meirion and Susie Harries, *The War Artists*, 1983. Commissioning the War Artists was among Buchan's duties first as Director of the Department of Information at the War Office and subsequently as Director of Intelligence at the newly-created Ministry of Information; Buchan was also responsible for commissioning the moving films of the Somme and Arras. Together with his history of the war, the images produced by the War Artists are perhaps the most lasting result of a war career which was, Buchan wrote, a "continuous struggle with small-mindedness and pettiness".

THE BREAKING OF THE
BARRIERS

In his preface to Buchan's first volume Lord Rosebery wrote: "Europe quakes to the tramp of armed races . . . There must be nearer thirty millions than twenty millions of armed men clutching each other's throats this year".

EARLY ON the morning of Sunday, June 28, 1914, the little city of Sarajevo, the capital of Bosnia, was astir with the expectation of a royal visit. The heir to the throne of Austria, the Archduke Francis Ferdinand, had been for the past week attending the manoeuvres of the 15th and 16th Army Corps, and had suddenly announced his intention of inspecting the troops in the capital. It was a military occasion; the civic authorities were given short notice, and had no time to organize a reception; and the Archduke and his wife, the Duchess of Hohenberg, were met at the railway station only by the local Governor and his staff. The party drove in motor cars through the uneven streets of the Bosnian city, which, with its circle of bare hills and its mosques and minarets, suggests Asia rather than Europe. There was an exceptional crowd in the streets, for the day was a Serbian fête – Catholic Croats, with whom the Archduke was popular; Orthodox Serbs, with whom he was very much the reverse; Mussulman Serbs, whose politics were not of Christendom; and those strange wildly clad gypsies that throng every Balkan town.

The Archduke Francis Ferdinand was a man in middle life, a lonely and saddened figure, oppressed by the imminence of a fatal disease. Almost alone of his countrymen he had the larger vision in statesmanship. He saw that Austria was succeeding badly in the government of her strangely varied races, more especially those Croat, Serb and Slovene peoples, numbering six and a half millions, whom we call the Southern Slavs. He had seen the rise of Serbia since the Balkan War, and realized that to her the Slavs of the Dual Monarchy looked as the emancipator of the future. But as a member of the House of Habsburg, he sought to counter the Greater Serbian ideal with that of a Greater Austria. His policy was the destruction of the Dualist system, and the establishment in its place of a true federation, under which different races should have a real local autonomy, and find union in a federal Parliament. Against such an ideal the military party of Vienna, represented by the Chief of the General Staff, Conrad von Hoetzendorff, and the Hungarians, under the leadership of Count Stephen Tisza, had set their faces like flint. To them the existing regime must be preserved at any cost, and they frankly acknowledged that their policy meant war. Indeed, early in the first Balkan War, von Hoetzendorff had contemplated an attack upon Serbia and Russia. The Archduke was, therefore, a voice in the wilderness, and his chief foes were those of his own household. Like Mirabeau, he was the only man who might have averted calamity, and his death, like Mirabeau's, meant that the arts of statesmanship must yield to the sword.

The royal party motored towards the Filipovitch Parade, where the inspection was to be held. Motoring in Sarajevo is a leisurely business, and the car moved slowly along the Appel Quay. Just before it reached the Chumuria Bridge over the Miliatzka, a black package fell on the opened hood of the Archduke's car. He picked it up and tossed it into the street, where it exploded in front of the second car, in which sat Count Boos Waldeck and the aide-de-camp to the Governor. The bomb was filled with nails and bits of iron, and the two occupants of the car and six or seven spectators were wounded. The would-be assassin was arrested. He was a compositor, called Cabrinovitch, from Trebinje in Herzegovina, who had lived for some time in Belgrade, and had, as he confessed at his trial, got the bomb from the Serbian arsenal of Kragujevatz. "The fellow will get the Golden Cross of Merit for this," was the reported remark of the Archduke. He knew his real enemies, and was aware that to powerful circles in Vienna and Budapest his death would be a profound relief.

The Archduke continued on his way to the Town Hall, and arrived in something of a temper. "What is the use of your speeches?" he asked the Mayor hotly. "I come here to pay you a visit, and I am greeted with bombs. It is outrageous!" The embarrassed city dignitaries read the address of welcome, and the Archduke made a formal reply. Then the whole entourage — Mayor, Governor, and Chief of Police — attempted to dissuade him from driving again through the city. There had been dark prophecies of evil, anonymous letters hinting at death had been frequent, and in those narrow streets amid the motley population no proper guard could be kept. The Duchess added her entreaties, but the Grand Duke was obdurate. He insisted on driving to the hospital to visit the aide-de-camp who had been wounded by the bomb.

About ten minutes to eleven the car was moving slowly along the Appel Quay, in the narrow part where it is joined by the Franz-Josefsgasse. Here a second bomb was thrown, which failed to explode. The thrower, a Bosnian student called Prinzip — like Cabrinovitch an Orthodox Serb and a member of the Greater Serbian party — ran forward and fired three shots from a Browning pistol. The Archduke was hit in the neck and the Duchess was terribly wounded in the lower part of the body, receiving the bullet in an effort to protect her husband. Both lost consciousness immediately. At Government House they rallied sufficiently to receive the last sacraments, but within the hour they were dead.

In an impassioned proclamation to the awed and silent city the Mayor laid the blame for the crime at Serbia's door.

* * *

On the 23rd July, nearly a month after the tragedy, the Austro-Hungarian Government presented its demands to Serbia. In their main lines they had been known unofficially a week before, and the full text had been communicated to, and had probably been drafted in collaboration with, the German Ambassador. The Austrian Note, which startled every Chancellery in Europe except the Wilhelmstrasse, was a lengthy document, embodying a number of drastic demands, devised partly as reparation for the Sarajevo murders and partly as a safeguard for the future. A reply was requested within forty-eight hours – that is, by six o'clock on the evening of Saturday, the 25th. While the reply was pending, significant events happened. The German ambassadors at Paris, London, and Petrograd (St Petersburg) called upon the French, British and Russian foreign ministers, and announced that Germany approved the form and substance of the Austrian Note, adding that, if the quarrel between Austria and Serbia were not localized, dangerous friction might arise between the Triple Entente and the Triple Alliance.

Serbia, faced with Austria's ultimatum, had recourse to Russia. The empire of the Tsar had made remarkable progress since the close of her war with Japan. Many of her institutions had been liberalized; the people had been given a new chance of participating in the government of the country; though her lost navy had not been yet replaced, her army organization had been completely remodelled, and she was now stronger on land than ever before in her history; her commerce and industries had grown immoderately, and she had become in some respects the richest of continental nations. She had recovered her self-respect, and was setting herself seriously and patiently to the work of national regeneration. Her policy was, from the nature of her interests, pacific. She desired no extension of territory, for her aim was intensive development. But, as the greatest Slav Power, she recognized certain obligations to the Slav peoples beyond her borders. She could not allow the little Balkan States to be swallowed up in a Teutonic advance towards the Bosphorus. Moreover, as the protector of the Greek Church, she resented any ill treatment of Orthodox believers in other lands. For some years there had been much ecclesiastical friction in Austria-Hungary, and frequent and bitter appeals had been made to Russia by Greek Churches in the Dual Monarchy to protect her co-religionists. Russia, who had no bellicose aims, could be drawn into war on three contingencies only – an assault upon a Slav nationality, the persecution of the Greek Church beyond her borders, or an attack upon her ally, France. The second had been long a cause of uneasiness to her statesmen, and the first was suddenly brought into prominence by the Austrian Note.

Acting on Russia's advice, Serbia replied within forty-eight hours, accepting all the Austrian demands in full with two reservations, on which she asked for a reference to the Hague Tribunal. These points concerned Articles 5 and 6 of the Note. Article 5 required Serbia "to accept the collaboration in Serbia of representatives of the Austro-Hungarian Government in the suppression of the subversive movement directed against the territorial integrity of the

Monarchy." Serbia replied that she did not clearly understand this request, but would admit such collaboration as agreed with the principles of international law and her own criminal procedure. Article 6 asked for judicial proceedings against the accessories to the Sarajevo plot, in which delegates of the Austro-Hungarian Government should take part. Serbia replied that she could not accept this, as it would be a violation of her constitution. Obviously this was so. The complete acceptance of the Austrian note meant that Serbia gave up her independent nationality and her rights as a sovereign state, and that Austria extended her authority to the Bulgarian and Greek frontiers. The Note was in the nature of a rhetorical question: it did not expect an answer; and at ten o'clock on the Saturday evening the Austro-Hungarian minister, after announcing that nothing short of a complete acceptance would satisfy his Government, asked for his passports and left Belgrade.

The following day there began that feverish week of diplomatic effort, the record of which will be found in the British White Paper, and which constitutes as dramatic an episode as our annals can show. The chief part was played by the British Foreign Secretary, Sir Edward Grey, whose labours up till the last moment for peace were of incalculable value in establishing the honesty of British purpose in the eyes of neutral peoples. His first step was to approach Germany, France and Italy, with a view to calling a conference in London to mediate in the Austro-Serbian quarrel. The two latter powers agreed, but Germany declined, on the ground that a conference was impracticable in the special circumstances of the two countries, adding that she understood that the Russian and Austrian foreign ministers were actually at the moment exchanging views, and that she was hopeful about the result. Again Sir Edward Grey, quick to seize the chance of Germany's admission, returned to the task, but was again put off.

Wednesday, the 29th, was the beginning of the final stage of the crisis. On that day the situation, apart from the diplomats, was as follows: Austria had declared war upon Serbia, and was bombarding Belgrade; Belgium had ordered a mobilization in self-defence; Germany had recalled her High Sea Fleet; and in the British fleet all manoeuvre leave had been cancelled, and concentration was proceeding. On that day we were informed that in consequence of Austria invading Serbia, Russia, while disclaiming any aggressive intentions against Germany, had ordered the mobilization of her southern commands.

✳ ✳ ✳

The weekend – Friday, 31st July, to Tuesday, 4th August – was such as no one then living had ever spent. For so widespread a sense of foundations destroyed and a world turned topsy-turvy we must go back to the days of the French Revolution. In Britain the markets went to pieces, the Bank rate rose to 10 per cent on the Saturday, and the Stock Exchange was closed. Monday, 3rd August, was a Bank Holiday, the strangest in the memory of man. An air of great and terrible things impending impressed the most casual visitor. Crowds hung about telegraph offices and railway stations; men stood in the street in little groups; there was not much talking, but many spells of tense silence. The country was uneasy. It had no desire for war; it suddenly realized the immensity of the crisis; but it was in terror of a dishonourable peace.

* * *

On Friday, 31st July, Germany issued an ultimatum to Russia, requiring immediate demobilization, and a reply next day by eleven o'clock. She also made final inquiry of France as to her attitude. On the same day Sir Edward Grey asked the German and French Governments if they would respect the neutrality of Belgium, provided it was not violated by another power. France gave a ready guarantee; Germany did not reply. Her views on the matter were already plain from the Imperial Chancellor's offer of 29th July. She had taken to heart Bismarck's famous dictum that "no people should sacrifice its existence on the altar of fidelity to treaty, but should only go so far as suited its own interests." Lastly, late in the evening, the French Ambassador was informed by his Government that the 16th Army Corps from Metz, the 8th from Trèves and Cologne, and the 15th from Strassburg, had closed up on the frontier, and that French territory had already been entered by German patrols.

Things now moved fast. On Saturday evening, about five o'clock, Germany declared war upon Russia. On Sunday our Naval Reserves were called out, and a moratorium proclaimed for the payment of certain bills of exchange. The Opposition offered to the Government their unqualified support in any measures they might take for the support of the Allied cause. Telegrams had been exchanged between the Tsar, the Kaiser, and our King, but the matter had gone too far for royal mediation, even if all three monarchs had desired it. On Monday, 3rd August, Sir Edward Grey expounded to the House of Commons, in a speech impressive from the entire absence of rhetoric or passion, the events which had led up to the situation, and the part which, in his view, Britain must play. We were bound by the most sacred treaty obligations to protect the neutrality of Belgium, and that very afternoon King Albert had appealed to Britain for help. We were not bound to France by any actual defensive and offensive alliance, though we had anticipated that joint action might some day be necessary, and had arranged for certain consultations between the two General Staffs. But the Government had given France the assurance that if the German fleet undertook hostile operations against the French coast or French shipping, the British fleet would protect it. The House of Commons received this declaration of policy with almost unanimous approval.

Next day, 4th August, the British Ambassador in Berlin was instructed to ask for certain information. It was reported that Germany had demanded of Belgium free passage through her territory, promising after peace to maintain the integrity and independence of the kingdom, and requesting an answer within twelve hours. Belgium had refused this categorically, and the British Government requested from Germany an assurance that Belgian wishes would be respected. Later in the day news came that German troops were at Gemmenich, and Sir Edward Grey wired again to Sir E. Goschen, asking for a reply before midnight, and instructing him, if it were not received, to return home. That telegram reached Berlin at 7 p.m., and the German Government, without waiting for the full time to expire, handed the British Ambassador his passports. Half an hour later the newsboys were shouting in every street that England had declared war. A state of war had already begun. That very night the German mine-layer, the *Koenigin Luise*, was busy off the British coast; the plain of Luxemburg was overrun by Uhlans; and the guns of the frontier guards in Lorraine were already making their reply to the Kaiser's challenge.

The German defence of the action which was the immediate occasion, though not the principal cause, of war, will be found in the subsequent speech in the Reichstag by the Imperial Chancellor:

> We are now in a state of necessity, and necessity knows no law. We were compelled to override the just protest of the Luxemburg and Belgian Governments. The wrong – I speak openly – that we are committing we will endeavour to make good as soon as our military goal is reached. Anybody who is threatened as we are threatened, and is fighting for his highest possessions, can only have one thought – how he is to hack his way through.

This doctrine, if put into general practice, would obviously make a speedy end of treaties and international conventions, and, indeed, of public faith. The best comment upon it is to be found in one of the latest interviews between Herr von Bethmann-Hollweg and Sir Edward Goschen. "Do you mean to say", the Imperial Chancellor asked, with scorn and incredulity, "that you are going to make war for a scrap of paper?" "Unfortunately, sir," the British Ambassador replied, "that scrap of paper contains our signature as well as yours."

(Vol. I pp. 13-17, 35-38, 40-41, 42-45)

THE MUSTER OF THE BRITISH EMPIRE

Buchan conveys vividly the inevitability and scale of events which followed the fatal shots at Sarajevo and led ultimately to the outbreak of a war which, in different ways, engulfed the world.

THE STATE of war with Germany, officially declared by Britain as from 11 p.m. of Tuesday, 4th August, did not in itself commit us to sending an Expeditionary Force to the Continent, and there is reason to believe that at first the Cabinet were far from unanimous on the desirability of such a step. But the unmistakable trend of public feeling, and the assurances of the French Government that they counted upon our military co-operation, made the expedition inevitable. On 3rd August the army had been mobilized; on 5th August Lord Kitchener, whose return to Egypt had been countermanded at the end of the previous week, was appointed Secretary of State for War; on 6th August the House of Commons in five minutes passed a vote of credit for £100,000,000 and sanctioned an increase of the army by 500,000 men. Urgent preparations were made for the departure of our force. The railways had been taken over by the Government, and troops were hurried down, mostly under cover of night, to various points of embarkation. A very proper secrecy was maintained, and the people of Britain knew nothing of the crossing of the Expeditionary Force till it was over, though full reports were published in American and Italian papers as early as the 9th August.

The embarkation began on the night of 7th August, as soon as Admiral Jellicoe had guaranteed the safety of the Channel passage. The Aldershot Division was the first to go, and within ten days the whole of the force, something between 150,000 and 160,000 men, had landed at various ports in France. This splendid feat of transportation was performed without the slightest hitch. The main port used was Southampton, but troops were also sent from the other Channel ports, from Avonmouth and the Bristol Channel, from Dublin, and from some of the ports on the south-east coast. Each vessel was in charge of a British naval officer. For the infantry most of the cross-Channel steamers were utilized, as well as the Holyhead-North-Wall steamers, the Fishguard boats, most of the vessels of the French, Harwich-Hook of Holland, Antwerp, and Hamburg lines, and a number of east-coast passenger steamers. One great Atlantic liner carried 3,000 men on one journey. The men were packed like Bank Holiday excursionists, for the weather was perfect. For guns, horses, and stores, tramps and minor passenger boats were collected from every

SIR JOHN LAVERY *Troops Embarking at Southampton for the Western Front, 1917*

port. The time of crossing varied from eight to fifteen hours. There was no covering fleet, the Grand Fleet in the North Sea being sufficient protection; but the British and French navies supplied a number of destroyers as scouts and messengers, and airships and seaplanes from the Naval Air Service kept watch in the sky.

A word should be said of the performance of the British railways. Take the case of the London and South-Western line. It was ordered to make ready within sixty hours to dispatch to Southampton 350 trains, each of thirty cars. It accomplished the work in forty-five hours. During the first three weeks of war there were dispatched and unloaded at the ships' sides seventy-three of such trains every fourteen hours. These trains arrived from every part of the country every ten minutes, and ran up to their scheduled times. It may well be claimed that this was a record in railway history.

The disembarkation on the French coast was managed with a like efficiency. Officers from the French General Staff journeyed to London upon the Tuesday, and the plan agreed upon worked to perfection. It had been arranged that the British force should take its place on the French left; and the first inland point of concentration was Amiens, though some of the later detachments were sent to places farther east as the advance of the French field army developed. On Monday, 17th August, it was officially announced in the English press that the whole of the Expeditionary Force was safely landed in France.

✳ ✳ ✳

The landing of the troops awakened wild enthusiasm. The geniality and fine physique of the men, and their gentleness to women and children; the cavalryman's care of his horses; above all the Highlanders, who are heroes of nursery tales in France, went to the hearts of the people. The old alliance with Scotland was remembered, the days when Buchan and Douglas led the chivalry of France. The badges and numbers of the men were begged for keepsakes, and homely delicacies were pressed upon them in return. Many a Highlander was of the opinion which Alan Breck expressed to David Balfour, "They're a real bonny folk, the French nation."

The dispatch of the Expeditionary Force was but the beginning of the great muster of the manhood of the British Empire. In Britain old political animosities were laid to sleep, and at a breath the differences not less deep which separated parties and races in the Oversea Dominions passed out of existence. In normal times our Empire is a loose friendly aggregation, more conscious of its looseness than of its unity.

✳ ✳ ✳

The response of the Empire is a landmark in our history, far greater, perhaps, than the war which was its cause. No man can read without emotion the tale of those early days in August, when from every quarter of the globe there poured in appeals for the right to share in our struggle. Canada had been passing through a time of severe economic troubles; these were forgotten, and all her resources were flung open to the Mother country. Sir Robert Borden and Sir Wilfrid Laurier united their forces, and party activity ceased. The Canadian defence scheme provided for a Regular force, called the Permanent Militia, with a peace strength of 270 officers and 2,700 of other ranks; the Active Militia, corresponding to our Territorial Force, with a nominal strength of 2,850 officers and 44,500 men; the North-west Mounted Police, with 650 men; and a large number of rifle associations and cadet corps. As in the South African War, a field force was promptly offered, and a division of all arms was accepted by the British Government. The call for volunteers was responded to with wild enthusiasm. In a few days more than 100,000 men had offered themselves. Old members of Strathcona's Horse and the Royal Canadians clamoured for re-enlistment; rich citizens vied with each other in providing equipment and batteries; and large sums were raised to provide for the dependants of those who were to serve. Every public man in Canada played his part. French-Canadians stood side by side with the descendants of the Family Compact; and the men of the western plains, the best shots and the hardest riders on earth, journeyed great distances to offer their services to the King. One instance may be quoted as a type of this determined spirit. Two hundred frontiersmen from Moosejaw could not be enlisted, as they wanted to go as cavalry, and the cavalry were full. Nothing daunted, they took the road at their own expense and came to Ottawa, where they purchased their own outfits, and announced that if they were not accepted for service they would hire a cattle-ship and sail for Europe. The United States had already displayed, through her press and the utterances of her statesmen, a warm friendship for the British cause; and it is pleasant to note that 60,000 of her citizens offered themselves for enlistment in the Canadian army, while American residents in Canada contributed liberally to relief equipment and funds. The various Canadian steamship companies offered their vessels to the British Government for transport. The Canadian cruisers *Niobe* and *Rainbow* were handed over to the Admiralty for purposes of commerce protection, and two submarines were offered for general service. Newfoundland increased her Naval Reserve strength to 1,000, and sent 500 men to the Expeditionary Force.

Australia and New Zealand, which possessed a system of national service, were not behind Canada in loyalty. That system was not yet fully developed to the point when it could provide a total of 150,000 trained men; but, in the words of Mr Fisher, Australia was ready to support Britain with her last man and her last shilling. She placed all the vessels of the Australian navy at the Admiralty's disposal, and undertook to raise and equip an Expeditionary Force of 20,000 men and a Light Horse Brigade of 6,000. The New Zealand Expeditionary Force was fixed at 8,000 of all arms, and 200 Maoris were accepted for service in Egypt. In South Africa the people had had unique experience of war, and both British and Dutch were eager to join the British field army. Many old officers of Boer commandos came to London to enlist, and the home-coming steamers were full of lean, sunburnt young men from Rhodesia bent on the same errand. The chiefs of the Basutos and the Barotses offered their aid; as did the East African Masai, the chiefs of the Baganda, and the emirs of Northern Nigeria. The Union Government released all British troops for service out of South Africa, and, amid immense popular enthusiasm, General Bòtha called out the local levies for a campaign against German South-West Africa, and put himself at their head. The most brilliant of Britain's recent opponents in the field had become a British general.

Besides these offers of men and money, help in kind was sent from every corner of the Empire. The smaller Crown colonies which could not provide troops could at any rate send supplies. The Canadian Government offered 98,000,000 pounds of flour, to which Manitoba and Ontario added further contributions; Alberta and Prince Edward Island sent oats, Nova Scotia coal, Quebec cheese, New Brunswick potatoes, British Columbia tinned salmon, and Saskatchewan horses. Australia sent wine, butter, bacon, beef, and condensed milk, and South Africa maize. From Barbados, the Falkland Islands, the Leeward Islands, and the Windward Islands came gifts of money; tea from Ceylon; sugar from British Guiana and Mauritius. No unit of the Empire, however small or however remote, was backward in this noble emulation.

But it was the performance of India which took the world by surprise and thrilled every British heart – India, whose alleged disloyalty was the main factor in German calculations. There were roughly 70,000 British troops on the Indian establishment, and a native army consisting of 130 regiments of infantry, 39 regiments of cavalry, the Corps of Guides, and ten regiments of Gurkhas, who were mercenaries hired from the independent kingdom of Nepal. The native army was composed of various race and caste regiments, representing the many Indian peoples who in the past century and a half had been brought under the sway of the British Raj. Chief among them were the Sikhs, that warrior caste of the Punjab who resisted us so fiercely at Aliwal and Sobraon, and since then have stood staunchly by our side in every Asian war. Next in numbers came the Punjabi Mussulmans, and the Pathan and Baluchi regiments, formed from the fighting hill tribes of the North-West Frontier. Among the high-caste Hindus we had the fine Brahman troops, the Dogras and the Mahrattas. The Gurkhas, the little square men in dull green, who could march tirelessly and shoot marvellously, were mountaineers from the Eastern Himalaya, and in creed might be described as Hindus without prejudices. Well-nigh a century of constant fighting, and the comradeship of British officers and men, had made of this army a fighting weapon equal to any of its size in the world. In a war for the existence of the Empire it was inevitable that the Indian army, one of the strongest of the Empire's forces, should be given a share.

(Vol. I pp. 115-17, 119-20, 122-26)

THE RETREAT FROM MONS

The first major engagement fought by the British Expeditionary Force was the Battle of Mons. In order to avoid encirclement by the German army, the BEF fell back and the Retreat from Mons took place between 24th August and 5th September. Casualties during the entire operation were considerable, and it is arguable that as a result, the old British regular army ceased to exist in a recognizable form.

THE FIRST stages of the retirement began on the Sunday evening. All heavy transport was sent to the rear to clear the roads, and a little later the ambulances began to move off, carrying with them as many of the wounded as they could accommodate. The sight of the retiring columns at once conveyed a melancholy warning to the local inhabitants. For three days they had seen the British force moving northward, and had welcomed them as deliverers. At every town, village, and farmstead the people had lavished little kindnesses upon our men. Now, as they saw the transport columns and ambulances streaming back towards France, the rumour spread that the battle of which they had heard the thunder through the afternoon had ended in disaster. With legends of German cruelty in their minds, the country folk fled from their houses, and the marching columns were encumbered by crowds of fugitives.

Though the general order was that the troops were to march at sunrise, more than one regiment received instructions towards midnight to begin to move. They had settled down to sleep in the trenches, and when the night march started many did not realize that they were moving back towards France. The Germans were close in front of the line, and some small British detachments missed their way, wandered to the enemy's outposts, and were taken prisoners. In the grey dawn of Monday morning, 24th August, the whole British force stood to arms. In order to carry out his retirement in the face of a superior enemy, who would not hesitate to press the retreat, Sir John French had determined to show a bold front.

The official dispatch tells simply that "the retreat was continued far into the night of the 26th," but the narratives of some of those who took part in it show that it was no less trying an experience than the battle itself. It was pitch dark, and guns, transport, and infantry were hopelessly confused in the narrow roads, for efficient Staff work was impossible. Thus, of the march of the 5th Division we are told how they were first informed that they were to push on as far as the village of Estrées, and bivouac there. The men were tired even at the start, but

GILBERT ROGERS *A B.R.C.S and Order of St John Motor Driver*

they marched steadily. "There was never a halt nor a pause, though horses dropped between the shafts, and men sat down exhausted by the roadside. A heavy gun overturned in a ditch, but it was impossible to stay and get it out, so it was rendered useless, and the disconsolate gunners trekked on. When the horses could draw their loads no longer, the loads were cast by the roadside. There could be no delay, for the spent and weary infantry were fighting in our rear, and every moment's delay had to be paid for in human lives."

"Darkness fell" (continues the narrator), "and still we marched. I dozed in the saddle, to waken with a start, but still nothing but the creak and rumble of wagons and guns, and the tramp, tramp, tramp of the men. I cannot give a connected account of that night. The overpowering desire for sleep, the weariness and ache of every fibre, and the thirst! I had forgotten to be hungry, and had got past food, but I thirsted as I have only thirsted once before, and that was in the desert near Khartoum. About midnight we reached Estrées, and I asked the Staff officer where the 14th Field Ambulance was camped. 'Camped!' he exclaimed, 'nobody camps here. Orders are changed, and there must be no halt.'"

The column pushed on, but the writer whom we have quoted tells how, after a while, he found it impossible to ride farther, and, sitting with another officer by the roadside, holding the bridles of their horses, slept for a little. Then he continues: "In two hours we wakened. Dawn was just breaking over the hills, and still the column creaked and groaned its way along the road, more asleep than awake, but still moving – a wonderful triumph of will over human frailty. But at how great a cost to nerves and vitality was revealed by one look at the faces of the men. I was noticing how worn and gaunt my companion looked. But the same thought was in his mind, and he said, 'Isn't it wonderful how this kind of thing tells upon a man! You look as though you were just up from a serious illness, and only three days ago you looked a hard as nails.'"

We may quote from the same writer a striking instance of the discipline and self-denial of the men. "Soon after sunrise," he says, "we came up with two of our ambulance wagons, and one of our filter water-carts. The wounded were in such a state of exhaustion with the long trek and the awful jolting of the wagons that Major Fawcett decided to halt and make some beef-tea for them, and rode on ahead to find some farm where water could be boiled. He had hardly gone when a battalion of exhausted infantry came up, and as soon as they saw the water-carts made a dash for them. Hastily I rode up to them, and told them that there was very little water left in the carts, and that it was needed for their wounded comrades. 'I am thirsty myself,' I said, 'and I am awfully sorry for you chaps, but you see how it is; the wounded must come first.' 'Quite right, sir,' was the ready response; 'didn't know it was a hospital water-cart.' And, without a murmur, they went thirsty on their way."

During the night the Germans had pressed closely on the rear of the retiring columns, and had secured numbers of stragglers and some small detachments which had missed their way. They made one important capture. After dark the 1st Gordons became separated from the 8th Brigade, and by some mischance took the wrong direction. Between one and two o'clock in the morning they were marching down a narrow lane, when they were suddenly fired on from the left. There was a halt, and the word was passed along that they had been fired on accidentally by a French picket. Earlier in the evening the rumour had spread that the retirement was being directed towards a French supporting force.

Colonel W. E. Gordon, V.C., who commanded the battalion, found a gap in a wire fence by the road, and made his way on horseback into the field on the left from which the firing came. The men heard him calling out, *"Les Anglais! Les Anglais!"* They could not hear the answer, but they heard the colonel again speaking in French, evidently still under the impression that the men who had fired were their allies. By this time some of the Gordons saw dark shadowy masses moving round them, and into the lane on their front and rear. At the same moment the colonel came riding back. Before he could reach them he was shot down, a rapid fire opening on the battalion from front and flanks. The Gordons now realized that they had been attacked by the enemy, and made a gallant attempt at resistance. But they fell in heaps under the fire poured into them at close quarters from three sides, and in a few minutes all were killed, wounded, or prisoners.

Through the long night the British army had been marching over the belt of low upland in which the streams of Scheldt and Sambre take their rise. On the morning of Thursday, 27th August, it came to a halt at last just north of St Quentin, where the land begins to fall to the green and smiling valley of the Oise.

(*Vol. II pp. 38-39, 57-61*)

THE BATTLE OF YPRES

There were altogether three Battles of Ypres fought respectively – and for the most part indecisively – in 1914, 1915 and 1917. It was the first battle, described here by Buchan, which established the so-called Ypres Salient, an incursion into the German front line. It was defended at great cost and with enormous tenacity by mostly British and Dominion troops throughout the war. Their trenches were often waterlogged and always overlooked by the enemy, who occupied the sparse high ground above both Ypres and the Salient.

THE LITTLE city of Ypres, now only the shell of its former grandeur, stands midway between the smoky industrial beehive of the Lys and the well-tilled flats of the Yser. Once it was the centre of the wool-trade of Flanders, and its noble Cloth Hall, dating from the twelfth century, testified to its vanished mercantile pre-eminence. No Flemish town could boast a prouder history. It was the red-coated burghers of Ypres who, with the men of Bruges and Courtrai, marched in July 1302 against Count Robert of Artois, and inveigled the chivalry of France into a tangle of dykes and marshes, from which few of the proud horsemen escaped. Seven hundred pairs of gilded spurs were hung in the Abbey church of Courtrai as spoil of battle, and the prowess of the burgher infantry on that fatal field established the hitherto despised footsoldier as the backbone of all future armies.

The town stands on a tiny stream, the Yperlée, a tributary of the Yser, which has long ago been canalized. A single-line railway passes through it from Roulers to the main Lille-St Omer line at Hazebrouck. An important canal runs from the Yser in the north to the river Lys at Comines, and two miles south of the town, at the village of St Eloi, turns eastward, bending south again in a broad angle between Hollebeke and Zandvoorde. To the east there are considerable patches of forest between Bixschoote and the Lys valley. A series of slight ridges rise towards the south, lying in a curve just inside the Belgian frontier from west of Messines to the neighbourhood of Zandvoorde. For the rest, the country is dead flat, so that the spires of Ypres make a landmark for many miles. On all sides from the town radiate the cobbled Flemish roads, the two main highways on the east being those to Roulers and to Menin, with an important connecting road cutting the latter five miles from Ypres at the village of Gheluvelt.

***

Ypres must rank as one of the most remarkable contests of the war; it is

PAUL NASH *The Ypres Salient at Night*

certainly one of the most remarkable in the record of the British army. Let us put the achievement in the simplest terms. Between Lille and the sea the Germans had not less than a million men. Six of their fourteen army corps were of the first line, and even the new formations were terrible in assault – more terrible than the veterans, perhaps, for they were still unwearied, and the edge of their keenness was undulled. The immature boys and elderly men, who often fell to pieces before our counter-attacks, came on with incredible valour in their early charges. They were like the soldiers of the Revolution – the more dangerous at times because they did not fight by rule. Against that part of this force which faced us we opposed numbers which began by being less than 100,000, and were never more than 150,000. In the actual salient of Ypres we had three divisions and some cavalry, during the worst part of the fighting, to meet five army corps, three of the first line. For the better part of two days one division held a front of eight miles against three army corps. In this mad mellay strange things happened. Units became hopelessly mixed, and officers had to fling into the breach whatever men they could collect. A subaltern often found himself in command of a battalion; a brigadier commanded one or two companies, or a division, as the fates ordered. At one moment a certain brigadier had no less than thirteen battalions under him. We can best realize the desperate nature of the struggle by quoting an order of Sir Henry Rawlinson issued to the 7th Division. "After the deprivations and tension," he said, "of being pursued day and night by an infinitely stronger force, the division had to pass through the worst ordeal of all. It was left to a little force of 30,000 to keep the German army at bay while the other British corps were being brought up from the Aisne. Here they clung on like grim death, with almost every man in the trenches, holding a line which of necessity was a great deal too long – a thin, exhausted line – against which the prime of the German first line troops were hurling themselves with fury. The odds against them were about eight to one; and, when once the enemy found the range of a trench, the shells dropped into it from one end to the other with terrible effect. Yet the men stood firm, and defended Ypres in such a manner that a German officer afterwards described their action as a brilliant feat of arms, and said that they were under the impression that there had been four British army corps against them at this point. When the division was afterwards withdrawn from the firing line to refit, it was found that out of 400 officers who set out from England there were only 44 left, and out of 12,000 men only 2,336."

The leadership of the corps commanders was beyond praise, and on Sir Douglas Haig fell the heaviest task. But Ypres was, like Albuera, a soldiers' battle, won by the dogged fighting quality of the rank and file rather than by any great tactical brilliance. There was no room and no time for ingenious tactics. Rarely, indeed, in the history of war do we find a great army checked and bewildered by one a fifth of its size. Strategically it can be done. Instances will be found in Napoleon's campaigns, and not the least remarkable was Stonewall Jackson's performance in the spring and summer of 1862. While McClellan with 150,000 men was moving against Richmond, and Banks with 40,000 men was protecting his right rear, Jackson with 3,000 attacked Shields at Kernstown. He was beaten off, but he returned to the assault, and for three months led the Federal generals a wild dance in the Shenandoah valley. As a result, Lincoln grew nervous: Shields was not allowed to co-operate with McClellan; McDowell's corps was detached from McClellan to support him; the attack upon Richmond ended in a fiasco; and presently Antietam was fought and the invasion of Virginia was at an end. In that campaign, in Colonel Henderson's words, "175,000 men were absolutely paralysed by 16,000." Ypres is not such a tale. The Allied strategy failed, and all that remained was a seemingly hopeless stand against a torrential invasion. It is to the eternal honour of our men that they did not break, and of their leaders that they did not despair.

A price must be paid for great glory, and the cost of Ypres was high. The German casualties cannot have been less than 250,000 in the three weeks' battle. The Allied forces from Albert to Nieuport lost well over 100,000 men, and in the Ypres fight alone the British lost at least 40,000. The total loss to the combatants was not far from the losses of the North during the whole of the American Civil War. Whole battalions virtually disappeared – the 1st Coldstream, the 2nd Royal Scots Fusiliers, the 2nd Wiltshires, the 1st Camerons. One divisional general, two brigadiers, nearly a dozen staff officers fell, and eighteen regiments and battalions lost their colonels. Scarcely a house famous in our stormy history but mourned a son. Wyndham, Dawnay, Fitzclarence, Wellesley, Cadogan, Cavendish, Bruce, Gordon-Lennox, Fraser, Kinnaird, Hay, Hamilton; it is like scanning the death-roll after Agincourt or Flodden.

Ypres was a victory, a decisive victory, for it achieved its purpose. The Allied line stood secure from the Oise to the sea; turning movement and piercing movement had alike been foiled, and the enemy's short-lived initiative was over. He was now compelled to conform to the battle we had set, with the edge taken from his ardour and everywhere gaps in his ranks. Had we failed, he would have won the Channel ports and destroyed the Allied left, and the war would have taken on a new character. Ypres, like Le Cateau, was in a special sense a British achievement. Without the splendid support of d'Urbal's corps, without the Belgians on the Yser and Maud'huy at Arras, the case would have, indeed, been hopeless, and no allies ever fought in more gallant accord. But the most critical task fell to the British troops, and not the least of the gain was the complete assurance it gave of their quality. They opposed the blood and iron of the German onslaught with a stronger blood and a finer steel. Where all did gallantly it is invidious to praise. The steady old regiments of the line revealed their ancient endurance; the cavalry did no less wonderful work on foot in the trenches than in their dashing charges at Mons and the Marne; the Household Brigade, fighting in an unfamiliar warfare, added to the glory they had won before on more congenial fields; the Foot Guards proved that their incomparable discipline was compatible with a brilliant and adroit offensive; our gunners, terribly outmatched in numbers and weight of fire, did not yield one inch; the few Yeomanry regiments and Territorial battalions showed all the steadiness and precision of first-line troops. "I have made many calls upon you," wrote Sir John French in a special order, "and the answers you have made to them have covered you, your regiments, and the army to which you belong with honour and glory." And again in his dispatch: "I venture to predict that the deeds during these days of stress and trial will furnish some of the most brilliant chapters which will be found in the military history of our times." It is no more than the truth. If fate had rendered the strategy of Marlborough impossible, Sir John French had none the less fought his Malplaquet.

Within hearing of the guns of Ypres, roaring their last challenge, the greatest British soldier passed away. Lord Roberts landed at Boulogne on 11th November on a visit to his beloved Indian troops. On the 12th he was at the headquarters of the corps, and went about among his old friends, speaking their own tongue, and greeting many who had fought with him in the frontier wars. To the Indian soldier he was the one Englishman who ranked with Nikelsaini

Sahib in the Valhalla of renown. The strain proved too great for the veteran; he caught a chill in the bitter weather; and while the Indian wounded waited in hospital on his coming, the news arrived that he was seriously ill. Pleurisy followed, and at eight o'clock on the night of Saturday, the 14th, the end came. It was fitting that the master-gunner should die within sound of his guns, that the most adored of British soldiers should have his passing amid the army he had loved so well. He had given his best to the service of his country, and had forgone his well-earned rest to preach the lessons of wisdom to dull ears. Such a career is a greater inspiration to his fellows, than a cycle of victories. *Felix opportunitate mortis*, he died, as he had lived, in harness.

(Vol. IV pp. 81-82, 114-20)

WILLIAM LIONEL WYLLIE *The Last of Scharnhorst & the Gneisenau*

THE WAR AT SEA

The Battle of the Falkland Islands, which took place towards the end of 1914, was the first major naval engagement of the war. It remains, in addition, an interesting reminder of continuities in history . . .

The German ships commanded by Admiral von Spee were lured to Port Stanley on the expectation of making an easy prey of the remnants of the British squadron commanded by Rear-Admiral Sir Christopher Cradock which was destroyed at the disastrous Battle of Coronel the previous month; the expedition of the British battle cruisers under Rear-Admiral Sturdee was, Buchan writes, "kept a complete secret".

ON THE morning of 7th December the British squadron arrived at Port Stanley, which lies at the eastern corner of the East Island. The Falklands, with their bare brown moors shining with quartz, their endless lochans, their prevailing mists, their grey stone houses, and their population of Scots shepherds, look like a group of the Orkneys or Outer Hebrides set down in the southern seas. Port Stanley is a deeply-cut gulf leading to an inner harbour on the shores of which stands the little capital. The low shores on the south side

almost give a vessel a sight of the outer sea. The entrance had been defended to some extent by mines. December the 7th was spent by the British squadron in coaling. The *Canopus*, the *Glasgow*, and the *Bristol* were in the inner harbour, while the *Invincible, Inflexible, Carnarvon, Kent*, and *Cornwall* lay in the outer gulf.

About daybreak on the morning of the 8th, Admiral von Spee arrived from the direction of Cape Horn. He sent one of his light cruisers ahead to scout, and this vessel reported the presence of two British ships, probably the *Macedonia* and the *Kent*, which would be the first vessels visible to a ship rounding the islands. Upon this von Spee gave the order to prepare for battle, expecting to find only the remnants of Cradock's squadron. The Germans advanced in line, the *Gneisenau* leading, followed by the *Nürnberg*, the *Scharnhorst*, the *Dresden*, and the *Leipzig*, and steered north-east towards the entrance of the port.

At 8 o'clock the signal station announced the presence of the enemy. It was a clear fresh morning, with a bright sun, and light breezes from the north-west. All our vessels had finished coaling, except the battle cruisers, which had begun only half an hour before. Orders were at once given to get up steam for full speed. The battle cruisers raised steam with fuel oil, and made so dense a smoke that the German look-outs did not detect them. The Germans fired a shell at the wireless station about 9, and the *Canopus* had a shot at the *Scharnhorst* over the neck of land, directed by signal officers on shore. At 9.30 von Spee came abreast the harbour mouth, and was able to see the strength of the British squadron. He at once altered his course and put to sea, while Admiral Sturdee's command streamed out in pursuit.

First went the *Kent* and then the *Glasgow*, followed by the *Carnarvon*, the battle cruisers, and the *Cornwall*. The Germans had two transports with them, the *Baden* and the *Santa Isabel* and these fell back to the south of the island, with the *Bristol* and the *Macedonia* in pursuit. The *Canopus* remained in the harbour. At about 10 o'clock the two forces were some twelve miles apart, von Spee steering about due east. The *Invincible* and the *Inflexible* quickly drew ahead, but had to slacken speed to 20 knots to allow the cruisers to keep up with them. At 11 o'clock about eleven miles separated the two forces. At five minutes to one we had drawn closer, and opened fire upon the *Leipzig*, which was last of the German line.

Von Spee, seeing that flight was impossible, prepared to give battle. So far as the battle cruisers were concerned, it was a foregone conclusion, for they had the greater speed and the longer range. His three light cruisers turned and made off to the south, followed by the *Kent*, the *Glasgow*, and the *Cornwall*, while the *Invincible*, the *Inflexible*, and the *Carnarvon* engaged the *Scharnhorst* and the *Gneisenau*. About 2 o'clock our battle cruisers had the range of the German flagship, and a terrific artillery duel began. The smoke was getting in our way, and Admiral Sturdee used his superior speed to get to the other side of the enemy. We simply pounded the *Scharnhorst* to pieces, and just after 4 o'clock she listed to port and then turned bottom upwards with her propeller still going round. The battle cruisers and the *Carnarvon* then concentrated on the *Gneisenau*, which was sheering off to the south-east, and at 6 o'clock she too listed and went under.

Meanwhile the *Kent, Glasgow,* and *Cornwall* were hot in pursuit of the three light cruisers, and here was a more equally matched battle. The *Dresden*, which was farthest to the east, managed to escape. The other two had slightly the advantage of speed of the British ships, but our engineers and stokers worked magnificently, and managed to get 25 knots out of the *Kent.* It was now a thick misty day, with a drizzle of rain, and each duel had consequently the air of a separate battle. The news of the sinking of the *Scharnhorst* and the *Gneisenau* put new spirit into our men, and at 7.27 p.m. the *Nürnberg*, which had been set on fire by the *Kent*, went down with her guns still firing. The *Leipzig*, which had to face the *Glasgow* and the *Cornwall*, kept afloat till 9 p.m., when she too heeled over and sank. As the wet night closed in, the battle died away. Only the *Dresden*, battered and fleeing far out in the southern waters, remained of the proud squadron which at dawn had sailed to what it believed to be an easy victory. The defeat of Cradock in the murky sunset off Coronel had been amply avenged.

The Battle of the Falkland Islands was a brilliant piece of strategy, for a plan, initiated more than a month before and involving a journey across the world, was executed with complete secrecy and precision. The honours must be divided between Sir Frederick Sturdee and the Admiralty at home, which conceived the enterprise. Technically, the sole blemish was the escape of the *Dresden*, which could scarcely have been prevented, for the *Carnarvon*, owing to her inadequate speed, could not join her sister ships in the pursuit of the lighter German vessels, and the *Glasgow*, the only ship which might have overhauled her, was busy with the *Leipzig*. The fight had a vital bearing on the position of Germany. It annihilated the one squadron left to her outside the North Sea, and it removed a formidable menace to our trade routes. After the 8th of December, the *Dresden* and the *Karlsruhe* were the sole enemy cruisers left at large, for the *Bremen*, never very fortunate in her efforts, seemed to have temporarily disappeared. These, with the armoured merchantmen, the *Kronprinz Wilhelm* and the *Prince Eitel Friedrich*, were the only privateers still at work on the High Seas.

(*Vol. IV pp. 218-24*)

TRENCH WARFARE

Back to the Western Front: Buchan describes the conditions that soldiers had to face in the front line, and says something about the support services which made life tolerable.

THE DISCOMFORTS of trench warfare can never be removed; at the best they can be mitigated. In the early days, before 20th November, when regiments were cooped up with their dead for a fortnight under constant fire in shallow mud-holes, the misery of it beggars all description. As the first violence of the attack ebbed and the Allies were given leisure to revise their trenches, many improvements were introduced, battalions were more frequently relieved, and the whole system was regularized. The strain and the ennui of the work remained, but the physical hardships grew lighter, the trenches were lined and drained, and the communication network was perfected. The British food supplies were excellent: good feeding will go down to history as a tradition of this army in Flanders, like hard swearing in the case of an earlier expedition. How much this means to the British soldier every one who remembers South Africa will bear witness, for there, when a man complained that he was "fed up", he generally meant that he was not fed up. Frequent relief and better provision for billets and baths in the rear did much to ease their lot. A battalion which came out of the trenches weary, lame, dishevelled, spiritless, and indescribably dirty, would be restored in a couple of days to a reasonable smartness and good humour. Perhaps the officers in the later weeks had the worst of it. For them war justified its old definition: "Months of acute boredom punctuated by moments of acute fear."

The worst part of the business was the wet. A dripping winter and the presence of a million men churned West Flanders into a gigantic mud-hole. Some parts of the Allied line were better than others. The Arras district was fairly dry; so was the Klein Zillebeke ridge and the country round Messines and Wytschaete; while in the Ploegsteert Wood – a stretch about two miles long by one mile wide – a fairly dry and comfortable forest colony was established, where men could move about with a certain freedom. But all along the Lys and the Ypres Canal the trenches were liable to constant flooding, and the approaches were seas of mire. It was worse still between Dixmude and the sea, where life became merely amphibious. Tons of wood laid for pathways disappeared in the sloughs. A false step on a dark night meant a descent into a quagmire, from which a man, if happily rescued by his fellows, emerged, as Trinculo said of Caliban, "No fish, but an islander that hath lately suffered by a thunderbolt." The Lys overflowed its banks, and inundated our trenches for

JOHN NASH *"Over the Top"*

eighty yards on each side. A brook at Festubert came down in flood, and several men in the neighbouring trenches were drowned. But far worse than any risk to life was the misery of standing for hours up to the waist in icy water, of having every pore of the skin impregnated with mud, of finding the walls of a trench dissolving in slimy torrents, while rifles jammed, clothes rotted, and feet were frost-bitten. It was a lesson in the extremes to which human endurance can go. But so efficient was our commissariat work, and so ample the provision of comforts and warm clothes, that the British sick rate was no more than 3 per cent, lower than that of many garrison towns in peace, and inconceivably lower than that of any war in the past.

(Vol. V pp. 27-29)

THE CAMPAIGN IN THE AIR

This chapter, which is reprinted in its entirety, represents the first instalment of the first history of war in the air to be written in English.

IN THE years before the war it had become the fashion to announce that the next European conflict would witness a phenomenal use of aircraft. Ingenious romancers had pictured an Armageddon in the clouds, and lovers of peace had clung to the notion that the novelty and frightfulness of such a warfare would make the Powers of the world hesitate to draw the sword. The results have been both below and in excess of expectation. The air was a realm of pure guesswork, for in the Tripoli and Balkan wars there was no serious aerial service, though various adventurers experimented in the new arm. What may be the ultimate outcome no man can tell, for aircraft are still in an early stage of development. But up to date we can say that they have not altered any of the traditional principles of war in their fundamentals, while, on the other hand, they have proved a far more manageable, precise, and calculable branch of the service than even their warmest supporters foretold.

France led the way in aerial experiment, and her government between 1909 and 1914 acquired the largest air fleet in the world. Her aviators were brilliant performers, especially in long-distance flights, but they were not thoroughly absorbed into the military machine. They had less knowledge of the tactical use of aircraft than of their mechanical capabilities, and the organization of the French Air Corps was severely criticized by the Committee of the Senate just before the war. It suffered, too, from having a somewhat heterogeneous collection of machines, many of an excellent type, but many indifferent. There was no government standardized pattern, and hence supply of spare parts and accessories became a difficulty. The French airmen had brilliant technical skill and endless courage – men like Garros and Pégoud had no rivals – but as a corps they were not so fully organized for war as their neighbours. The Germans had preferred at first to interest themselves rather in airships than in aeroplanes, but their military advisers were well aware of the value of the latter, and had prepared a strong corps. The German aviator could not fly as well as the French; on the whole he had not as useful a machine; but he understood perfectly his place in the military plan. He was thoroughly trained to reconnaissance work, and especially to the task of range-finding for the field guns. The Austrian air service was much inferior, though it contained some dashing pilots. The Russian had enormously improved, under the Grand Duke Alexander, but it suffered from a shortage of machines and a chronic difficulty in rapid manufacture. It possessed, however, several great biplanes, useful for destructive purposes, for each could carry over a ton's weight of explosives.

The British air service, the last to be started, had been so wisely and energetically developed by Sir David Henderson and his colleagues that on the outbreak of war it was probably the best equipped in the world. We had a good type of machine and enough of them, a number of highly qualified pilots and observers accustomed to go out in all weathers and under every condition of difficulty, and, above all, trained in tactical co-operation with other arms. We have rarely been successful in occupations which demand a peculiar and fantastic gift – in trick-flying and high-speed motoring we have been out-stripped easily by continental rivals; but we have the power of making a novel art subserve a prosaic and practical purpose, just as the British soldier brings to the business of bloodshed something of the homely atmosphere of his ordinary life. The British Royal Flying Corps contained a military and a naval wing. Each wing was divided into squadrons, consisting of twenty-four aeroplanes and twenty-four pilots, under a major or commander. The squadron was in turn divided into six flights, each flight comprising four machines commanded by a captain in the one case and a commander or lieutenant in the other. The squadron was a self-contained unit, having its own transport in the shape of motor wagons calculated to maintain on good roads a speed of twenty miles an hour. Armed motor cars were also attached to it.

The uses of aircraft, so far as the war has revealed them, are principally two – for reconnaissance in its many forms, and for destruction. The latter purpose, from the strict military point of view, is exemplified by the destruction of enemy troops, fortresses and fortified bases, ships, transports, communications, and munitions of war. To these uses the Germans have added a third – the destruction of civilian life and property with a view to intimidation; but in this sinister departure they have happily not been followed by the Allies. There is also the important duty of driving off and, if possible, destroying hostile aeroplanes, for it is now clear that the only real weapon against one aeroplane is another. Let us glance at these different functions and the main instances of their performance during the first six months of war.

The reconnaissance of aircraft has, as we have seen, worked a revolution in strategy. More rapid and comprehensive than cavalry, the aeroplane makes surprises on a grand scale an impossibility except in a densely-wooded land or under weather conditions so bad that no aviator can ascend. Instances are endless. It was the German aviators who revealed to the German generals the weakness of the Allied line along the Meuse and the Sambre. It was an air reconnaissance that inspired the first abortive advance of the French into Alsace. From our Flying Corps we first learned of von Kluck's wheel to the south-east – a fine performance, of which General Joffre wrote: "The precision, exactitude, and regularity of the news brought in by its members are evidence of their perfect organization and also of the perfect training of pilots and observers." Aircraft gave the Germans news of our enveloping movement from the Aisne, and gave us information of their counter-movement which led to the race for the sea. In the long struggle between Arras and Nieuport we were able from the reports of aviators to follow the track of the German reinforcements and strengthen our own thin lines. Aircraft told Japan all that she needed to know about the fortress of Tsing-tau; they warned us of the Turkish movement across the desert against the Suez Canal; they told us of the coming of the Prussian Guard at Ypres. In the East it was by aeroplanes that von Hindenburg found out the weakness of Samsonov's position; aircraft gave the Grand Duke Nicholas early news of the first assault upon Warsaw, and of the Austrian *revanche* from Cracow. Now and again the service was at fault. It did not tell us soon enough of the four new German formations advancing on Menin about 15th October, nor did it inform von Hindenburg of the Russian trans-Vistula movement which drove him back from Warsaw, or the Grand Duke Nicholas of the dash against Lodz, or the later assault from East Prussia, when he lost his 20th Corps. But, generally speaking, the commanders of all the great armies have had early knowledge of the main hostile movements, and have been able to provide against them. Without aircraft there would have been fewer battles, perhaps, and more manoeuvring on the defensive, but when a disaster came it would have been more crushing. Foreknowledge, shared pretty well by all sides means a slow war.

The work of aircraft has been well described in an official note by the French Government: "They give information to our commanding officers, who find in them an invaluable auxiliary, concerning the movements of the enemy and the progress of columns and supplies. They are not liable to be stopped like cavalry by the uninterrupted lines of trenches. They fly over positions and batteries, enabling our forces to aim with accuracy. They drop bombs on gatherings of troops, convoys, and staffs, and are an instrument of demolition and demoralization." Of this varied programme the most important item is the first. In half a dozen hours an aviator will scan many hundreds of miles of country, and if the air is clear, the odds are that no important enemy movement will escape his notice. He may misjudge it, as the Russian airmen misjudged von Hindenburg's activity before Tannenberg, but that is a risk in all reconnaissance, aerial or otherwise.

In the blue weather of the late summer and early autumn the Allied aircraft went far afield. The famous French airmen, Pégoud and Finke, flew 200 miles into German territory. During the twenty days previous to 10th September the British Flying Corps maintained a daily average of more than nine reconnaissance flights over a hundred miles each. Then the only danger came from the enemy's fire. The aviator flew every now and then into a zone of peril, where the bullets from rifles and anti-aircraft guns rattled on his machine and his planes, and where bursts of shell engendered a hundred odd currents. In such circumstances he had to rise to an altitude of some 6,000 feet to be secure from the enemy. But observation cannot be carried on at that height, and he had to descend again, picking his way in sharp zigzags. When the weather broke in October the work became harder. Mists and winter gales often made flights

J. McGILCHRIST *Sopwith Camel Attacking Hanoveranger Bi-Plane*

impossible; but whenever there was a sporting chance our airmen went out, for movements on land do not wait on the weather in the clouds. On 15th November, for example, it was bitterly cold, and rain fell in torrents. "Nevertheless," wrote the British "Eye-witness", "in spite of all difficulties our aviators carried out a successful reconnaissance, observing the emplacements of batteries, and searching the roads for hostile columns in the midst of a storm of driving snow and sleet." A pilot, strapped to his seat 5,000 feet in the air during a north-east gale, is one of the least protected of God's creatures. Yet in spite of the immense appearance of risk, the service was, in results, the least dangerous of all. About a dozen casualties made up the total of the British Flying Corps during the first six months of the war. Just as our seamen, freezing in the North Sea, commiserated their unfortunate brothers in the trenches, so an airman was often heard to express his shame at being engaged in so secure and well-sheltered an occupation.

When the campaign became a war of positions the most vital duty of aircraft was to detect the positions of big guns – especially the howitzers, with their high-angle fire, which could be concealed miles away behind a hill. Without such an aid it is difficult to see how hostile artillery could be fairly met. The Germans showed in the early days of the fighting an extraordinary mastery of this tactical use of aircraft, but the Allies speedily learned the game, and established what the official report calls "an individual ascendency". They drove back the reconnoitring "Taubes", and themselves performed some remarkable feats of intelligence work. At the Aisne, and in the first weeks in Flanders, they located the German trenches; and later, when the trench lines were only too well known to both sides, they did admirable service in fixing the emplacements of the big howitzers. Such work was far more risky than long-distance reconnaissance, for they had to fly at a low elevation, and they were exposed to the fire of the enemy, and not infrequently to that of their own side. Often an aeroplane returned from its trip to be welcomed by rifle shots from the troops it was safeguarding.

In this work the most vital task was that of the observer; the most difficult, too, for, while the pilot had the excitement of manipulating his machine, the observer sat still to see and to be shot at. British observers proved themselves amazingly efficient. They seemed to have a natural eye for country, and to pick out a movement as a stalker picks out a stag on a hill which he has known from childhood. The most skilled aviator in the world may not have this talent; it is a gift as specific as a turn for rock-climbing, and its prevalence among our officers may perhaps be attributed to the national training in field sports. "Eye-witness" has well described it. "The temperament of the observer", he wrote, "is of the greatest importance. He must be cool and capable of great concentration in order to keep his attention fixed upon his objective in spite of all distractions – such as, for instance, the bursts of shell close to him, or the noise of rifle bullets passing through the planes of his machine. He must withstand the temptation to make conjectures, or to think that he has seen something when he is not absolutely certain of the fact, since an error in observing or an inaccuracy in reporting may lead to false conclusions, and cause infinite harm."

> "The really first-rate observer", we are told, "must possess extensive military knowledge, in order to know what objects to look for and where to look for them; he must have very good eyesight in order to pick them up, and he must have the knack of reading a map quickly, both in order to mark correctly their positions and to find his way. To reconnoitre is not easy even in fine weather; but in driving rain or snow, in a temperature perhaps several degrees below zero, or in a gale, where an aeroplane travelling with the wind rocks and sways like a ship in a heavy sea and may attain a speed of one hundred and fifty miles an hour, the difficulties are immense. In these circumstances, and from the altitude at which it is necessary to fly in order to escape the projectiles of anti-aircraft guns, columns of transport or of men are easily missed. Indeed, at a first attempt, an observer will see nothing which is of military value, for it is only after considerable practice that the eye becomes accustomed to scouring a great stretch of country from above and acquires the power of distinguishing objects upon it."

Mr Roosevelt in one of his books defines scouting as the art of seeing wherein a bit of landscape differs from the ordinary. An old hunter can tell that a wapiti is on a hillside, because he knows the normal look of that hillside from long experience, and sees in a second the minute difference caused by the presence of the deer. But this experience was impossible for our observers. They had never cast eyes before from a great elevation upon the slag heaps and canals and chessboard fields of Flanders, or the broad green valleys of Oise and Aisne. The art had to be learned, and an Admirable Crichton had to be produced who combined the gifts of a lookout man, a Polar explorer, a Staff-College professor, and Patience on a monument. After our island fashion we did not know we possessed him till the crisis came.

The second task of aircraft – destruction of enemy troops and materials – had to take second place so far as the military wing was concerned, for most aeroplanes were busied with the more urgent duty of reconnaissance. We hear of various incidental successes by both French and British – an ammunition convoy blown up during the Marne battles, bombs dropped on the railway station at Freiburg and the airship sheds at Metz, a park of transport severely damaged at La Fère, the killing of artillery horses, the demolition of rolling stock on the railway at Laon, the destruction of two food trains, the burning of six German aeroplanes found in one shed. Both French and German aviators made use of steel arrows, called *flêchettes*, dropped in batches of five hundred (an aeroplane being able to carry a stock of four thousand). Such darts would undoubtedly have pierced a man's skull if they had happened to hit him, but the aiming must have been difficult, for we heard of few successes. The aircraft of no army was so organized as to be capable of great and continued damage to troops. For that five times the number of machines was needed, and a strategy of attack which no General Staff had yet elaborated. In this direction, perhaps, we may look for the main future development of aircraft as a fighting arm. In the destruction of *matériel* an aeroplane is hampered by the comparative smallness and fewness of the bombs it can carry. It can never work the damage caused by a shell from a great howitzer. It must seek out places containing delicate structures or explosives – gasworks, magazines, airship and aeroplane sheds – for it is of little use against normal fortifications.

The chief destructive work was done, as we should expect, by the naval wing of the Royal Flying Corps, on whom fell no daily duty of reconnaissance. During the crossing of the British force to France the seaplanes had scouted to east and west of the Channel, and on 27th August, when Ostend was occupied by British marines, a strong squadron was sent there. It presently removed its headquarters to Dunkirk, whence many bold raids and reconnaissances were made. Between 4th and 23rd September successful skirmishes of both aeroplanes and armed motor cars took place; and on 16th September, near Doullens, Commander C.R. Samson, with a force of armed cars, annihilated an Uhlan patrol. On 22nd September a naval airman, Flight-Lieutenant C.H. Collet, flew 200 miles in misty weather to Düsseldorf, and descending to a height of 400 feet, dropped bombs upon the airship shed. His machine was hit, but he returned safely. At the same time two other British airmen had visited Cologne, but the fog was too thick to enable them to locate the Zeppelin sheds, and they refrained for honourable reasons from dropping bombs upon the civilian part of the city. We do not know the actual damage done at Düsseldorf, but the moral effect was great. "The importance of the incident", ran the Admiralty announcement, "lies in the fact that it shows that, in the event of further bombs being dropped into Antwerp or other Belgian towns, measures of reprisal can certainly be adopted."

On 8th October four or five aeroplanes, under Squadron-Commander D.A. Spencer Grey, set out for Germany. The party divided, one section making for Düsseldorf and the other for Cologne. At the first place bombs were dropped on the airship shed by Lieutenant Marix, and an outburst of flames and the collapse of the roof showed that their object had been attained. The attacking aeroplanes were badly hit, but the airmen succeeded in reaching the British lines in safety. The Cologne party circled for some time above the city at a height of 600 feet, and although heavily fired upon, succeeded in wrecking a large part of the military railway station. The boldness and skill of these raids deserve the highest praise; and as an instance of the spirit of our naval airmen another incident may be quoted. During some patrol work it became necessary to change a propeller blade. This meant that the machine must descend, but to avoid loss of time two of the crew volunteered to carry out the work in the air. At a height of 2,000 feet they completed their task, climbing out on the bracket which carried the propeller shafting.

On 1st November bombs were dropped by a British aviator on Thielt, then the German headquarters, which the Emperor had only just left. Next day, by way of a return, the Germans dropped bombs on Furnes, which President Poincaré was believed to be visiting. The chief aerial feat of November was the raid of British naval airmen on Friedrichshafen, the town on the Lake of Constance where the Zeppelins are largely built. On 21st November Commander E.F. Briggs, Lieutenant J.T. Babington, and Lieutenant S.V. Sippe flew from Belfort, 250 miles distant, and dropped bombs on the airship factory and an adjacent gas factory, which they seriously damaged. All three machines were hit, and that of Commander Briggs was brought down through shrapnel bullets striking his petrol tank, and its occupant taken prisoner. The Cross of the Legion of Honour was awarded to the bold adventurers.

In the beginning of December the wild weather kept the aeroplanes at home. But on the 20th Commander Samson visited Brussels, where the Germans had erected airship sheds, and dropped bombs on the flying ground at Etherbeek, damaging many machines. Four days later Squadron-Commander R.B. Davies flew to the same city, and dropped twelve bombs on the airship sheds, probably destroying a Parseval machine. But the great expedition of the month came on Christmas Day. Seven seaplanes flew early in the morning from England, and rendezvoused at a point described as "in the vicinity of Heligoland". Thence, escorted by cruisers and submarines, they advanced to the Schillig roads off Cuxhaven, where some German warships were lying. On these and on the shore defences they dropped their bombs, with what result it is still uncertain, for the morning fog was dense, but there is good reason to believe that one or more of the Zeppelin sheds were destroyed. According to arrangement, the escorting warships waited for the return of the airmen, and while so doing were sighted from Heligoland and attacked by four German seaplanes, two Zeppelins, and several submarines. The bombs of the seaplanes fell near our ships, but failed to hit them, and the Zeppelins were easily put to flight by the guns of the *Arethusa* and the *Undaunted*. For three hours the cruisers maintained their station, and returned home after picking up three of the aviators. Three others who came back later destroyed their machines, to prevent them falling into the enemy's hands, and were taken on board the submarines. The fate of the seventh, Flight-Commander F.E.T. Hewlett, was for a day or two uncertain, his machine having been seen broken and derelict about eight miles from Heligo-land. He was, however, picked up by a Dutch trawler, and returned safely. Lastly – to bring the record to the end of the first six months of war – Squadron-Commander R.B. Davies and Flight-Lieutenant R. Peirse on 22nd January flew over the new German naval base at Zeebrugge, and dropped bombs on the artillery and two submarines, one of which they destroyed. Commander Davies was at one time surrounded by seven hostile aeroplanes, but he managed to elude them, and returned, slightly wounded, to his base. Seldom in history have more adventurous deeds been done with fewer losses than in our air campaign from August to January. By this time the German anti-aircraft guns were becoming very formidable, especially at places like Antwerp, Zeebrugge, and Ostend, where they had frequent practice.

The German aircraft have also a long record of destruction. Their pet invention, the Zeppelin, proved, indeed, something of a fiasco. It had revealed itself as a highly delicate and vulnerable contrivance in peace time, and it was not less so in war. Stories of the misadventures of the huge airships were published daily; but though perhaps half a dozen cases can be authenticated, we must be sceptical about most of them. Human nature believes what it wants to believe – a gift which makes for happiness but not for truth; and just as every German aeroplane was a Taube and every howitzer a 42 cm. gun, so in the popular mind every German airship was a Zeppelin. On 16th September the British Headquarters stated that the Royal Flying Corps, who had been out on reconnaissance every day since their arrival in France, had never seen a Zeppelin. One – No. VIII, the largest of all – was brought down by artillery in Alsace on 22nd August, when it was flying from Strassburg, and the pieces were exhibited in Paris; the same fate befell another which a few days later was engaged in dropping bombs on the railway station at Mlawa; and a third seems to have been captured by the Russians about 6th September, and sent to Petrograd. One may have been destroyed at Friedrichshafen and one at Düsseldorf; but we shall not be far wrong if we put half a dozen as the outside number of Zeppelins which were demolished by the Allies.

The Zeppelins – and indeed all the large airships – were singularly unhandy weapons, and they served a better use as a popular bogey than as instruments of offence, though they were undoubtedly present at various times at Antwerp, at Nancy, and at Warsaw. Far more effective for destruction were the German aeroplanes. They destroyed the railway station at Charleroi; they did considerable execution among the French cavalry; they dropped bombs upon Ghent, Ostend, Dunkirk, Calais, Lunéville, Pont-à-Mousson, Nancy, Paris, and Warsaw; and towards the end of October killed over a hundred persons close to the headquarters of the Russian General Staff. At Hazebrouck in December nine British soldiers and five civilians were killed by bombs from aircraft, and during January Dunkirk suffered severely. In these visitations no precautions were taken to attack only objects of military significance. Populous streets and suburbs in Paris and Warsaw were assaulted, for the distinction between soldiers and civilians is a quibble unknown to the German doctrine of war. A Zeppelin raid upon London was the most cherished of German dreams; for on this theory any place which possesses a single trooper or an antique gun is a fortress, and therefore a legitimate object for destruction.

Of such a type – aimless from a military point of view, and useful only as a practice flight and as an inspiration of panic – was the raid upon England on 19th January. Ten days before a fleet of aeroplanes, estimated at sixteen, had been sighted in the Channel, but the stormy weather drove them back from our coasts. The raid of Tuesday, the 19th, seems to have been carried out by two craft; but whether they were Zeppelins or airships of another pattern, or merely big aeroplanes, is not yet clear. They reached the coast of Norfolk about 8.30 in the evening, dropped bombs on Yarmouth, and then steered north-west across country towards King's Lynn, dropping bombs there, and on several villages *en route*. As these are not populous places, and by no conceivable definition military stations, it is possible that the aim of the invaders was the royal residence of Sandringham. At Yarmouth two persons were killed and some damage done to property; at King's Lynn the death-roll was the same, but more buildings were injured. The accounts of eyewitnesses differed widely. Some declared that they saw four ships, an account from Holland spoke of the return of three, and the German report spoke of them in the plural; but it is unlikely that there were more than two. The view that they were Zeppelins rests partly upon the general impression as to their size, and partly on the weight of the bombs dropped. A few weeks later a single aeroplane visited the Essex coast and dropped a bomb at Colchester, the result being the destruction of a child's perambulator.

Destruction, except in the special case of gasworks, airship sheds, and magazines, must rank at present far behind reconnaissance in the tale of the work of aircraft. But one other task falls to the aviator – the duty of engaging an enemy machine, for it has been abundantly proved that the true weapon of offence and defence against an attack from the air is a counter-attack in the same element. Airmen have instructions to engage at once a hostile aeroplane or airship; and though a duel between a Zeppelin and an aeroplane has not yet been witnessed, almost every day of the war saw a fight between two aeroplanes.

It is curious that the most modern device should have restored to the campaign the old single combat of the Middle Ages with both armies looking on. In such duels the individual ascendency of the Allies brilliantly revealed itself. The manoeuvring for position, the sudden crack of pistol or rifle, the wounding of the pilot or the crippling of the machine, the momentary disappearance of the foe into a bank of cloud, the ever-present possibility of being dashed to a violent death, make up a tale of sensations which no duello of the past has ever equalled. The two foes struggle to get the higher position till they are mere specks in the heavens, and the upper drives his opponent in zigzags and whorls to earth like a hawk circling above a finch. The grim business may even have its humorous side. In December there was an encounter between a British and a German airman, in which the former emptied his pistol at the enemy without any visible result. He then proceeded to take a photograph, and the sight of the camera drove the German to incontinent flight.

(*Vol. V pp. 54-73*)

THE GALLIPOLI LANDING

The ill-fated Gallipoli expedition of 1915, undertaken in theory at least to relieve pressure on the Western Front, was in its earlier stages a successful example of combined operations. The landing on an inhospitable shore under enemy fire was accomplished; but Allied troops soon became bogged down, and despite their gallantry the enterprise ended in failure when the peninsula was evacuated in January 1916.

Buchan describes the problems and the initial landing in which the Australia and New Zealand Army Corps (ANZAC) began forging a military tradition which has proved enduring.

LET US examine briefly the military elements of the Gallipoli peninsula. One of the difficulties of the task before us was that it was impossible to surprise the enemy. Surprise is the essence of most schemes of invasion. If Britain lost command of the sea and our coast lay open to attack, the enemy could count upon surprise as his chief asset. It is true that the attack would be expected, but there are so many possible landing-places on our coasts that no man could tell where the blow would fall. Our plan of defence would necessarily be a careful watch along our shores by a great chain of outposts, while our main forces were held in reserve at points inland where they could easily be moved to the zone of invasion. If, however, the attack were well directed, it might for long be doubtful where the chief effort was being made. There would be feints at several places, and troops landed only to be withdrawn, till the defence was in that condition of nervous confusion which gives the chance to the enemy with the bold initiative.

But in the Dardanelles expedition there was no room for such ingenuities. From the start the element of surprise was wholly eliminated. This was nobody's blame; it was due, not to the premature naval enterprise of February and March, but to the nature of the Gallipoli peninsula. The possession of that peninsula was essential to the control of the Straits, and this was clear to the Turco-German Staff before the first shot was fired on 3rd November. To master Gallipoli meant an assault from the Aegean, and the possible landing-places were few in number, small in extent, and clearly defined by the nature of the ground. Gaps must be found in the screen of yellow cliffs which fringe the sea. If we take the peninsula west of the line drawn north and south across the upper end of the Narrows, there were only two places where troops could be disembarked. One of these was the various beaches round about Sedd-el-Bahr and Cape Helles. The other was on the Gulf of Saros, near Gaba Tepe, where the sandstone hills leave a narrow space at the water's edge. Neither was good, and both were believed by the Turkish Staff to be wholly impracticable. Nevertheless they left no stone unturned in their defence.

The mere landing of the Expeditionary Force would not affect much. The hills of the Gallipoli peninsula may be said to form a natural fortress defending the rear of the Narrows forts. Behind the point of Kilid Bahr a rocky plateau, which is more than 600 feet high, extends inland for some five miles. Its highest ridge runs up to the summits known to the Turks as Pasha Dagh. These hills are a salient with the point towards the Gulf of Saros, and the sides curving back to the Dardanelles above and below Kilid Bahr. North the high ground continues, and is pierced by a pass, through which a rough track runs from Krithia to the town of Maidos, on the channel opposite Nagara.

But to an invader coming from the west and aiming at Maidos the Pasha Dagh is not the only obstacle. West of it and south of Krithia rises the bold peak of Achi Baba, nearly 600 feet high, which sends out rocky spurs on both sides to the Dardanelles and the Gulf of Saros, and forms a barrier from sea to sea across the narrow western point of the peninsula.

The problem before Sir Ian Hamilton was, therefore, simple enough in its general lines. He must effect a landing at the apex of the peninsula and at Gaba Tepe, in the Gulf of Saros. It would then be the business of the force landed at the first point to fight its way to Krithia, and carry the Achi Baba ridge, while the second force would advance from Gaba Tepe against the pass leading to Maidos. It might then be possible for the left wing of the first to come in touch with the right wing of the second, and together to force the Pasha Dagh plateau. If that movement succeeded the battle was won. We could bring up artillery to the plateau, which would make the European forts untenable. Moreover, we would dominate at short range the enemy's positions on the Asiatic side, and a combined attack by land and sea would give the Narrows to our hands.

The Expeditionary Force was assembled in Egypt during the first half of April. Sir Ian Hamilton had arrived at Tenedos on March 17th, but he found that the transports had been wrongly loaded, and had to send them back to Alexandria. Lemnos was chosen as the advanced base, and by the middle of the month the expedition began to arrive in the Bay of Mudros. Part of the force was landed on the island, and the rest remained on board the ships, where day and night, under the direction of naval officers, they practised the landing of men, horses, and guns. Germany was well aware of our intentions, and on 22nd April published an announcement that 20,000 British and French troops had landed at Enos at the mouth of the Maritza, a place some sixty-four miles from Bulair by a bad road. This was a legend, but we experimented during these days in small landings and bombardments in the Gulf of Saros as feints to distract the enemy. Meanwhile, by the 20th of April Sir Ian Hamilton had perfected his plans, and the first attack was fixed for Sunday, 25th April.

That Sunday morning was one of those which delight the traveller in April in the Aegean. A light mist fills the air before dawn, but it disappears with the sun, and all day there are clear skies, still seas, and the fresh, invigorating warmth of spring. Round about Cape Helles there are five little beaches. Beginning from the left, there is Beach Y, and, a little south of it, Beach X. Rounding Cape Tekke, we come to Beach W, where a narrow valley opens between the headlands of Tekeh and Helles. Here there is a broad, semicircular stretch of sand. South of Helles is Beach V, a place of the same configuration as Beach W, but unpleasantly commanded by the castle and village of Sedd-el-Bahr at its southern end. Lastly, inside the Straits, on the east side of Morto Bay, is Beach S, close to the point of Eski Hissar. The landing at Gaba Tepe was entrusted to the Australian and New Zealand troops; that at the Helles beaches to the 29th Division, with some units of the Naval Division. It was arranged that simultaneously the French should land on the Asiatic shore at Kum Kale, to prevent the Turkish batteries from being brought into action against our men at Beaches V and S. Part of the Naval Division was detached for a feint farther north in the Gulf of Saros.

Let us assume that an aeroplane, which miraculously escaped the enemy's fire, enabled us to move up and down the shores of the peninsula and observe the progress of the different landings. About one in the morning the ships arrive at a point five miles from the Gallipoli shores. At 1.20 the boats are lowered, and the troops line up on the decks. Then they embark in the flotillas, and the steam pinnaces begin to tow them shorewards in the hazy half-light before dawn. The Australians destined for Gaba Tepe are carried in destroyers which take them in close to the shore. The operations are timed to allow the troops to reach the beaches at daybreak.

Slowly and very quietly the boats and destroyers steal in towards the land. A little before five an enemy's searchlight flares out. The boats are now in shallow water under the Gaba Tepe cliffs, and the men are leaping ashore. Then comes a blaze of rifle fire from the Turkish trenches on the beach, and the first comers charge them with the bayonet. The whole cliff seems to leap into light, for everywhere trenches and caverns have been dug in the slopes. The fire falls most heavily on the men still in the boats, who have the difficult task of waiting as the slow minutes bring them shoreward. The first Australians – the 3rd Brigade, under Colonel Sinclair Maclagan – do not linger. They carry the lines on the beach with cold steel, and find themselves looking up at a steep cliff a hundred feet high. In open order they dive into the scrub, and scramble up the loose yellow rocks. By a fortunate accident the landing is farther north than we intended, just under the cliffs of Sari Bair. At Gaba Tepe the long slope would have given the enemy a great advantage in defence; but here there is only the forty-foot beach and then the cliffs.

He who knows the Aegean in April will remember the revelation of those fringed sea walls and bare brown slopes. From a distance they look as arid as the Syrian desert, but when the traveller draws near he finds a paradise of curious and beautiful flowers – anemone, grape hyacinth, rockrose, asphodel, and amaryllis. Up this rock garden the Australians race, among the purple cistus and the matted creepers and the thickets of myrtle. They have left their packs at the foot, and scale the bluffs like chamois. It is an achievement to rank with Wolfe's escalade of the Heights of Abraham. Presently they are at the top, and come under the main Turkish fire. But the ground gives good cover, and they set about entrenching the crest of the cliffs to cover the boats' landing. This is the position at Gaba Tepe at 7 a.m.

As we journey down the coast we come next to Beach Y. There at 7 a.m. all is going well. The three cruisers, *Dublin, Amethyst*, and *Sapphire*, have covered the landing of the King's Own Scottish Borderers and the Plymouth battalion of the Naval Division, who have without difficulty reached the top of the cliffs. At Beach X things are even better. The *Swiftsure* has plastered the high ground with shells, and the landing ship, the *Implacable*, has anchored close to the shore in six fathoms of water. Without a single casualty the Royal Fusiliers have gained the cliff line. There has been a harder fight at Beach W, between Tekke and Helles, where the sands are broader. The shore is trenched throughout, and wired and mined almost to the water's edge, and in the scrub of the hinterland the Turkish snipers are hidden. The result is that, though our ships have bombarded the shore for three-quarters of an hour, they cannot clear out the enemy, and do not seem to have made much impression on the wire entanglements. The first troops landed to the right under the cliffs of Cape Helles, and reached the top, while a party on the left scaled Cape Tekke. But the men of the Lancashire Fusiliers who landed on the shore itself had a fiery trial. They suffered heavily while still on the water, and on landing came up against unbroken lines of wire, while snipers in the valley in front and concealed machine guns and quick-firers rained death on them. Here we have had heavy losses, and at 7 a.m. the landing has not succeeded.

But the case is more desperate still at Beach V, under Sedd-el-Bahr. Here, as at Beach W, there are a stretch of sand, a scrubby valley, and flanking cliffs. It is the strongest of the Turkish positions, and troops landing in boats are exposed to every type of converging fire. A curious expedient has been tried. A collier, the *River Clyde*, with 2,000 men of the Hampshires and Munster Fusiliers on board, as well as eight boatloads towed by steam pinnaces, approached close to the shore. The boatloads – the Dublin Fusiliers – suffered horribly, for when they dashed through the shallows to the beach they were pinned to the ground by fire. Three lines of wire entanglements had to be forced, and a network of trenches. A bank of sand, five or six feet high, runs at the back, and under its cover the survivors have taken shelter. In the steel side of the liner doors have been cut, which opened and disgorged men, like some new Horse of Troy. But a tornado of shot and shell rained on her, and few of the 200 gallant men, who leaped from the lighters to the reef and from the reef to the sea, reached the land. Those who did have joined their fellows lying flat under the sand bank on that beach of death.

At Beach S, in Morto Bay, all has gone well. Seven hundred men of the South

NORMAN WILKINSON
Troops Landing on C Beach, Suvla Bay, Later in the Day, 7th August, 1915

Wales Borderers have been landed from trawlers, and have established themselves on the cliff tops at the place called De Totts Battery.

Let us go back to Gaba Tepe and look at the position at noonday. We are
prospering there, for more than 10,000 men are now ashore, and the work of
disembarking guns and stores goes on steadily, though the fire from inland is
still deadly. We see a proof of it in a boat full of dead men which rocks idly in
the surf. The great warships from the sea send their heavy shells against the
Turkish lines, seaplanes are "spotting" for them, and wireless stations are being
erected on the beach. Firing from the ships is not easy, for the morning sun
shines right in the eyes of the gunners. The Royal Engineers are making roads
up the cliff, and supplies are climbing steadily to our firing line. On the turf on
the cliff top our men are entrenched, and are working their way forward.
Unfortunately the zeal of the Australians has outrun their discretion, and some
of them have pushed too far on, looking for enemies to bayonet. They have
crossed three ridges, and have got to a point above Eskikeni within sight of the
Narrows. In that "pockety" country such an advance is certain death, and the
rash attack has been pushed back with heavy losses. The wounded are being
brought in, and it is no light task getting them down the cliffs on stretchers,
and across the beach and the bullet-splashed sea to the warships. Remember
that we are holding a position which is terribly conspicuous to the enemy, and
all our ammunition and water and food have to be dragged up those breakneck

cliffs. Still the first round has been won, Indian troops are being landed in support, and we are firmly placed at Gaba Tepe.

As we move down the coast we find that all goes well at Beaches Y and X, and that the troops there are working their way forward. The *Implacable* has knocked out of action a Turkish battery at Krithia which gave much annoyance to our men at Beach X. At Beach W we have improved our position. We have cleared the beach and driven the Turks out of the scrub at the valley foot, and the work of disembarking men and stores is proceeding. Our right wing – Worcesters and Lancashire Fusiliers – is working round by the cliffs above Cape Helles to try and enfilade the enemy who are holding Beach V, where our men are still in deadly jeopardy.

The scene at Beach V is strange and terrible. From the deep water the *Cornwallis* and *Albion* are trying to bombard the enemy at Sedd-el-Bahr, and the 15-inch shells from the *Queen Elizabeth* are screaming overhead. The Trojan Horse is still lying bow on against the reefs, with her 2,000 men unable to move, and the Turkish howitzers playing on her. If a man shows his head he is picked off by sharpshooters. The troops we have landed lie flat on the beach under cover of the sand ridge, unable to advance or retreat, and under a steady tornado of fire. Brigadier-General Napier has fallen, and Lieutenant-Colonel Carrington Smith, commanding the Hampshires. At Beach S things are satisfactory. Meantime the French landing at Kum Kale has achieved its purpose. Originally timed for 6 a.m., it did not take place till 9.30. They had a skirmish with the Turks, partly on the height at Kum Kale, and partly on the Trojan plain. Then they advanced along the swell of ground near the coast as far as Yenai Sheri. Next evening they re-embarked, and joined our right wing at Beach S. They took 500 prisoners, and could have taken more had there been room for them in the boats. The Turk, who showed himself a dauntless fighter when fighting was the order of the day, surrendered with great complaisance and good humour when the game was up. He had no crusading zeal in the business.

As darkness fell on that loud Sabbath, the minds of the Allied Staff may well have been anxious. We had gained a footing, but no more, and at the critical point it was but a precarious lodgment.

(Vol. VI pp. 183-93)

THE FIRST YEAR OF THE WAR

The completion of the first year of the war gave Buchan a chance to survey the first year's fighting.

IT IS desirable in the chronicle of a campaign to halt now and then and look backwards over the path we have travelled. This work is the more necessary in a history written at a short distance from events, and therefore compelled to take the form of annals, where facts must be set down in their temporal sequence, and no grouping is possible according to logical significance. It may be a help to a true perspective if we attempt a summary and an estimate of the doings of the year of war, which we may reasonably date from that Sunday, the 28th June, when the heir to the Austrian throne was murdered at Sarajevo.

The military results of the year must have seemed to any man, casting up the account on paper at some distance from the atmosphere of strife, an indisputable German triumph. Belgium, all but a small western fraction, lay captive, and was in process of Germanization. The rich industrial district of Lille, and all north-eastern France between the Oise and the Meuse, were occupied by her troops. She had battered down with ease the northern fortresses. She had driven a wedge across the Upper Meuse. The Woëvre was in her hands. Her battle front was only thirty miles from the gates of Paris. To set against this, the Allies had penetrated German territory for a small distance in Upper Alsace, but Alsace was not Germany in the sense that Picardy was France. Again, she held her conquests with a line of trenches which for eight months the Allies had endeavoured in vain to break. She had the high ground from Ypres to La Bassée; she had the crest of the Falaises de Champagne; and even positions which seemed precarious, like the St Mihiel salient, had proved so far impregnable. In August she had defeated the Allies in a series of great battles; and though thereafter her progress had been less positive, it was difficult to point to any counterbalancing Allied gain. It was true that her first plan had shipwrecked at the Marne, and her second on the bastion of Ypres; but she had made a third, and the third had prospered mightily. She was holding the Western front with fewer men than her opponents, and she was holding it securely. The much-vaunted efforts of Champagne, Les Eparges, the Artois, Neuve Chapelle, and Festubert had made only inconsiderable dints in her battle line. Moreover, she possessed, as she believed, the vantage ground for a fresh attack upon the Channel ports when she cared to make it. She had reaped the full benefit from the territory she had occupied. Belgium and north-eastern France had been bled white in her interests, and she was using their wealth and industrial organization to forge new weapons against her foes. The situation in the West, an impartial observer might have decided, was wholly advantageous to Germany. There she could keep off the enemy with her left hand while she struck with her right elsewhere.

But if German eyes could turn westward with a modest comfort on that 28th day of June, they looked eastward with something like exultation. There, surely, the age of miracles had dawned. The early disasters in East Prussia had been gloriously atoned for at Tannenberg. Von Hindenburg, after one failure, had secured all Western Poland. Austria had blundered at the start and lost the better part of Galicia, and for some months there had been anxious hearts in the Oder valley. But since the opening of the New Year all failures had been redeemed. East Prussia was inviolate, and German armies were hammering at the gates of Riga. Galicia had been won back, its great oil fields had been regained, and all menace to the cornlands of Hungary had gone. Further, with immense slaughter, the armies of Russia had been driven inside their own frontiers; the Warsaw triangle was being assailed, Warsaw seemed doomed, and it looked as if all Poland would soon be in German hands. Even if Germany was granted no Sedan in the East, she would have broken the Russian offensive for a year, and would presently be free to use half her Eastern armies to compel a decision in the West.

Her Allies had not distinguished themselves; but in the grip of the German machine even Austrian and Turk could march to victory. The threat from Italy did not disturb her. She knew the strength of the Austro-Italian frontier, and, even if Trieste fell, small harm would be done. The Allies were committed to an impossible enterprise at Gallipoli, where even success, in her eyes, would not atone for their desperate losses. She noted with approval that the Balkan States still maintained their uneasy neutrality. After her victories of the summer there would be small inducement for Romania, Bulgaria, and Greece to pledge their fortunes to a drooping cause. Even if they lost their heads, it would matter little. Germany had a supreme contempt for subsidiary operations. When she had crippled Russia, and broken France and Britain, she could deal at her leisure with any foolish Balkan princeling.

The naval position was less satisfactory. It was true that the German fleet was still intact in the sanctuary of the Heligoland Bight, but it was a weapon that might rust for want of use. The Allied navies had cleared her mercantile shipping from all the seas of the world. Her coasts were blockaded, and her breaches of international law had compelled Britain to rewrite the maritime code and to bear hard upon those neutrals in whom she had trusted. She had no ships of war anywhere except in her home waters, and the few occasions on which she had tried conclusions with Britain had not ended prosperously. Her submarines had, indeed, done marvels, but they were fruitless marvels. They had sent to the bottom a large number of Allied and neutral merchantmen, and had exasperated her enemies; but they had not seriously interfered with the sea-borne Allied commerce, and they had done nothing to relieve the blockade of

Germany. No doubt they had destroyed several Allied ships of war, and they had driven the big battleships from the Dardanelles; but thoughtful people in Germany were beginning to look with some disfavour on the submarine worship of which Admiral von Tirpitz was the hierophant. It was daring and brilliant; but it had not weakened the Allied navies or interfered with their operations, and it was raising ugly difficulties with America. On the general question of the rival Grand Fleets there was little difference of opinion. The war must be decided on land, and the victor there would impose his own terms as to the future of the seas. The British fleet had destroyed Germany's overseas trade, and there its activity ceased. If, in spite of it, Germany could obtain the requisite supplies, then the boasted naval predominance of Britain came to nothing. She would give Britain no occasion for a Trafalgar, and all the battleships on earth could not interfere with the decision on the Vistula or the Oise.

Her economic position, which some months earlier had occasioned much searching of heart, had now been clearly determined. Germany could still, through the complaisance of her enemies, receive certain foreign supplies, such as cotton, and for the rest she could make shift with her own productions. The Teutonic League was virtually self-supporting. All the mechanical skill of her engineers, all the learning and ingenuity of her chemists, were utilized. Her industrial life down to the smallest fraction was mobilized for war. Substitutes were invented for former imports, food supplies were organized and doled out under Government supervision, and all the machinery of her recent commercial expansion was switched on to the making of munitions. She was confident that she could maintain a far greater output than the Allies for a long enough period to ensure victory. As for her finances, she was living upon the certainty of that victory. Her internal credit, which was all that was needed, would last out the war. If she were beaten, then, indeed, she would be bankrupt on a colossal scale; but defeat did not enter into her calculations.

The position of the Teutonic League and Turkey, its ally, was gloomy enough outside Europe. The Turks, though they were doing well under German supervision in the Dardanelles, had been beaten in the Caucasus and in Mesopotamia, and their invasion of Egypt had ended in a fiasco. In the Far East the great German fortress of Tsing-tau, on which millions had been spent – her one foothold on the continent of Asia – had fallen to Japan. Her Pacific possessions had melted away like a mirage. In Africa the dreams of von Wissmann and Nachtigal were vanishing. Togoland was a British colony. The vital parts of the Cameroons were in British and French hands, and its German garrison had been forced far up into the inhospitable hinterland. In East Africa she was holding her own; but she could get no reinforcements there, and it could be only a question of time till her enemies pressed in the sides of the quadrilateral. In South Africa, on which she had counted, the situation was farcical. The rebellion had been a flash in the pan; General Botha had overrun and conquered German South-West territory; and the land which she had looked upon as a likely ally was preparing to send an expeditionary force to France. But she might well comfort herself with the reflection that the ultimate fate of those outland possessions would follow the decision of the European conflict, and she did not doubt what that decision would be.

The summary which we have given would have represented the view of an impartial outsider on 28th June, and, a little more highly coloured, that of the average thinking German. On the whole – the conclusion would have been – the honours of the first year of war lay with Germany. But if we are to judge the situation rightly, we must look beyond the bare facts to the policies of which they were the consequence. An outlook may seem roseate enough to everybody except the man who bears the responsibility. Mere successes do not signify much unless they represent stages in the realization of the central purpose. How far had Germany achieved her desires? Were the victories she had won bringing her nearer to that kind of result which alone would serve her purpose?

Germany's first plan of campaign had assumed a speedy decision. The Allies in the West were to be crushed by the Day of Sedan; and then, with France prostrate under her heel, she could turn eastwards and compel Russia to sue for peace. That dream of a "battle without a morrow" had died on the day in September when her great armies recoiled to the Aisne plateau. Then had come a new plan. The second offensive was to seize the Channel ports, take Paris from its northern side, terrorize Britain, and compel a settlement before winter had fully come. That scheme, too, had to be relinquished when, in the first week of November, odds of five to one failed to force the West Flanders gate. Thereupon, with admirable courage and amazing vitality, Germany adopted a third course. She consented in the West, and presently in the East also, to a war of attrition which went directly against her interests, for it wore down the one thing she could not replace – her numbers of men. But meanwhile she was busy piling up a weight of munitions which far exceeded the total complement of the Allies. The exact point of this policy should be noted. *It would enable her to hold her front, and even to take the offensive, with far fewer men than her enemies.* With its aid she could, though outnumbered, hold the front in the West, while she could destroy the Russian lines. It nullified not only the superior numbers of the Allies, but their superior fighting qualities. She could destroy them from a distance, as an undersized mechanic in an aeroplane might with bombs destroy a regiment of heroes. She had grasped with extraordinary precision the exact bearing of modern science upon modern warfare.

If we are to do justice to Germany's achievement, we must realize that this policy was the reverse of that with which she started. She began with an attempt to destroy her foes in manoeuvre battles. When that failed, she calmly and methodically revised her calculations, and adopted a new, difficult, and laborious scheme, which required immense efforts to set it in working order. That is the essence of a performance whose magnitude it is folly to decry.

This new plan of war involved a revision of her national purpose. The dream of sweeping like a new Timour over East and West, and dictating terms in a halo of glory was promptly relinquished. She saw herself condemned to a slow war which would give her enemies the chance of increasing their strength, of making that effort which she had made years before the first shots were fired. She resolved to turn the odds against her to her advantage. Russia and Britain might add millions to their first levies, and multiply their war supplies by twenty; but the business would be slow, for the Allies had not patiently organized themselves for war. If she could hold her own for two years, rifts would appear in the Allied lute. The populations, faced with unfamiliar problems involving novel sacrifices, would grow restive. Criticism would flourish, ministries and governments would fall into discredit, and half their efforts would be dissipated in idle quarrels. There was a chance, too, of serious differences arising between the Allied governments. One power would carp at the supineness of another; recriminations would follow, and then a division of energy. Germany hoped for much from the old difficulties that confront an alliance of equals. Her allies would give her little trouble, for they were not equals, and she was carrying their burden as well as her own.

Britain was the most dangerous enemy, because of her wealth and her manpower. But the longest purse will some day empty itself, and Germany noted with pleasure that Britain, who had to finance much of the Allied preparations, was conducting her expenditure with a wastefulness which must soon impoverish even her deep coffers. As for the British levies, however numerous and sturdy they might be, she comforted herself with the reflection that the British Staff had in the past been trained to handle only small forces, and would in all likelihood find the ordering of millions beyond its power. Her aim, it is clear, was no longer a sweeping conquest, but a draw which would leave her in possession of certain vantage points. This "white peace" would find her much depleted in men and money, but with a universal credit as by far the greatest military power in history. There would follow some years of recuperation, and then a second and successful stroke for the dominion of the world.

These calculations were not ill founded, and on the 28th day of June might well have seemed to impartial observers a just forecast. It is always hard to estimate fairly the achievement of an enemy. Our judgement is apt to follow our inclination till the moment of panic comes, when it follows our fears. In Germany we saw for the first time in history a great nation organized down to the humblest detail for war. No atom of national energy was dissipated in irrelevancies; every channel was tributary to one main purpose. The very faults of Prussianism in peace — its narrowness, its officialdom, its contempt for individual freedom — became assets in strife. If Germany fell it would be no fault of hers, for she had done all that mortal could do to deserve success.

But while it is right to estimate her achievement high, it is easy to put it too high. The machine had taken long years to create. If you have a docile people and a centralized and autocratic Government, and bend all your energies to the preparation for conquest, then you will create a far more efficient machine than your enemy, who has no thought of conquest and only a hazy notion of defence.

In a struggle such as this the only side which could be fully prepared was the side which had always contemplated war. The perfection of German methods stood out in relief against the unprofessional ways of the Allies rather than because of their intrinsic virtues, though these were great. As the campaign developed, evidence accumulated to prove that Germany had willed just such a war of conquest for more than two decades, and through years of peace had been toiling without rest to prepare the path. Her machine had been in working order for a generation, and against it there came only improvisations.

A few of Germany's preparations had grossly failed, and had defeated their own end. For nearly half a century her teachers had been endeavouring to get Europe to accept an idea of the Teutonic race as God's chosen people. Racial generalities are not an exact science, and this crusade led to some sad nonsense. But it made many converts. Historians in Britain and America fell victims to it, and decried for its sake the Slav and the Latin, and even in Italian schools under German influence there was an attempt to inculcate the worship of *Germanenthum*. The first whiff of grapeshot shattered these whimsies, and the laborious efforts of the pedants – outside Germany – went for nothing.

So, too, with the attempt on the part of the German governing class to infect the world with a new morality. The Nietzschean doctrine of force, which in peacetime was poisoning the springs of the world's thought, suddenly lost its appeal when war began. It lost its appeal even in Germany. The prophets of the new morality tumbled over each other to prove that they were still devotees of the old. Britain was blamed for actions which, if true, would have been precisely those which Treitschke and von Bernhardi had recommended to their countrymen; and the latter teacher was compelled to explain that he had been misunderstood, and had always been on the side of the old-fashioned angels. The German people were made to believe that they had Right on their side – copy-book, Scriptural Right – and they died confident in the same cause for which the Allies fought, and which to the later fashionable German moralists had been as foolishness.

The German preparation, then, was of small value, except that part of it which was the military machine. But it had had its effects, and the chief was to bring into being an antagonism which could not be measured merely by the Allied fleets and armies. The German leaders might persuade their obedient people that they stood for truth and righteousness, but to the eyes of the world their writings, their speeches, and above all their deeds, remained damning evidence to the contrary. There lay the chink in the shining German armour. No conquest in history has ever endured unless the conquerors brought to the conquered substantial benefits. The Romans gave law and security, Charlemagne gave peace, even the Turkish dominion in the late Middle Ages brought some order and comfort for the plain man. Still more true is it of the modern world, where education has disposed the majority of men to a critical habit. For Germany to win, she had to persuade not only neutrals but belligerents that an endless and terrible war was more dreadful than her victory. She had persuaded the world of the opposite. To three-fourths of mankind no price seemed too great to pay for her ruin. Even those who retained some kindliness for the rank and file of the German people were being driven to the conviction that their only hope of ultimate salvation was to endure a crushing defeat. Germany was playing now for a one-sided peace, but to win any kind of peace you must convince your opponents that the prospect is at least tolerable. She had by her conduct of the war and by her avowed purpose convinced the Allies that it was of all prospects the most intolerable. This indisputable truth, of which she seemed to have no recognition, vitiated all her plans. She had nothing to offer to the world as the price of acquiescence. She stood glaringly bankrupt in all that the better instinct of our mortal nature desires. The tragedy of Germany was far deeper than the tragedies of Poland and Belgium.

The position of the Allies on 28th June has already been sketched by implication in the preceding pages. There was no slackening of resolution, but to the ordinary man there was a very real dashing of hope. In Britain especially, where the contest had been entered upon in a spirit of exuberant optimism, the truth about the German machine had been slow to dawn upon the popular mind. We had sacrificed so much, we had raised and lost so many men, and now it seemed as if the effort had been fruitless. The talk about "organization", which political mentors used, perplexed and frightened the nation. To some timid souls it seemed Prussianism under another name. Could we beat our enemy only by adopting what we had been led to regard as that enemy's vices? And even those who desired to make the ultimate sacrifice did not know how to set about it. We clung to old constitutional watchwords about the "freedom of the individual", and attempted the ancient impossibility of crossing an unbridged river dryshod. The lack of any conspicuous national leadership intensified the confusion. The British people are not slow to recognize facts when they are once pointed out, but the recognition of facts is the rarest of virtues among politicians, who are accustomed to a particular game, and object to any tampering with the rules and counters. In a democracy such as ours the mass of the people are quicker to learn and wiser in the results than their professional leaders, who, accustomed to wait for a popular "cry" and "mandate", are rarely capable of that thinking and doing in advance which is the true function of leadership. But for opinion to percolate up from below takes time, and in the urgency of a crisis there is sore need of statesmen to initiate and lead. A democracy is rarely fortunate in its normal governors. That is why in the hour of need it is apt to seek a dictator.

The British people during a season of military set-backs had two difficulties to face which their Allies did not share. Both sprang from their previous lack of interest in military questions. A prosperous businessman will rarely take his adversary to the lawcourts. He will prefer to compromise even at some loss to his own pocket, for litigation is a waste of time and may give an undesirable publicity.It is the same with commercial nations like Britain and, in a far greater degree, the United States. They will always prefer, except in the very

C.R.W. NEVINSON *Dog Tired*

last extremity, to pay Danegeld rather than fight the Danes, and if they have to fight they regard their wealth as their principal asset. But conceive the case of a businessman who has unwillingly gone to law, announcing that if money can do it he will crush his opponent. Conceive the position of such a man when he suddenly finds that the litigation will deplete his balance, and that he may have great difficulty in paying the fees of the eminent counsel on whom he has set his heart. Yet about midsummer that was not unlike Britain's position. She realized in a blinding flash the enormous outlay to which she was committed, and understood that even her vast resources would be strained to meet it.

A second source of discouragement came from the extreme popular ignorance of the conditions of war. In every campaign there are critical, and even desperate moments, times of black uncertainty, obstacles which seem at the time insuperable. It is unnecessary to refer to the position of the North during the first two years of the American Civil War. Take even so small and simple a campaign as the Sudan War of 1898. The situation after the seizure of Berber, the chance of a night attack before Omdurman, and the position of Macdonald's brigade during the actual battle, were all matters to cause grave uneasiness to those in authority. In the ordinary campaign these anxious hours are experienced only by the Commander-in-Chief and his Staff. The public know nothing of them till long afterwards, when detailed histories are published. But in a war like the present, in spite of the paucity of official information, the movements were on so gigantic a scale that they stood out like large type. Every man understood when Paris or Warsaw was in peril, when the Allies failed, and when the Germans succeeded. Moreover, the movements were so long drawn out that instead of critical hours, as in other campaigns, they involved critical weeks. In France and Russia the ordinary educated man had the rudiments of military knowledge which the average Briton lacked. He was aware that war has its ups and downs, that what seem gigantic losses may have little influence on the ultimate decision, and that what seems a glowing success is often the preliminary to failure. In Britain we did not know these things, civilians having rarely interested themselves in the science of war, and consequently the inevitable chances and mischances of the campaign presented themselves to us in darker colours than the truth.

One thing all the Allies had in common – an organization far less perfect than the Germans, and less natural capacity for such organization. There lay their weakness, which no taking thought could wholly remedy. We have seen what Germany did with her unequally-yoked allies, putting precision into the Turks and homogeneity into the Austrian legions, and turning every economic advantage of her colleagues to the profit of the whole. France, Russia, Italy, and Britain, though in spirit far more united than the Teutonic League, had by 28th June still failed to pool their assets scientifically, and to make full use of their advantages of position. The buying of war stores by the different Powers was still often at cross purposes. Events proved that the different strategic plans had not been perfectly harmonized, and that the vital matter of munitions was not treated as one problem, concerning not Russia and Britain as individuals, but the whole Allied front. It is true that much had been done by conferences to make the financing of the war uniform; but even in this sphere Germany would have carried the policy further. She would have devised that which Pitt appealed for in the House of Commons in 1783, "a complete economic system adapted to the new features of the situation." Had France, Russia, Italy, Britain, Japan, Belgium, and Serbia formed themselves into an economic league to control all matters of international commerce, a formidable weapon would have been prepared against their enemies and a powerful lever to influence the policy of hesitating neutrals.

The great asset of the Allies was their unity of purpose and singleness of heart. They had agreed to make peace as one Power, and they were wholly resolved to make no peace which should be indecisive. When Charles XII of Sweden was faced, at the age of eighteen, with an attack by three armies, he told his council: "I have resolved never to engage in an unjust war, but, on the other hand, never to conclude a just one but by the ruin of my foes." In that spirit all the Allies now faced the future. Their situation was far stronger than could be gathered from a map of rival positions. Every day was adding to the numbers of their armies, while very soon every day must lessen the numbers of the enemy. They were moving towards the construction of a machine as strong as the German – gropingly and slowly, it is true, but steadily. Time was still on their side. No one of their armies had been destroyed. Their losses, great as they were, had been made good. More and more, in the eyes not only of soldiers but of politicians and peoples, it was clear that Germany would be defeated only by the destruction of her field armies, and that all her gains of territory were irrelevant except in so far as they postponed that purpose. Hence the conquests which exhilarated Berlin were borne by the Allies – even by those at whose expense they had been made – with a certain robust philosophy. A lion is the less dangerous to an African village when it has gorged itself upon a portion of the herds.

What Germany had fondly counted upon had not come to pass. The Allies were working harmoniously, in spite of the most strenuous Teutonic efforts to stir up strife. Peripatetic German agents in Britain attempted to set labour and capital by the ears; their cousins in France whispered to the French people how infamous it was that Britons should be going on strike in such a crisis, and insisted on the shortness of the British line; while others in Russia, helped by the dregs of the Baltic-German bureaucracy, quoted certain unfortunate witticisms of French generals, pointed to the stagnation in the West, and observed that France would resist no doubt to the last drop of blood, but that that blood would be Russian. On the surface it looked as if the field for mischief-making were clear. But three forces combined to make the seeds of strife sown by Germany fall upon unreceptive ground. The first was the gravity of the crisis and the intense antagonism which Germany had inspired. Men engaged in what they believe to be a holy war are the less inclined to be captious about their colleagues. The second was the goodwill between the Allied armies brought about by the sincere admiration felt by each for the performance of the others. The memories of the Marne and Ypres and Le Cateau, of Rava Russka, Augustovo, and Przasnysz, were the best preventives of a carping spirit. Most important of all, each of the Allies was profoundly conscious of its short-comings, and was more disposed to criticize its own unpreparedness than that of its neighbours. Each was busy setting its house in order. In Britain, as we have seen, the Government was reconstructed, and there was a zealous inquest for administrative ability. In Russia certain effete and corrupt elements were ruthlessly weeded out. In France there was least change, for the great change had been made on that August day when Paris was threatened and government migrated from the politicians to the soldiers. Since then the rock-like figure of General Joffre had been enthroned in the confidence of his countrymen.

This modesty, admirable in itself, might, if carried too far, have conduced to those evil results on which Germany counted. She cunningly hoped that a spirit of doubt and disquiet would go abroad among the Allies, and lead to the fall of Ministers and the "ungumming" of generals. In Britain, where, since the popular voice was most easily audible, criticism might have been most expected, we sinned little in this respect. Indeed, under the influence of Lincoln's saying about "swapping horses in the middle of the stream", we were inclined to be almost too tolerant of proved administrative incompetence and too chary of even well-informed and patriotic criticism. It is a mistake to change horses in the middle of the ford; but if the horse can only lie down, change is necessary to avoid drowning. The fact that competent critics were patriotically silent left the necessary task of public watchfulness to men who had small authority in the nation.

The position of neutral states on that 28th of June was still obscure. Italy had joined the Allies, but the Balkan nations – the only ones remaining whose decision from a military point of view was vital – were still perplexed by contradictory interests. In Greece, though M. Venezelos had won a victory at the polls, he was not yet in office, and his country was as yet uncommitted. Bulgaria had come to a railway agreement with Turkey, but had shown no signs of joining the Teutonic League. Nor had she settled those territorial difficulties with Greece and Serbia, which might have brought her in on the Allies' side. Romania, though undoubtedly influenced by Italy's decision, was still keeping an anxious eye on Bulgaria. She did her best to preserve a strict aloofness, and refused to allow officially the passage of war munitions to Turkey through her territory.

Germany had counted on her victories in Galicia and Poland to fix for ever Balkan neutrality. But it is probable that she calculated wrongly, and that von Mackensen's sweep to the San had the opposite effect from that which she hoped for. No one of the neutral Balkan states desired war. Each would have preferred that the Allies should do all the fighting. But the one prospect they could not face with equanimity was a triumphant Germany. That would mean the end of Romania's hopes of Transylvania, of Bulgaria's Macedonian aspirations, of Greece's dreams of the hegemony of the Aegean. In all likelihood it would mean at no distant date the end of the little Balkan nationalities altogether, for

ERIC KENNINGTON *The Kensingtons at Laventie*

Austria and Germany would create a Teutonic belt to the Persian Gulf.

The United States, whose markets provided the Allies with war materials, was finding her position one of great and growing difficulty. President Wilson's policy, though expressed by him in an academic phraseology which seemed curiously inept in such a crisis, was based upon a judicial view of American interests. The pitfalls which beset her path were not fairly estimated by European observers. But Germany seemed determined to make neutrality impossible. The sinking of the *Lusitania* drew a strong protest from the American Government. This protest brought about the resignation of the Foreign Secretary, Mr Bryan, who had spent his life in a world of emotional verbiage. To this protest on behalf of neutrals against the barbarity of her submarine practices, Germany replied defiantly. Several Notes were exchanged, and – to anticipate a little – in the middle of July Mr Lansing, Mr Bryan's able successor, presented what would have been regarded by the older diplomacy as an ultimatum. He laid down three uncontrovertible principles: that the high seas are free to neutral ships; that this freedom can only be interfered with after the character and cargo of the ship has been ascertained; and that the lives of non-combatants can only be lawfully endangered if the vessel seeks to escape after summons or attempts resistance. A repetition of the breaches of these principles of which Germany had been guilty would, said the Note, be regarded as an unfriendly act. Germany, through her Press, replied with an arrogant disdain; and a few days after the receipt of the Note her submarines sank an American steamer off the Orkney Islands. The atmosphere was electric, but what with another Power would have meant an immediate declaration of war did not necessarily involve such a consequence in the case of the United States. Her diplomatists had never regarded "terms of art" in the European way, and the phrase "unfriendly act", which elsewhere was the wording of an ultimatum, was with her only a strong type of protest.

Relations with Britain were also, in spite of very real goodwill on both sides, moving to an impasse. In March, it will be remembered, the British Government declared a blockade of Germany – a blockade which, since it could not be made fully effective, was not in accord with the accepted principles of international law. It decreed the seizure and confiscation of non-contraband goods of German origin, ownership, or destination carried in neutral ships to neutral ports, though Britain did not propose to apply the rule with any technical rigour. This practice involved a considerable breach of the recognized code of maritime law, a breach which Britain justified by the exceptional character of the circumstances and by the international anarchism of Germany, and defended on the precedent of the novel methods adopted by America during the Civil War . . . There was a great deal to be said for the British contention; there was much to be said for the American counterplea. But obviously so grave a matter could not depend only on the argumentation of international lawyers and the Foreign Offices which employed them. The plain facts were that America was seriously affected by British policy in perhaps her most vital interest – her cotton export. She saw her trade with enemy countries and to some extent with neutral countries hampered, and this on a plea which was manifestly at variance with accepted international practice. It did not convince the Southern planter to be told that the North in the Civil War also had done something in the way of rewriting international law. America was on strong ground, and she knew it, and she pressed her claims with much force during the summer months. It was gradually becoming apparent that the British plan, though reasonable enough in itself, would have to be modified.

Cotton was the chief difficulty, and three steps were pressed upon the Government as a solution. The first was to declare cotton contraband. It was clear that it was a most vital munition of war, since it was practically essential to the manufacture of nitro-cellulose, the basis of most modern propellent charges. It was perfectly true that to declare cotton contraband would have given us no weapon to restrict its import to Germany beyond what we had at present, though we should have been able not only to stop but to confiscate cargoes. But, combined with the doctrine of continuous voyage, it would have given us an authority which America could recognize. She herself had declared cotton contraband in her Civil War, and on the facts it was now a military munition like sulphur and saltpetre in former days. In the second place, it was suggested that neutral states might be put on rations, and that we might permit only a certain amount of cotton to be consigned to them, based on their average consumption for the three years before the war. Finally there was a proposal to purchase that portion of the American cotton crop which was normally exported to the enemy countries, and to hold it till after the war. The cost was usually estimated at some £30,000,000.

The importance of the question was as great as its intricacy. On 28th June it was the foremost problem we had to face in connection with our policy towards neutrals, and, since America was the munitioning ground of all the Allies, it vitally affected the whole Allied cause. The wheels of diplomacy move slowly, and the months passed without a solution. Happily the goodwill of the majority of the American people, and the genuine anxiety of the Ministers on both sides of the Atlantic to reach an agreement, prevented the controversy reaching the stage of crisis.

In reviewing a year of war we look naturally to see what new military doctrines have justified themselves, what novel methods in tactics and strategy have appeared in the various theatres. We find nothing revolutionary, nothing at variance with the accepted practices of war. Strategically, all the German prepossessions about envelopment, if they ever existed, had died a sudden death with the opening of trench warfare. Of the main German doctrines, one only was clearly justified, and by those who had reflected on the subject it had never been seriously denied. That doctrine was the crushing effect of artillery both against forts and field positions. The German practice of massed infantry attacks had nothing in itself to recommend it; when it succeeded it was only because of the artillery preparation which preceded it. It was less a device deliberately selected than a *concessio propter infirmitatem*, necessary to armies which had to absorb into their ranks, as the war went on, much inferior fighting material.

Even as regards artillery the special German merit was not their tactical handling of it, but their ample supply. Heavy field pieces and machine guns in great quantities involve certain tactics, as inevitably as the length of reach of a boxer determines his method. The supreme achievement of the German Staff was that they saw precisely the part modern science could be made to play in modern warfare, and that they kept their eyes resolutely fixed on it. Since they were organized for war not only militarily but industrially, they could concentrate as a nation upon a single purpose in a way impossible to the freer civic organisms of their opponents. Germany made use of all her assets; her blow was weighted with her full national strength – that, in a sentence, was the gist of her excellence.

Some of the details of her machine were open to serious criticism not only on moral but on military grounds. Poison gas and liquid fire had momentarily a great success, but it may well be questioned whether they did not defeat their own ends. Apart from the fact that there was no special skill required in their use, and that the Allies if they chose could retaliate in kind, the fact that Germany was a pioneer in such methods was bound to exacerbate the feelings of her opponents – an unfortunate result for a Power which in the long run must play for a draw. On the general moral question it is foolish to dogmatize. Gas and fire were innovations, and seemed atrocious devices to the Allies. But it is doubtful whether the suffering they caused was greater than the suffering from shell-fire. A man who died in torture under chlorine might have suffered equal agony from a shrapnel wound. All the arguments against them might have been used with as much force by the mediaeval knight against gunpowder, by the old footsoldier against high explosives, by the savage warrior against Maxims. The true point is that the innovation was not so much barbarous – all war is barbarous – as impolitic. Unless his weapon is so powerful as to break down all opposition, the innovator may find that he rouses a storm of resentment which nullifies the value of his devices. Again, Germany's machine had this further drawback, that it disposed her soldiers to trust too much to it, and thereby weakened individual initiative and stamina. Here, again, if Germany were to be for all time the sole owner of such a machine, this defect would hurt her little. But if her opponents could sooner or later create a similar machine, then the struggle would lie between the human factors, and hers would *ex hypothesi* have been weakened.

The Allies on the whole might claim that their theories of war had been justified whenever it had been possible to apply them. The attack in open order, and their high standard of individual rifle-fire, provided good results whenever the enemy's guns allowed fighting at close quarters. Man for man, the average Frenchman, Russian, and Briton had demonstrated his superiority to the German soldier. It was not a question of courage, for the bravery of the German ranks could not be over-praised, but rather of dash, fortitude, stamina, and that indefinable thing which we might call temperamental predominance. This was conspicuously proved in bayonet work, in bomb-throwing, and especially in our most daring and successful aerial reconnaissance. Wherever individual qualities were demanded there the Allies were conspicuous. Our fighting machine, too, so far as it concerned the human element, was at least as good as the German. It was only in material, in the scientific aids to war, that we were excelled, and then only in one class of weapon, which, however, happened to be the most vital.

Summaries are apt to be fallacious, but if we were to summarize the military position on 28th June – the true military position independent of territorial gains – we might say that Germany possessed a machine strong in material but declining in manpower, while the Allied mechanism was conspicuous in its

AUSTIN O. SPARE *After an Attack*

manpower, and weaker, but slowly moving towards an equality, in its material. On the 28th of June optimism was out of fashion; but none the less, on a dispassionate survey of the case, the conclusion for the Allies would have been optimistic.

At the heart of the matter lay the question of numbers. Germany in that respect was on the crest, or had already passed it, of her maximum effort. Her wonderful organization might add indefinitely to the number of her shells, but it could not call the dead from their graves. She must inevitably decrease, the Allies must increase, and, though her artillery machine would allow her yet awhile to hold her front with fewer men, this possibility would shrink as the Allies perfected their equipment. The true estimate of the position on 28th June involved some understanding of the losses of the combatants, and the numbers still available. Unfortunately, even for the high commands, this question was still in the realm of conjecture. A few figures were certain. According to the British Prime Minister, the British casualties up to the middle of July, excluding the operations in German South-West Africa, were 330,995, of which some 70,000 were killed. France published no statement, but an unofficial estimate up to the end of June gave 400,000 killed, 700,000 disabled, and 300,000 prisoners, a total of 1,400,000. The Russian casualty list was very large, and if we are to credit German figures, after making all allowance for their notoriously swollen estimates of prisoners, we should probably put it at well over 3,000,000. The personal losses of the Allies for the year would seem to have reached a figure greater than 4,500,000 but less than 5,000,000. The German losses, according to the calculation of the French Staff, would in the same period have been something over 3,000,000. But the figure only allowed for the normal rate of wastage – 260,000 a month – and in May and June this must have been more than doubled, what with the fighting in the Artois and the great Galician advance. We should probably not be far wrong in putting Germany's permanent loss as between 3,500,000 and 4,000,000. The Austrian casualties were only guesswork, but we know that Russia and Serbia had 700,000 prisoners, and a cautious estimate gave the dead loss in killed and wounded as 1,500,000. Leaving out Turkey, we should probably have been justified in putting the losses – the irreplaceable losses – of the Teutonic League up to 28th June at well over 5,000,000, and those of the Allies at something less than 5,000,000.

But the real question was not how many had fallen, but how many remained? France, on the admission of her General Staff, was able to fight for another year, allowing for her normal wastage, without weakening any of her field units. Britain could in the next year at least double her forces in the field, and supply all necessary drafts. It was announced that Russia at the beginning of July had, apart from her field armies, a reserve for new formations and drafts of over 6,000,000 untrained and partially trained men. If we allow Italy to balance Turkey – an allowance which scarcely does justice to our ally – we reach the conclusion that after a year of war the Teutonic League, in spite of all its artillery preparation, had lost absolutely more men than the Allies, and had nothing like the vast Allied reservoirs from which they could be replaced. The few people who in the end of June cared to work out the calculations found a reasoned justification for their confidence in the Allies' future.

The naval position demands a very brief note. It was wholly in favour of the Allies. In all the seas of the world German merchantmen and German ships of war had disappeared. In the north-eastern corner of the Adriatic, Italy held the Austrian fleet; in the Aegean, the British and French fleets were operating against the Dardanelles. The one German success, the Battle of Coronel, had been promptly redeemed by von Spee's destruction at the Falkland Islands. The German Grand Fleet lay behind the shelter of the Frisian Islands. The battle of the Bight of Heligoland showed that Britain could carry the war inside German territorial waters, and the one serious German raid had been checked and defeated in the battle of 24th January. The boasted German submarine campaign had effected nothing of a military purpose, except the withdrawal of the larger British battleships from the Dardanelles. Up to a date early in July it had sunk 98 British merchantmen – or 195 if we include trawlers – 30 Allied ships, and less than 50 neutrals, and had thereby raised international difficulties for Germany which far out-balanced these trivial successes. The British losses by submarines were only about 1 ¼ per cent of our total shipping, and the new risk did not raise insurance rates or affect in the slightest degree the nerve of our merchant seamen. The boasts of the German Press were conclusively answered by Mr Balfour in a letter to an American correspondent – a letter which states with admirable clearness and justice the achievements of the British navy.

The British Grand Fleet during the year was, like the country of the proverb, happy in that it had no history. Without any of the great battleships firing a shot it had fulfilled its task. Its mere existence gave security to our commerce and a free hand to our lighter squadrons, and kept the enemy inside his harbours. Its potent inaction was not idleness. It was ready and anxious to meet its opponent as soon as he ventured forth. But till that day came it held the seas and waited, as Nelson's fleet for two years before Trafalgar watched the coasts of the enemy. How great a strain this duty involved is beyond a civilian's estimate. Day and night the great ships kept the sea, in the stormy winter months steaming without lights in black darkness, with the perpetual menace of mines and submarines around them. They were hidden from the nation's gaze. No achievements filled the papers. There was nothing to relieve the tedium of their toil or key the spirit of their men to that high pitch which is the reward of war. In months of danger and heavy labour they had to endure something worse than the monotony of peace. Yet we know that the Grand Fleet kept its health unimpaired, its nerves steady, its eagerness unabated. Such a moral achievement was not the least of the triumphs of the year, for he that ruleth his spirit is better than he that taketh a city.

In modern warfare it would seem that the period of waiting must be longer, for modern warfare sinks the individual in the machine. Just as industrialism tends to turn the craftsman into a mere machine-tender, so the latest developments of war transform the soldier into a kind of operative. Till the other day we were accustomed to speak of "fighting races" – of men like the tribesmen of the Indian frontier, or the Boers – whose life had given them a natural hardihood, an eye for country, quick senses, and great bodily endurance, and to contrast with them the products of urban civilization who were born with none of these gifts. But it looks as if we must revise our views. Our new war machine abolishes, or at any rate greatly modifies, the distinction between martial and non-martial peoples. The ideal soldier would appear to be the skilled mechanic, who gets his fortitude partly from a high discipline and partly from confidence in his machine. The noble savage with the spear has fallen before the lesser physique of civilization armed with a rifle. Now it would seem that the soldier, trained in the various branches of the military art, and full of valour and self-reliance, must yield to the pasty operative who can handle at a distance the levers and bolts of a great gun.

In the same way modern warfare gives small chance for individual generalship. Surprises, night marches, ingenious feints are seldom possible. The conditions are rigidly prescribed, and can rarely be dominated and altered by the most fertile mind. The general has also become a machine-tender. The brains – the genius, if you will – are to be found in the construction of the machine, for its use is more or less a mechanical task. Some men will be more skilled in it than others, but the highest skill is not the same thing as generalship in the old sense. A Marlborough, a Caesar, even a Napoleon, would beat ineffectual wings against the new barriers.

All this is true, and those who declaimed during the campaign against the absence of genius in generalship forgot that generalship, like other arts, needs the proper occasion. Supply will scarcely be forthcoming if the demand is nil. In former days war was three-fourths an art and one-fourth a science. Now it is at least three-fourths science, and the human element is circumscribed . . . Yes, but not wholly, and not in the last resort. For a machine is not immortal. It may break down through internal weakness, or because it is confronted with a machine of equal strength. When that day comes war will become an art once more, and individual generalship and individual fighting quality will recover their old pre-eminence.

✳ ✳ ✳

The year which ended on 28th June had revealed a war less of the high commands than of subordinate leaders. Trench fighting and the importance of artillery combined to annul all major strategy, and put the main burden on the brigadiers, the battalion and company commanders, and even on the subalterns. There were many chances for individual gallantry, but few and rare were

WILLIAM HATHERELL *The Last Message*

the occasions when officers, from subalterns to generals, could earn distinction by initiative or special military knowledge. In the stalemate on the West war was reduced to very primitive elements, and the débâcle in the East submerged human skill under a shower of shell. Such was the inevitable result of modern scientific war in its early phases.

But the wheel came full circle, and that very science, which depressed the human factor, contrived in its extreme developments to make it the more conspicuous. For a sphere where courage and brains found full scope we must look to the most expert warfare of all — the work of the submarine and aeroplane. There the possession of one kind of machine took a man out of the grip of the Machine, and set him adventuring in a free world, as in the old days of war.

(Vol. VIII pp. 9-45, 51-52)

THE SUMMER'S WAR IN THE AIR

This extract continues Buchan's almost day-by-day history of the war in the air, covering the summer of 1915

SPRING AND summer brought easier conditions for the air services of the belligerent Powers; but the comparative stagnation in the Western theatre, where the service had been most highly developed, prevented any conspicuous action by this arm. The work of the winter in reconnaissance and destruction went on, and the story is rather of individual feats than of any great concerted activity. The importance of the air had revealed itself, and all the combatants were busied with new construction. In Britain we turned out a large number of new machines. We experimented with larger types, and we perfected the different varieties of aerial bomb. The Advisory Committee on Aeronautics, containing some of the chief scientists of the day, solved various difficult problems, and saw to it that theory kept pace with practice. We added largely to the number of our airmen. At the beginning of the war we had only the Central Flying School, capable of training at one time twenty pupils; by midsummer we had eleven such schools, able to train upwards of two hundred. The enemy aeroplanes began to improve in speed and handiness, but where Germany advanced an inch we advanced an ell. Admirable as was the air work of all the Allies, the British service, under its brilliant Director-General, Sir David Henderson, had reached by midsummer a height of efficiency which was not exceeded by any other branch of the Army or Navy.

To a student of military affairs it seemed amazing that a department only a few years old, and with less than one year's experience of actual war, should have attained so soon to so complete an efficiency and so splendid a tradition. Perhaps it was the continuous demand upon nerve and intelligence. Young men gathered from all quarters and all professions became in a little while of one type. They had the same quiet voices, the same gravity, the same dull blue eyes, with that strange look in them that a man gets from peering into infinite space. The air, like the deep sea, seemed to create its own gentility, and no service had ever a more perfect breeding. Its tradition, less than a year old, was as high and stiff as that of any historic regiment. Self-advertising did not exist. In the military wing, at any rate, no names were mentioned; any achievement went to the credit of the corps, not of the aviator, unless the aviator were killed. Its members spoke of their profession with a curious mixture of technical wisdom and boyish adventure. The flying men made one family, and their *esprit de corps* was as great as that of a battleship. To spend some time at their headquarters at the front was an experience which no one could forget, so complete were the unity and loyalty and keenness of every man and officer. To be with them of an evening when they waited for the return of their friends, identifying from far off the thresh of the different propellers, was to realize the warm camaraderie born of a constant facing of danger. In the air service neither body nor mind dared for one second to be stagnant, and character responded to this noble stimulus.

The most vital task of aircraft was reconnaissance – the identification of gun positions, the mapping of enemy entrenchments, the detection of the movement of troops. This work was important as a preliminary tc any Allied attack. By its means artillery could be concentrated against an enemy position, while the concentration passed unobserved because of the ascendency established by our airmen. The actions of Neuve Chapelle, Festubert, and the Artois were all preceded by an elaborate aerial reconnaissance. Photography was brought into use, and maps taken from the air revealed the nature of the enemy's defences. As the weeks passed, certain imperfections, inevitable imperfections, were apparent in the results thus obtained. Photographs could only be taken from a fairly high elevation, and, while they showed the main lines of a hostile position, they could not provide the details with any certainty. For example, they could not show which trenches were occupied and which were not, and they could not distinguish between a trench and a watercourse. On the second day at Festubert our troops found themselves faced during a night attack with a stream fifteen feet broad and ten feet deep, for which the most careful aerial reconnaissance had failed to prepare them.

But in spite of defects, which were the fault of the conditions and not of the service, the Allied air work was splendid both in its boldness and in its fruitfulness. Its keynotes were complete resolution and absolute devotion. No risk was considered too high. An enemy when he appeared was engaged, whatever the odds. In this sphere, where individual nerve and skill were predominant, there could be no question of the Allied superiority. But as our skill and boldness increased, the enemy's defences multiplied. His anti-aircraft guns made good shooting, and hits could be made at an elevation of two miles. These, of course, were outside chances, but it was observed that wherever the guns had frequent opportunities of practice – as at places like Nieuport, Dixmude, and Ypres – their accuracy became remarkable. A French aviator reported: "They waste a lot of ammunition against us, as every time we go out they fire between 300 and 400 shells at each of us. But as a rule they place all their shots within 100 or 150 yards of our machines." The risk of our airmen was rather from guns on land than from enemy aeroplanes, which rarely showed much enterprise or skill. An airman was in danger of having his control wires cut or his petrol tank pierced and being compelled to descend behind the German lines; in which case his escape was unlikely, for it was not easy to re-start an engine single-handed.

Considering the multiplicity of dangers, it is wonderful how few were the casualties of the corps. A letter from an airman gives a picture of what were everyday occurrences: "I was flying a rotten old machine, with an engine that ran very badly, and was missing from the time I left the ground. Under ordinary circumstances I should have landed again immediately, but it was an important reconnaissance, so I had to do it. The highest I could get the machine to was 4,700 feet, and then as I flew towards the lines I could see our other machines up getting a hot time from 'Archie'. [The British soldiers' name for the anti-aircraft gun.] They were flying between 7,000 and 8,000 feet, and as soon as I was within range the Germans opened on my machine; and then during the whole of the reconnaissance, which consisted of circling about a small area, they didn't give me a moment's peace. I had shells bursting around my machine the whole time; simultaneously flashes of flame and loud bangs, sometimes on one side and sometimes on the other, below the machine, above it, behind, and in front, and some of them bumped the machine about unpleasantly. It was thoroughly uncomfortable. I twisted the machine about this way and that, made side-slips outwards, and did everything I could to spoil their aim, but they kept me guessing the whole time. One shell exploded just in front, and I saw some bits of things flying off the engine, and thought the propeller was gone. I was very glad when the reconnaissance was over. On landing, I found that the machine had been hit by rifle-fire as well as by shrapnel . . . Yesterday I was up for over an hour trying to get a reconnaissance, but there was mist from 400 feet up, and from 3,000 feet thick clouds, in which I was awfully knocked about by bumps. After flying some time at a bit under 5,000 feet, I thought I was behind our lines, and shut off the engine and glided down to 3,000 feet, and, when I could see the ground, found I was well behind the German lines. They must have laughed when they saw the machine unsuspectingly appearing out of the clouds, and they greeted me with a tremendous fusilade of rifle-fire and some 'Archies', that didn't, however, come very near. I got into the clouds again as soon as I could, but had a warm time in doing it. They only succeeded in hitting the machine once or twice."

To watch the work in the air over any section of our trench lines was on most days an exciting experience. Far behind, flying at an altitude of 7,000 feet, would appear a British aeroplane. As soon as it crossed the front the bombardment began from rifles, machine guns, and anti-aircraft guns. White clouds with yellow hearts dotted the blue sky around the aeroplane – generally fairly distant, if it was flying high, but sometimes seeming to obscure it altogether. Unperturbed, the aviator kept on his way to Belgium. An hour or two later, his reconnaissance completed, he returned to the accompaniment of the same fusilade, and disappeared in the direction of some flight or squadron station behind the British lines. Presently a German *aviatik* would appear on the same errand. As it crossed our trenches it was saluted by our "Archibalds" and Maxims. Then suddenly from the west, driving up into the heavens with swift bounds, came a British plane. The two manoeuvred for the upper position, but the superior handling of our machine gave it the victory. The invader turned

C.R.W. NEVINSON *Archies*

and made for his own lines, followed by the Briton, and from far above, till it was drowned in the roar of the trench Maxims, could be heard the sound of the conflict in the air. If our man was lucky the German machine might suddenly head for the ground, the pilot killed, or the engine broken, and land a wreck behind the German lines. It was difficult to judge the result of these combats, for the invaders came so small a distance into British territory that, when crippled, they usually managed to descend on their own ground. But of the Allied superiority, both in defence and attack, there was never the slightest doubt. It is said that a young German airman in the early days of the war asked how he would know a British machine if he met it. "Oh, you'll know it right enough," was the reply. "It will attack you."

An instance of the skill and intrepidity of our airmen was the performance of Captain L. G. Hawker. Captain Hawker, who had received the Distinguished Service Order for his bombardment of a German airship shed at Gontrode on 19th April, fell in on 25th July with three enemy aeroplanes. All three were armed with machine guns, and each carried a passenger as well as a pilot. The first managed to escape eventually; the second was driven to the ground in a damaged condition; and the third, which he attacked at a height of 10,000 feet, was completely destroyed, both pilot and observer being killed. Captain Hawker received the Victoria Cross.

The French activity in the air corresponded in its main lines to the British. Their aviators made reconnaissances daily along the 500 miles of front. During eight months of war it was calculated that the French had made 10,000 reconnaissances, corresponding to 18,000 hours of flight, and representing a distance equal to forty-five times round the world. On 2nd April, for example, apart from seven bombardments, their work included forty-five reconnaissances and twenty range corrections. Just as the submarine and airship bases at Flanders were the main British objective, so the French directed their chief efforts to the bases of south-eastern Germany.

The main feats of destruction may be briefly chronicled. On 8th February, in a heavy gale, a French airman dropped bombs on an ammunition column near Middelkerke, and then bombarded the Kursaal at Ostend. In order to escape the searchlights and the German guns he was driven out to sea, and descended low enough to feel the spray of the waves. Early in March the powder works at Rottweil were destroyed – a fine achievement, for the place is on the other side of the Black Forest, and nearly 100 miles from Belfort as the crow flies. On 26th March the airship sheds of Frescaty and the station of Metz were bombarded from the air. During the April fighting in the Woëvre, Vigneulles, the nodal point of German communications and an important air station, was constantly attacked by French aeroplanes; while on 19th April a single airman attacked the airship shed near Ghent and caused a heavy explosion. At the same time Pégoud was busy in Champagne, and brought down his third German aeroplane in the neighbourhood of St Menehould. On 28th April Friedrichshafen was attacked, and a Zeppelin damaged in its shed.

On 27th May an important raid was undertaken. A French squadron composed of eighteen aeroplanes attacked the chemical factory at Ludwigshafen, the Badische Anilin und Soda Fabrik, the most important factory of explosives in Germany. The aviators dropped eighty-five bombs, and kindled three enormous fires, which must have destroyed a large part of the works. June was a busy month in the air. On 3rd June, very early in the morning, twenty-nine French airmen bombarded the headquarters of the Imperial Crown Prince. On 9th June there was a raid on Brussels, and on 15th June, as a reprisal for the bombardment of open French and British towns, an attack was made upon Karlsruhe, the capital of the Grand Duchy of Baden. Twenty-three French aeroplanes arrived above the city just before 6 a.m.; 130 bombs were dropped on the castle, the arms factory, and the railway station. Many fires broke out, and a wild panic was created. The German Press fell into transports of fury over the episode, and the Kaiser telegraphed his "deep indignation at the wicked attack on beloved Karlsruhe." Karlsruhe had a garrison of 4,000 men, and so was infinitely less of an open town than Scarborough or Whitby. The French enterprise was definitely undertaken as a reprisal, and does not appear to have infringed the accepted rule as to reprisals, that they should not be disproportionate to the offence committed by the enemy.

In July the chief episodes were determined by the nature of the land campaign. During the Crown Prince's attack in the Argonne all the hinterland was heavily bombarded, especially such vital points as Vigneulles and Conflans. Colmar station was also attacked as an incident in the Vosges campaign. Later in the month French aeroplanes bombarded a factory in Alsace engaged in the production of asphyxiating gas, the station of Freiburg, the petrol works between Hagenau and Weissenburg, the station at Dettweiler, and the aviation sheds of Pfalzburg.

The French losses during the summer were small considering their constant activity. The brilliant aviator, Jean Benoist, was accidentally killed on 29th July. On 19th April Roland Garros, perhaps the most famous figure in the French service, was forced to land behind the German lines in West Flanders. Three days before he had performed one of his most remarkable feats. A German aeroplane had been reported to be heading for Dunkirk, and Garros gave chase. Reserving his fire until he was within twenty yards of the enemy, he shot both pilot and observer dead with two shots, and the derelict German machine was presently dashed to fragments. Late in August, to the profound regret of all lovers of gallant men, Pégoud was killed in Alsace by a shot in the air. For twelve months he had served continuously, and no man had ever a nobler roll of achievements.

* * *

The summer was punctuated with Zeppelin raids, which vied with the submarine exploits in their fascination for the German public. With its curious grandiosity of mind, that public chose to see in the sudden descent of the mighty engine of destruction out of the heavens a sign of the almost supernatural prowess of their race. A great mystery was made of the business in the hope of exciting among the civilian population of the Allies a dread commensurate with German confidence. In this Germany was disappointed. The French and British peoples took the danger with amazing calmness. It was a war risk, unpleasant in its character, but very clearly limited in its scope. There was a moment in Britain when the peril was overestimated; there were also moments when it was unduly minimized; but for the most part the thing was regarded with calm good sense. There were four types of German airship in use – the Zeppelin, the Schütte-Lanz, the Parseval, and the military ship known as the "M" type – but the term Zeppelin was used popularly to cover them all. During the war Germany went on building at the rate of perhaps one a month, a rate which more than made up for losses. Her main difficulty was the supply of trained crews, for her reserves at the beginning of the campaign were speedily absorbed.

The raids on England began on 19th January, when the coast of Norfolk was bombarded. On 14th April came a more serious attack on our north-eastern coast, which seems to have been aimed at the industrial and shipping regions of Tyneside. The Zeppelin was first sighted at Blyth about eight o'clock in the evening, and moved over Wallsend and South Shields. Numerous bombs were dropped, but the destruction of property was small, and there appears to have been no loss of life. Next night an airship visited the coast of East Anglia and dropped bombs on Lowestoft and Maldon. According to the German Press it aimed at destroying the Lowestoft fishing fleet, as a retaliation for the English blockade of German foodstuffs. Next day, in the afternoon, a biplane paid a futile visit to Kent, dropping bombs on Faversham and Sittingbourne. On 23rd April a Zeppelin attempted to reach Blyth, but failed. Early on the morning of 30th April another passed over Ipswich, and dropped bombs there and at Bury St Edmunds, destroying a few shops and cottages, but causing no loss of life.

On 10th May the watering-place of Southend-on-Sea on the Thames estuary was bombarded by an airship, several houses being struck and one woman killed. On the 13th a Zeppelin attacked Ramsgate, but after dropping six bombs was driven off by British machines. On its way back it was met by Flight-Commander Bigsworth off the Flemish coast. Four bombs were dropped on it, and its tail seemed to have been blown off, for it steered homewards on a very drunken course. On the night of 26th May another attack was made on Southend by two Zeppelins, which resulted in one death and several injuries.

London was first visited on the night of 31st May. The airships came by way of Ramsgate and Brentwood, and their object seems to have been the Thames riverside docks. There were a certain number of casualties but little material

SIR JOHN LAVERY *Kite Balloons, Roehampton, 1915*

destruction. The raid caused wild jubilation in Germany. "Great God, at last!" wrote one newspaper. "Like an organ tone in the sky is the hum of the propellers. This is no ordinary war; it is a crusade, a holy war. There lies a giant city, in which for fifty years they have worked only evil against us. London lies beneath us, the heart of the British world-empire! A moment which sets the keystone to the life-work of Count Zeppelin." Such extreme heroics were scarcely warranted by the modest results, but the Zeppelin had become an obsession for the German mind.

During June the east and north-eastern coasts were repeatedly raided. One visit fell on the night of 4th June, a second on the night of 6th June, a third on the night of 16th June. In these attacks there was a considerable loss of civilian life, but no military purpose of the remotest kind was effected. The British authorities very wisely discouraged the publication of details, and the good sense of the people prevented this silence from breeding wild rumours. No risk of war had ever been more calmly accepted. The threatened localities pursued their ordinary avocations, and people went holiday-making as usual to parts of the coast in the direct track of the invaders. In a letter to a correspondent Mr Balfour summarized the Zeppelin results during a year of war. Seventy-one civilian adults and eighteen children had been killed, one hundred and eighty-nine civilian adults and thirty-one children had been injured. "No soldier or sailor has been killed; seven have been wounded; and only on one occasion has damage been inflicted which could by any stretch of language be described as of the smallest military importance."

The French Press published, in the middle of June, a complete list of raids made by German aeroplanes and airships on open towns. From this it appeared that such towns in France and England had up to that date been bombarded eighty-three times by German aeroplanes, and twenty-one times by Zeppelins. The principle French centres thus assailed were Paris and Calais. On 20th March, early in the morning, two Zeppelins dropped bombs on Paris, but were driven off by the anti-aircraft guns. On their way back they attacked Compiègne and some of the adjoining villages. One of them was probably hit, and during the summer Paris was little molested. Its aerial defence had been so carefully prepared that there was little chance of a hostile airship being able to stay long enough to do much damage. As soon as a raider arrived he was received by fire from the forts and the anti-aircraft batteries. The great searchlights flashed into the sky, and a squadron of aeroplanes rose to meet him. Bugles warned the inhabitants, and every light in Paris was turned off. Into this hornet's nest the boldest aviator thought twice before entering. Calais was an easier matter. It was bombarded on 21st February, and again on the morning of 18th March, when a number of railway employees were killed. A Zeppelin appeared on the night of 16th May, when there were four victims, three children and an old lady.

The Zeppelin campaign was undertaken for two purposes, both strategically sound. The first was to destroy works of military value, such as arsenals and barracks; the second was to inspire in the civilian population that nervous dread which in the long run would weaken the Allies in the field. It failed, failed almost ludicrously, in both purposes. In Mr Balfour's words, "Zeppelin raids have been brutal; but so far they have not been effective. They have served no hostile purpose, moral or material." The resolution of the Allied nations was confirmed, not weakened, by these efforts of blind terrorism. As for the first aim, no military or naval work was damaged. Little shops and the cottages of the working classes alone bore the brunt of the enemy's fury. It was very different with the Allied air work. The yellow smoke of burning chemical factories and the glare of blazing Zeppelin sheds attested the fruitfulness of their enterprises. The truth was that the boasted Zeppelin proved an unhandy instrument of war. Its blows were directed blindly and at random. This was not to say that it might not achieve a surprising result, but that achievement would be more by accident than design. In the darkness of night its aim was handicapped. It was highly sensitive, too, to weather conditions, for a layer of snow equivalent to one-twenty-fifth of an inch on its surface would mean a weight of four tons, and would inevitably bring it down. Weather forecasts in Britain were rigorously suppressed, but it seems certain that the Germans found some means of obtaining barometrical information; otherwise their losses would have been a hundred-fold greater.

It is difficult to estimate with any accuracy the casualties among German airships. During the first six months of war probably at the outside half a dozen Zeppelins were demolished by the Allies. In February two of the largest, L 3 and L 4, were wrecked on the coast of Denmark owing to their encounter with snowstorms. In March L 8 came to grief in the neighbourhood of Tirlemont, and seems to have become a total wreck. In April one of the Zeppelins lent by Germany to Austria fell into the Adriatic and was lost. In May another broke loose from its moorings near Koenigsberg, and disappeared into the void. There were unverified reports of other losses, and a certain number – not less than four – were destroyed by the Allied aircraft in their sheds.

A fight between a Zeppelin and an aeroplane had been long looked forward to as, sooner or later, inevitable, and the Allied aircraft had instructions to engage a German airship whenever it appeared. It was not till the morning of 7th June that such a duel took place. About 3 a.m. Flight-Sub-Lieutenant R. A. J. Warneford, an officer of the Naval Air Service, discovered a Zeppelin between Ghent and Brussels. He was flying in a very light monoplane, and managed to rise above the airship, which was moving at a height of about 6,000 feet. Descending to a distance of about 50 feet, he dropped six bombs, the last of which burst the envelope, and caused the whole ship to explode in a mass of flame. The force of the explosion turned the monoplane upside down, but the skill and presence of mind of Sub-Lieutenant Warneford enabled him to right it. He was compelled to descend in the enemy's country, but was able to re-start his engine and return safely to his base. The Zeppelin fell in a blazing mass to the ground, and was destroyed with all its crew.

The hero of this brilliant exploit had only received his flying certificate a few months before. It would be hard to overpraise the courage and devotion which inspired such an attack, or the nerve and fortitude which enabled him to return safely. Sub-Flight-Lieutenant Warneford's name became at once a household word in France and Britain, and he was most deservedly awarded the Victoria Cross and the Cross of the Legion of Honour. His career was destined to be as short as it had been splendid, for on 17th June he was accidentally killed while flying in the aerodrome at Versailles.

(*Vol. VIII pp. 88-95, 99-102, 105-112*)

THE HOME FRONT

In this short piece, Buchan shows how Britain continued to organize for a long war, and incidentally shows himself aware of the radical change in women's social role brought about by the war.

NO SURVEY of British effort is complete without some reference to the work done by voluntary bodies and by individuals in the thousand and one paths of charity which the war revealed. The British Red Cross Society, the Order of St John of Jerusalem, and the Voluntary Aid Detachments provided a nursing organization which could not be paralleled in the world. Private hospitals were sent to Serbia, where they grappled with the insoluble problem of an army ill supplied with medical comforts and with various deadly epidemics, and lost many devoted members of their staffs. Nurses and ambulances went to the French, Russian, and Belgian fronts, and the civilian population of France and Belgium were cared for by special organizations. The immense business of dealing with the refugee Belgian population was skilfully handled, and they were temporarily absorbed into the social life of Britain, while with the assistance of a commission of neutrals food supplies were sent to Belgium itself. Large sums were raised for the relief of distress in Poland and for a dozen other charitable purposes. Happily there was little immediate distress in Britain, and the energies of her people could be devoted to war purposes and the succour of the invaded lands. Our own troops were amply supplied with the small luxuries and comforts which are not included in rations. Scarcely a household in the Empire but did its part. The remotest cottages in the Highlands, the loneliest farms in Alberta and Queensland, were connected by strange threads with the far-away theatres of war.

During the later months women began to appear in many novel employments. As ticket collectors, tram conductors, chauffeurs, bill posters, postmen, and in a score of other tasks, they released men for the fighting line. Never had the women of Britain shown to finer advantage. Of all who were compelled to remain at home, they were the chief sufferers, for they had given sons and brothers, husbands and lovers, to the field of danger. From the beginning they realized the gravity of the struggle. The women's movement of recent years had given to a large class a special organization and discipline, which was turned to admirable purpose. The leaders of that movement in the Press and on the platform did a great work in rousing the nation, and none dealt more trenchantly with counsels of supineness and peace. The women of Britain asked only for the chance of service, and when the munitions difficulty revealed itself

VICTORIA MONKHOUSE *A 'Bus Conductress*

J. BARNARD DAVIS *The Workroom of the Gerrard's Cross War Hospital Supply Depôt*

they were foremost in offering their work. What had happened in Germany and France was beginning to take place in Britain. The barriers of sex were falling, like the barriers of class, before the trumpet call of the national need.

(Vol. VIII pp. 136-37)

EDITH CAVELL

The execution in October 1915 of Nurse Edith Cavell caused a fury of anti-German feeling in Britain and allied countries. She had been working in Brussels since 1906, and elected to remain there after the city was occupied by the German army in 1914. Early in August of the following year she was arrested and charged with helping Allied servicemen to reach the safety of neutral Holland. She signed a confession to this effect, but let it be known that she regarded her actions only as doing her duty to suffering humanity. The German commandant in Brussels had her tried by court martial and shot. In doing so, he created a martyr for the Allied cause at the time, and a legend for posterity.

IT WAS the death of one Englishwoman in Brussels which did more than any other incident of the war – more than the sinking of the *Lusitania* or the tragedy of Belgium – to key the temper of Britain to that point where resolution acquires the impetus of a passion. Miss Edith Cavell, a lady of forty-three, and the daughter of a Norfolk clergyman, had been since 1906 the head of a nursing institute in Brussels. When the war broke out she was in England, but she returned at once to Belgium, and transformed her institute into a hospital for wounded soldiers. There she nursed without discrimination British, French, Belgians, and Germans. During her year's work she succeeded, with the help of friends in Brussels, in conveying many of the wounded Allied soldiers into Holland, whence they could return to their armies, and also in assisting the escape of Belgian civilians of military age. Her activities were discovered by the German authorities, and on 5th August she was arrested and lodged in the military prison of St Gilles.

Here she was kept in solitary confinement, and no word of her arrest reached her friends till three weeks later. On 26th August Sir Edward Grey asked the American Ambassador in London to request Mr Brand Whitlock, the American Minister at Brussels, to inquire into the case. Mr Whitlock took up the matter energetically, and on 31st August addressed an inquiry to Baron von der Lancken, the chief of the political department of the German Military Government in Belgium. He waited ten days without receiving an answer, and then wrote again. On 12th September he was informed that Miss Cavell by her own confession had admitted the offence with which she was charged, that her defence was already in the hands of a Belgian advocate, and that as a matter of principle no interview could be permitted with accused persons. Upon this M. de Leval, the legal adviser to the American Legation, took action. With admirable assiduity he endeavoured to get in touch with Miss Cavell and her so-called advocates, but found endless difficulties in the way. It was not till 4th October that he was informed that the trial was fixed for the following Thursday, 7th October. On that date – nine weeks after the arrest and without the production to the defence of any documents of the prosecution – the trial of the thirty-five prisoners began. Miss Cavell by frankly admitting the charge had given the prosecution evidence which could not have been otherwise obtained. Under the German Military Code, paragraphs 58, 90, and 160, the offence was treason and punishable by death, and the penalty was applicable to foreigners as well as to German citizens. The Court rose next day, and judgement was reserved.

During the weekend M. de Leval tried in vain to find out what was happening. On Monday Mr Hugh Gibson, the young Secretary of the American Legation, spent the whole day interrogating the German authorities, and as late as 6.20 p.m. he was officially informed that the decision of the Court had not been pronounced. At 8 p.m. M. de Leval heard by accident that sentence had been passed at 5 p.m., and that Miss Cavell was to be shot at 2 a.m. on the following morning. The American Legation made a last gallant effort. Two pleas for mercy were drawn up, addressed to Baron von der Lancken and to Baron von Bissing, the German Governor-General. Mr Whitlock was ill in bed, but he wrote a personal letter to von Bissing, and Mr Gibson, M. de Leval, and the Spanish Ambassador, the Marquis de Villalobar, called on Baron von der Lancken about 10 p.m. The only power to grant a reprieve belonged to Baron von Bissing, a military pedant of the narrowest type, and the deputation, after an earnest appeal, was dismissed about midnight.

That night at ten o'clock a British chaplain, Mr Gahan, was admitted to Miss Cavell's cell. From him we have an account of her last hours. She asked him to tell her friends that she died willingly for her country, without fear or shrinking, and in the true spirit of Christian humility she forgave her enemies. "This I would say, standing as I do in view of God and eternity, I realize that patriotism is not enough. I must have no hatred or bitterness towards any one." At two in the morning she died, her courage and cheerfulness, on the admission of the German chaplain, being unweakened to the end. Some difficulty was found in providing her executioners, and there is reason to believe that a number of German soldiers were put under arrest for refusing to assist in the barbarity.

Miss Cavell's execution was a judicial murder. It was judicial since, on the letter of the German military law, she was liable to the extreme penalty. But in the case of a woman and a nurse who had ministered to German sick and wounded the pedantry which exacted that penalty was an outrage on human decency. That the German authorities were uneasy about their work is shown by the secrecy which they insisted upon, and which Sir Edward Grey in his letter to Mr Page rightly denounced. There was little comment in the German Press, and there is evidence that the incident was by no means applauded by

Germany at large. Herr Zimmermann, the German Under-Secretary for Foreign Affairs, could only defend it by a legend of a "world-wide conspiracy", and by the familiar plea of the necessity of "frightfulness" in a crisis "to frighten those who may presume on their sex to take part in enterprises punishable with death." In France and Britain, in Holland and America, the murder woke a profound horror, and revealed as in a flashlight the psychology of that German "culture" which proposed to regenerate the world. Von Bissing and his colleagues stood clear in all their lean and mechanical poverty of soul, cruel by rule, brutal by the textbooks, ruthless after a sealed pattern, but yet without the courage of their barbarity, for their policy was furtively pursued and safeguarded with deceit.

Against that dark background the spirit of the lonely Englishwoman shone the brighter. We would not tarnish so noble a deed with facile praise. Her heroism had led captivity captive, and for her death was swallowed up in victory. She was not the least of the sisterhood of great-hearted women who have taught the bravest men a lesson in courage. M. Clemenceau spoke the tribute of the people of France. "The profound truth is that she honoured her country by dying for what is finest in the human soul – that grandeur of which all of us dream but only the rare elect have the chance of attaining. Since the day of Joan of Arc, to whose memory I know that our Allies will one day seek to erect a statue, England has owed us this return. She has nobly given it."

(Vol. XI pp. 62-66)

CHARLES DIXON *The Sinking of L.15*

THE ZEPPELINS

By the end of May 1916 a good deal of Eastern Britain from Scotland to Kent had either been raided or overflown by enemy airships, known as Zeppelins, and there had been a number of civilian casualties. In the following extract several early air raids are described.

THE ZEPPELIN was not a weapon of precision. Though, unlike an aeroplane, it could steer a course at night by the compass and by wireless, yet it had the formidable difficulty of its size to face, and to pass unnoticed needed fog or a cloudy sky. Consequently it was very easy for it to miss its objective. Again, it could not drop bombs with any accuracy at a mark, for air currents in the higher spaces deflected its course, and if it came lower it became an obvious target. Hence it was usually compelled to drop its bombs blindly from some height like 10,000 feet, and to trust to fortune to hit something valuable.

But it was one thing to recognize the working limits of a Zeppelin, and quite another to provide adequate defences. Reconnaissance might give early warning of its approach and searchlights reveal when it arrived, but the weapons of offence were terribly limited. Quick-firing guns of large calibre, firing first luminous and then explosive shells, were the natural protection for any locality likely to be the object of Zeppelin attacks. But such guns could not be distributed over the whole country, and the Zeppelin had an immense area to manoeuvre in. The "swarm of locusts", which Mr Churchill had predicted, was hard to use, even if the machines had been there, for aeroplane flights on a dark night over a great city were more risky to the aviator than to the enemy. The best hope lay in attacking the monster on the out or return journey, either by battle-planes or by the fire of ships at sea. The other alternative, a counter-attack by Zeppelins, was impossible, since the Allies had none ready.

In August 1915 there were two Zeppelin raids on the eastern and south-eastern coasts of Britain. On the evening of 7th September Zeppelins attacked the suburbs of London, and next night a serious assault was made on the heart of the city. The raiders came between 10 and 11 p.m., while the theatres and music-halls were full, and dropped bombs in the City and the central districts. There were 106 casualties – 20 killed and 86 injured; but the people of London behaved with praiseworthy composure, and the fires kindled were quickly subdued by the admirable work of the London Fire Brigade. The next raid came upon 13th October, early in the evening, when the streets were thronged, and the tale of casualties was the largest yet recorded – 56 killed and 114 injured. The area which suffered most was a suburban residential district, and, except for one or two soldiers who happened to be in the streets, the list was civilian, mainly women and children. There were no further raids during the rough weather of November and December, but on the last day of January 1916 at least six Zeppelins made landfall on the East Coast, and went inland over East Anglia and the Midland counties. The raiders seemed to be searching for Birmingham and Liverpool, but the bombs they dropped fell mainly in rural districts and in some of the lesser Midland industrial towns. Sixty-seven were killed and 117 injured, and of these casualties two-thirds were women and children. The brutality of the business was only equalled by its aimlessness. The raiders seemed to have lost their way, and, since no danger had been anticipated in those parts and there were no defences, they wandered about for hours unmolested. One of them, the L19, sank in the North Sea on her return voyage. On the previous night Zeppelins had raided Paris, and did some damage in a working-class northern suburb. They stayed only a short time, and were hunted back by the French battle-planes.

The next raid on Britain fell on 5th March, in a storm, when three Zeppelins visited the East Coast from Yorkshire to Kent, and left seventy killed or injured. The month was wet and boisterous, but with its close came the period of still weather which often marks the transition from March to April. On 31st March the eastern coast was again attacked, on 1st April the north-eastern counties, and on 2nd April the Scottish Lowlands, which had been thought to lie far beyond the danger zone. In the first two attempts 59 were killed and 166 injured, and in the third there were over a score of casualties. The Zeppelin L15, which took part in the first raid, was brought down off the mouth of the Thames and her crew made prisoners. Out of these adventures the Germans wove wonderful fairy tales, of great ports wrecked, munition factories in flames, camps destroyed, and a people in abject terror. The plain fact was that no military or naval damage of the slightest consequence was effected, only the killing and maiming of innocent civilians in undefended hamlets and suburbs.

(Vol. XIII pp. 73-77)

THE FIRST BATTLE OF VERDUN

Between February and December 1916 the battles for possession of Verdun took place. The Germans were intent upon capturing this fortress town in Eastern France, and the French were determined to hold it. By the end of the fighting, casualties on both sides were very nearly one million. Verdun was held, but the surrounding country devastated. It was partly to relieve the French army that the attack on the Somme was undertaken. In these short extracts, Buchan sets the scene, discusses the problem of supplying the battlefield, and pays tribute to the French soldier.

VERDUN SINCE the days of the Romans had been a famous city. A prince-bishop had his seat there in the Middle Ages, when the place was under the German Empire. The Constable de Montmorency in the time of Henry II conquered it for France, and under Louis XIV Vauban fortified it with his system of bastions, revelines, and ditches. In 1792 it surrendered readily to the Duke of Brunswick, and was consequently the indirect cause of the September massacres in Paris. But in the war of 1870 it made a stout resistance. Waldersbach in vain tried to batter his way in; but the place held out for ten weeks, and fell only when the investment was complete and supplies failed. After the loss of Alsace-Lorraine it became, along with Belfort, Toul, and Epinal, one of the eastern bulwarks of France, and was a vital point in the defensive plans of Seré de Rivières. In 1875 the entrenched camp of Verdun formed the left wing of the fortifications of the Heights of the Meuse. It barred the crossing of that river on the main line of advance from Metz to the passes of the Argonne and the Upper Marne valley. It was the meeting-place of the great road from Paris eastwards, and the highway which followed the Meuse. It was the junction of five railway lines. It was only a day's march from the German frontier and the fortress of Metz.

✳ ✳ ✳

The French transport was now almost wholly by road and motor, and an endless chain of convoys passed and repassed between Verdun and railhead. It was a task which involved a terrific strain for the men. A letter from a French mechanical transport driver gives some notion of the work:

> Each outing represents for us from fifteen to twenty-five hours at the wheel – when it is not thirty – and for our lorries 150 to 200 kilometres. This night and day. On arriving here, we did the journey twice almost

C.R.W. NEVINSON *French Troops Resting, 1916*

without stopping – that is to say, forty-eight hours without sleep, and almost without food. It was so hard that it was decided that there should be only one chauffeur per lorry, and that we should take it in turns. Can you imagine what it means to drive one of these lorries, weighing five tons, and carrying an equal weight of shells, either during a descent of 12 or 14 in the 100, and with a lorry just in front and one just behind, or driving during a frosty night, or without lights for short intervals when nearing the front? Can you see the driver alone on his lorry, whose eyes are shutting when a shock wakes him up suddenly, who is obliged to sing, to sit very upright, to swear at himself, so as not to sleep, or throw his lorry into a ravine, or get it stuck in the mud, or knock the one in front to pieces? And then the hundreds and hundreds of cars coming in the contrary direction, whose lights blind him!

Conspicuous among the merits of the French infantry were the discipline and initiative of the smallest units, even of individuals. Men had constantly to act without orders, at any rate in the first days of the battle, and they showed that austere conscience as to what was personally required of them which belongs to an army which is no mechanism but a living weapon.

(Vol. XIII pp. 125-26, 162-63, 198)

THE SECOND YEAR OF THE WAR

In writing a summary of the second year of the war, Buchan allowed himself a guarded optimism. The German outlook, he thought, "had appreciably darkened". So it had; but the outbreak of the Somme battles in July 1916 and their ending in November brought lengthening casualty lists and little optimism on either side.

As our narrative approaches the end of the second year of war, and reaches the second anniversary of those murders at Sarajevo which opened the flood gates, it is desirable to halt and review the position. Only in this way can a campaign whose terrain was three continents and every sea, and whose battle fronts were reckoned in thousands of miles, be seen in its full purpose and its right perspective.

At the end of June 1915 Germany's aims to a superficial observer seemed to be everywhere crowned with success. It was true that her original scheme had failed, and that she had been compelled to revise her ideas, and adopt a plan for which she had small liking. But with admirable patience she had performed the revision, and the new policy had won conspicuous triumphs. She held the Allies tightly in the West, held them with the minimum of men by virtue of an artillery machine to which they could not show an equal, and fortifications of a strength hitherto unknown to the world. Using her main forces in the East, she had driven Russia from post to pillar, had won back Galicia, had penetrated far into Poland, and had already in her grip the great fortresses whose cession meant for Russia not only a crushing loss in guns, but an indefinite further retreat. She held vast tracts of enemy soil in Poland, Belgium, and France, and so far these gains had not diminished, but were daily growing. The Central Powers had a completely unified command, and all their strength could be applied with little delay and friction to the purpose of the German General Staff.

Nor was the full tale of the Allied misfortunes yet told. Bulgaria, though the fact was still secret, had entered the Teutonic League, and that must presently mean the annihilation of Serbia, and German dominion in the Balkans. Turkey had so far held the Allied advance in Gallipoli, and was soon to bring it to a melancholy standstill. There were tragedies waiting to be enacted in Mesopotamia. What had the Allies to show as against such spectacular triumphs? The conquest of one or two outlandish German colonies, a few miles gained on the Isonzo and in the Italian hills, the occupation of the butt-end of a Turkish peninsula, an advance up the Tigris, where the difficulties loomed greater with every league, a defensive action in Egypt, and one or two costly failures on the Western front. To the German observer it seemed a mirage as contrasted with the solid earth.

Nor was the prospect less pleasing when viewed with another eye than the strategist's. In the struggle of military bureaucracies against democracies, it would seem that the bureaucracies must win. Fifty years before Abraham Lincoln had said, "It has long been a grave question whether any Government, not too strong for the liberties of its people, can be strong enough to maintain its existence in great emergencies." That question seemed to have been answered against the democracies. Germany and her allies looked abroad, and saw Britain still perplexed with old catchwords, still disinclined to turn a single mind to the realities of war. The air was full of captious criticism. Her people had willed the end, no doubt, but they were not wholly inclined to will the means. Again, while the Teutonic command was unified, the Allies were still fumbling and wasting their strength on divergent enterprises. There seemed to be no true General Staff work done for the Alliance as a whole. Each unit fought its own campaign, and was assisted by its colleagues only when disaster had overtaken it. Their assets, potentially very great, could not be made actual. They had far more men, but those men could not be made soldiers in time. They had a great industrial machine, but that machine would not adapt itself quickly enough to military needs. They commanded the sea, but their fleets could not destroy Germany's unless Germany was willing to fight. Their blockade, while it might annoy, could not seriously cripple the energies of Central Europe, which in the greater matters was economically self-sufficing. As for morale, had not a bureaucracy shown that it could elicit as splendid a resolution and as whole-hearted an enthusiasm as those Powers which worshipped the fetish called popular liberty?

Nevertheless an impartial critic, looking around him in June 1915, might have noted chinks in the Teutonic panoply. So far the Allied blockade had had no very serious effects; but might it not be tightened? Germany had occupied much land; but could she hold it? She was spending herself lavishly and brandishing her sword far afield in the hope of intimidating her enemies; but what if those enemies declined to be intimidated? Unless Germany achieved her end quickly, it was possible that the Allies might set their house in order. They were fighting for their national existence, and they saw no salvation save in a complete and unquestionable victory. Was it not possible that, as the urgency of the need sank into their souls, there might come such a speeding up and tightening of energies that Germany's offensive would be changed to a defensive? For the one hope of Germany lay in a successful offensive which would break up the Alliance by putting one or other of its constituent armies out of action. If this was not done speedily, could it be done at all?

The intelligent German would probably have assented to the premises, but denied the possibility of failure. The German offensive was on the eve of decisive success. The Kaiser had told his people that they were drawing very near to a victorious peace.

Let us suppose that a man, wounded at the close of June 1915, had been shut off from the world for the space of a year. As he became convalescent he asked for news of the war. Was the Russian army still in being? and if so, in what ultimate waste, far east of Petrograd and Moscow, did it lie? for in the absence of Russian equipment the German advance could not have been stayed short of those famous cities? To his amazement he was told that von Hindenburg's thrust had first weakened, and then died away, and that the winter in the East had been stagnant. More, Russia had had her breathing space, and was now advancing. All the Bukovina had been recovered, and the Volhynian Triangle, and Brussilov was well on the road to Lemberg, with three-quarters of a million Austrians out of action. In the Balkans, Serbia and Montenegro had been overrun, and Bulgaria had joined the enemy; but an Allied army – French, British, Serbians, Russians, and Italians – was holding the Salonika front, and waiting for the signal to advance. The Gallipoli adventure had failed, but the force had been extricated, and was now in France and Egypt and Mesopotamia. Egypt had laughed at the threat of invasion, and had easily subdued the minor ferments on her borders. On the Tigris one British fort had fallen, and a weak division had been made prisoner; but it had detained large Turkish forces, and allowed the Grand Duke Nicholas in Transcaucasia to take Erzerum, Trebizond, and Erzinghian, and to threaten the central Anatolian plain. Italy had flung back the invader from the Trentino, and was now beginning her *revanche*. In the West there had been one great effort to pierce the German front, and after its failure the Allies had sat down to perfect their equipment and increase their armies. The convalescent heard with amazement of the tornado that had swept on Verdun, and of the unequalled stand of the thin French lines. He was told of the desperate assault then being delivered against Fleury and Thiaumont, but he was told also of the great Allied armies mustered on the Somme for the counterstroke. Above all, he heard of the miraculous work of Britain, of ample munitions, of seventy divisions in the field and great reserves behind them. He heard, too, of a unified strategical and economic purpose among the Allies, of attacks conceived and directed with a single aim. As the manifold of these facts slowly shaped itself in his consciousness, he realized that he had awakened to a new world.

What is the test of military success? The question has often been asked, and the popular replies are innumerable; but the soldier knows only one answer. The test is the destruction of the enemy's power of resistance, and that power depends upon his possession of an adequate field army. Success is not the occupation of territory, or of successive enemy lines, or of famous enemy fortresses. These things may be means, but they are not in themselves the end. And if these things are won without the end being neared, the winner of them has not only not advanced; he has gone backward, since he has expended great

EDGAR SELIGMAN *Belgian Steel Factory, Goldhawk Road, W.12 – Women at Work*

forces for an idle purpose, and is thereby crippled for future efforts. Early in 1916, when the German Press was exulting in the study of the map of Europe, von Hindenburg is said to have described Germany's military position as "brilliant, but without a future". If the veteran field-marshal was correctly reported, he showed in the remark an acumen which observers would not necessarily have gathered from his exploits in the field.

Strategically, Germany had long ago failed. Her original strategic purpose was sound – to destroy one by one the Allied field armies. Her urgent need was a speedy and final victory. The Marne and First Ypres deprived her of this hope, and she never regained it. The Allies took the strategical offensive, and, by pinning her to her lines and drawing round her the net of their blockade, compelled her to a defensive war. In the largest sense the Allied offensive dated from the beginning of 1915. But it was an offensive which did not include the tactical initiative. So long as the Allies were deficient in equipment Germany was able to take the tactical offensive. Instances were the Second Battle of Ypres, and the great German advance in the East. "A weakening Power", in the words of General Foch, "must be always attacking", and these various movements were undertaken in the hope that tactical success might gradually restore the strategic balance. This hope was doomed to disappointment. Victories, indeed, were won, brilliant victories, but they led nowhere. By and by came the last attempts, the onslaughts on Verdun and the Trentino; and the failure of these prepared the way for the Allies themselves to take the tactical initiative. Germany was now tactically as well as strategically on her defence.

The essence of German tactics was their reliance upon guns. For them artillery was the primary and infantry the secondary arm. They looked to win battles at long range, confident in an elaborate machine to which their opponents could provide no equivalent. Their whole strategical plan was based upon this tactical calculation. It miscarried; but at the beginning of the war there was some ground for their confidence. To improvise an equivalent machine might reasonably have been considered beyond the power of France and Russia. But three things combined to frustrate the hope – the stubborn fight against odds of all the Allies, their command of the sea which allowed them to import munitions till their own producing power had developed, and the industrial capacity of Britain which enabled her to manufacture for the whole Alliance. Faced with an artillery equipment of anything like equal strength, the German tactics were ineffective, and when the day came that the Allies had a stronger munitionment than their enemy, they were both futile and perilous. That is the danger of fighting behind the shelter of a machine. Men accustomed to a long-range contest will be helpless when the battle comes to close quarters. How can infantry trained as a secondary arm stand against infantry which has been taught that on it primarily rests the decision? The quality can never be the same. At first the defect may be met by greater quantity, but as effectives decline quality will come by its own.

The Battle of Verdun may be taken as the final proof of the fallacy of German tactics. They were intrinsically wrong, and could only have succeeded if the whirlwind fury of the first German assault had immediately achieved its object. So soon as Germany was reduced to a strategical defensive they became a signal danger. For sooner or later her artillery was bound to be met by an equal or greater equipment, and then she could only retrieve the tactical inferiority of her infantry by the use of superior numbers. When numbers failed her it would appear that, sooner or later, she must accept defeat.

It was the fashion among the Allies towards midsummer 1916 to blame von Falkenhayn for serious blunders. But the blame really attached to Germany's pre-war preparations, and to the whole theory of war which the patient industry of her General Staff had elaborated for so many years. They had placed their money on a horse of surprising pace but of indifferent staying power over a long course. It is a little difficult to see what other road von Falkenhayn could have taken. He had to speed up the conflict and attack somewhere. To him the centre of gravity lay in the West, and it is not easy to say that he was wrong. If he could put France out of action, it would be impossible for Britain alone to conduct the war on that front, and the Alliance must crumble. Von Hindenburg, it was understood, while agreeing on the necessity of an offensive somewhere, preferred the Eastern theatre. He would have had Germany remain strictly on the defensive in the West, while he endeavoured to obtain a real decision against Russia. It may fairly be said that both schemes were impossible, and it is idle to determine degrees of impossibility. An assault on Russia in the spring and summer of 1916 would undoubtedly have failed, as the march through Poland had failed the year before. Since von Falkenhayn's plan miscarried, the exponent of the untried plan increased his reputation, but there is no reason to believe that one was wiser than the other. The time had gone by for a decisive German offensive, and her tactical misconceptions were exacting their penalty. A new offensive indeed she must undertake, but its chance of forcing a decision had gone.

The special blunder of Germany at this stage did not lie only with the General Staff, but with the whole German authorities, civil, naval, and military, and with the German people. Since she was clearly on the defence, it would have been well to take the measures proper to a defensive campaign. She was holding far-flung lines with too few men, and the path of wisdom was obviously to shorten them. There is some evidence that after the failure at Verdun the wiser brains in her General Staff favoured this view. But in the then state of German opinion it was impracticable. When the people had been buoyed with hope of a triumphant peace and a vast increase of territory, when the fanatics of Pan-Germanism were publishing details of how they intended to use the conquered areas, when the Imperial Chancellor was lyrically apostrophizing the map, a shortening of the lines in East and West would have tumbled down the whole edifice of German confidence. She could not do it; her political commitments were too deep; her earlier vainglory sat like an Old Man of the Sea on her shoulders.

Yet beyond doubt it was her best chance. Had she, before the Allied offensive began, drawn in her front to the Vistula and the Meuse, she would have had an immensely strong line, and adequate numbers wherewith to hold it. She would have offered the Allies the prospect of an interminable war, under conditions which they had fondly hoped they had made impossible. Her one chance was to weaken the Alliance internally, to weary this or that Power, to lengthen out the contest to a point where the cost in money and lives would induce a general nervelessness and satiety. Moreover, by shortening her lines her food problem would have become far less urgent, and the deadliness of the blockade would have been lessened. But she let the moment for the heroic course slip by, and when the first guns opened in the combined Allied advance that course had become for ever impossible.

The position at sea in midsummer 1916 had not in substance changed from that of the preceding year. The waterways of the world were still denied by the Allies to the enemy, and used by them for their own military purposes. There had been several bursts of submarine violence, but it is fair to say that the submarine as a serious weapon had during the year decreased in importance. Its brutality was enhanced, but its efficiency had declined. Its moral effect in the way of shaking the nerves of British merchant seamen was *nil*. The result of the year's experience had been to induce a high degree of popular confidence in the measures taken to meet the underwater danger – a confidence not wholly justified, and soon to be rudely shaken. One great incident had broken the monotony of our maritime vigil. The German High Sea Fleet had been brought to action, and in the battle of 31st May off the Jutland coast had been conclusively beaten and driven back to harbour. But that great sea-fight did not change the situation; it only confirmed it. "Before Jutland, as after it," in Mr Balfour's words, "the German fleet was imprisoned; the battle was an attempt to break the bars and burst the confining gates; it failed, and with its failure the High Sea Fleet sank again into impotence."

The British navy, viewing the position while they swept the North Sea and the bells rang in Berlin and Hamburg to celebrate von Scheer's return, were convinced that they would see the enemy again. They had reason for their view. The Battle of Jutland was fought because politics demanded that the German fleet should do something to justify its existence in the eyes of the German people. That demand must be repeated. As the skies darkened over Germany it was certain that von Scheer would make further efforts, and the nearer came the day of final defeat the more desperate those efforts would be. For the navy of a Power is like a politician who changes sides: it counts two on a division. If the Power is conquered, its fleet will be the spoil of the conqueror. Far better that the German battleships should go to the bottom, with a number of British ships to keep them company, than that they should be doled out ignobly to increase the strength of the Allied victors.

While Germany's military and naval situation had a certain clearness, it was far otherwise with her domestic affairs. If differences of opinion were rumoured within her General Staff, there were open and flagrant antagonisms among her civilian statesmen. Two main strains of opinion had long been apparent. One was that held by the Kaiser, possibly by von Falkenhayn, by the Imperial Chancellor, and by the bulk of the civilian ministers. They believed – with occasional lapses into optimism – that the contest must end in a stalemate, and they were willing to abate their first arrogance and play for safety. Above all, they were anxious to avoid any conflict with the more powerful neutrals, for they knew that only by neutral help could Germany set her shattered house in order. They still talked boldly about victory, but these utterances were partly a concession to popular taste, and partly a desire to put their case high in order to enhance the value of future concessions. These people were the *politiques*, and they were not agreed on the details of their policy, some looking towards a *rapprochement* with France or Britain, others seeing in Russia a prospective ally. But they differed from their opponents in being willing to bargain and concede, and in allowing prudential considerations to temper the old German pride.

Arrayed against them were the fanatics of Pan-Germanism of the Reventlow-

Tirpitz school, who still clung to the belief in a complete victory, and were prepared to defy the whole round earth. To this school Prince Bülow by a curious metamorphosis seemed to have become attached. Neck or nothing was their maxim. They were advocates of every extreme of barbarism in method, and refused to contemplate any result of the war except one in which Germany should dictate to beaten foes. They had a considerable following, and they used the name of von Hindenburg as their rallying-cry, not because that eminent person was an adherent of their views – for he had in all probability not troubled his mind with questions outside his profession – but because he loomed big in the popular imagination as the strong, implacable soldier.

We can trace the strife of these two schools through German speeches and writings till the late spring of 1916. And then something happened which convinced both that their forecasts were wrong – which took from the *politiques* their hope of bargaining, and from the fanatics their certainty of triumph. Suddenly, with one of those queer illuminations which happen now and then to the most self-satisfied, the masters of Germany realized that their case was getting desperate. They saw that the Allied command was now unified, and that the Allied efforts were about to be quadrupled. They saw that the Allies would accept no terms but unconditional surrender. And they saw, moreover, that the contest could not end with the war, for their enemies were preparing a conjoint economic policy which would insure that their gains in battle should not be lost in peace. They saw at the same time that their military position was losing its brilliance, and had even less future than when von Hindenburg coined his epigram. The alternative now was not between a complete victory and an honourable draw, but between victory and annihilation – *Weltmacht oder Niedergang*.

This sudden realization induced a new temper. The people had been deluded, but there must some day be a stern awakening. Let that awakening come from the enemy, was the decision of the German High Command. The people must learn that their foes would not stop short of their utter destruction, the ruin not only of Germany's imperial dream, but of that laborious industrial and economical system which brought grist to the humblest mill. The boldest course was the safest. Concessions to humanity brought no reward, so let barbarism rule unchecked. It was only on the grim resolution of the whole nation that they could count for the life-and-death struggle before them, and the nation must be brought to this desperate temper by the proof that their leaders possessed it. Germany proceeded accordingly to burn her boats.

The first evidence of this calculated insanity was the murder of Captain Fryatt. Early in June the Great Eastern steamer, *Brussels*, plying between Harwich and Holland, was captured in the North Sea by a German torpedo boat and taken to Zeebrugge. Captain Fryatt was imprisoned at Bruges, and brought to trial as a *franc-tireur*, on the ground that in an encounter with a German submarine on March 28, 1915, he had defended himself by trying to ram his enemy, and had compelled her to dive. He was condemned to death on

Thursday, 27th July, and shot that evening.

***

At the end of June the economic situation of the Central Powers was becoming serious. The immediate food stringency was the least part of it. That stringency was very great, and till the harvest could be reaped in August it would continue to increase. A Director of Food Supplies was appointed in the person of Herr von Batocki; but no rationing and no ingenious manipulation of stocks could add to an aggregate which was too small for the comfort of the people. The British blockade had been greatly tightened, and every day saw its effectiveness growing. In June the unfortunate Declaration of London had been totally and finally abandoned. However good the German harvest, it could not make up all the deficit, and its results would cease early in 1917; nor could it supply the animal fats, the lubricating oils, and the many foreign necessaries which the British navy had forbidden. As for finance, further loans might be raised on the security of the Jutland "victory", though such loans were at the mercy of some sudden popular understanding of the true position. But the darkest part of the picture was the situation which must face Germany after the war, assuming that a crushing victory was beyond her. Her great commercial expansion had been largely due to the system of favourable treaties which under Caprivi and Bülow she had negotiated with foreign countries. Even before the war it was clear that the signatory nations would seek to recover their freedom, and a tariff struggle was in prospect when at the end of 1916 all the treaties were liable to denunciation. Now not only was there no hope of their renewal on good terms, but there was the certainty that all the Allies after the war would unite in boycotting Germany and developing commercial relations between themselves. At a conference held in Paris in the middle of June it was agreed that in the reconstruction period the enemy Powers should be denied "most-favoured nation" treatment, that enemy subjects should be prevented from engaging in vital industries in Allied countries, and that provision should be made for the conservation and exchange of the Allied natural resources. It was further resolved to render the Allied countries independent of the enemy countries in raw materials and essential manufactured articles. Unless Germany won the power to dictate treaties to her foes, as she had dictated to France in 1871, it looked as if the self-sufficiency of which she had boasted would be all that was left to her.

How nervous was Germany's temper on this subject was shown by the extravagant popular joy which greeted the voyage of a German submarine to America, and its safe return. On 9th July the U boat *Deutschland* arrived at Baltimore from Bremen with 280 tons of cargo, mostly dye-stuffs, and an autograph letter of the Kaiser. She had sailed under a commercial flag, and, being held by the American authorities to be technically a merchantman, was allowed to leave, and returned safely to Germany. It was what is known as a sporting performance, and nobody grudged the crew and captain their meed of honour; but the voyage involved no naval difficulty, its commercial results were infinitesimal, and the popular joy in Germany was based upon the erroneous idea that a means had been found of meeting the British blockade. She hoped that she had re-established trading relations with the chief neutral Power. It was a vain whimsy; there was nothing which the British navy more desired than that a hundred *Deutschlands* would attempt to repeat the enterprise. A submarine or two in the vast expanse of the Atlantic might escape detection, but a submarine service would be gently and steadily drawn into their net.

The one hope for Germany – and it was slender at the best – was that dissension would creep into the Allied councils. She could not look to draw any one of her foes to her side, but she might weaken their affection for each other, and so lessen their united striking power. She used her Press and her connections in neutral countries to play the part of the sower of tares in the Allies' vineyard. France was praised for her gallant exploits, and was advised not to count on the alliance of perfidious Britain. It was hinted that the Channel ports would never be restored to her; that Normandy had once been joined to England, and that history might repeat itself. What, it was asked, had become of the British during the long Verdun struggle? The overgrown improvised armies of Britain were simply mobs, too untrained to influence the war. "The value of the English infantry", wrote the *Vossische Zeitung*, "is not exactly to be considered as diminished, for we must think of the old English army as a perfect thing apart; the present infantry has never had any value." The legend of Britain's commercial ambitions was zealously preached. Russia was warned that after the war she would soon pray to be delivered from her friends. Happily this game was destined to fail for two good reasons. It was most blunderingly played, for German diplomacy was a clumsy thing, and her backstairs efforts were betrayed by the tramping of her heavy feet. Again she underrated the depth and gravity of the Allied purpose, which was faced with far too desperate an issue to have time for pettishness and vanity. There was rivalry, indeed, between the Allies, but it was a noble emulation in gallantry and sacrifice.

When we turn to the position of Germany's opponents, we find by midsummer 1916 that in every respect the year had shown a change for the better. Britain had enormously increased her levies, and had provided the machinery for utilizing her total manpower. France, though she had suffered a terrible drain at Verdun, had all her armies in being, and, with the assistance of Britain, who had taken over a large part of the front, would be able to supply the necessary drafts for many a day. Russia had trained huge numbers of her new recruits, and was stronger in men than before her great retreat began. In munitionment the change was amazing. France was amply provided for, Russia had at least four times greater a supply than she had ever known, and Britain, though still far from the high-water mark of her effort, had performed the miraculous. In a speech in the House of Commons, Mr Montagu, who had succeeded Mr Lloyd George as Minister of Munitions, drew a contrast between the situation in June 1915 and June 1916. The report of the work of the department read like a fairy tale. In shells the output which in 1914-15 it took twelve months to produce could now be supplied from home sources in the following times: field-gun ammunition, 3 weeks; field howitzer ammunition, 2 weeks; medium shells, 11 days; heavy shells, 4 days. Britain was now manufacturing and issuing to the Western front weekly as much as the whole pre-war stock of land-service ammunition in the country. In heavy guns the output in the year had increased sixfold, and would soon be doubled. The weekly production of machine guns had increased fourteenfold, and of rifles threefold – wholly from home sources. In small-arm ammunition the output was three times as great, and large reserve stocks were being accumulated. The production of high explosives was 66 times what it had been in the beginning of 1915, and the supply of bombs for trench warfare had been multiplied by 33. These figures were for British use alone, but we were also making colossal contributions to the common stock. One-third of the total British manufacture of shell steel went to France, and 20 per cent of our production of machine tools we sent to our Allies. Such a record was a triumph for the British workman, who in his long hours in dingy factories was doing as vital a service to his country as his brothers in the trenches of France and Salonika, on the hot sands of Mesopotamia and Egypt, or on the restless waters of the North Sea.

The economic linchpin of the Alliance was Britain, and on her financial stability depended its powers of endurance till victory. All the Allies had to make vast purchases abroad, and these had to be supported by British credit. The foreign exporter had to be paid for his goods in the currency which he would accept, and hence, while Germany's only problem was internal payments which could be met by an indefinite issue of paper, Britain had to find large quantities of gold or marketable securities for her daily purchases. So far as internal finance was concerned, her position was sound. In a speech in the House of Commons on 10th August, the Chancellor of the Exchequer calculated that by March 31, 1917, if the war lasted so long, our total indebtedness would just about equal the national income, "a burden by no means intolerable to contemplate", and that our national indebtedness would be less than one-sixth of the total national wealth. But the question of foreign payments – something between one and two millions a day – remained an anxious one, and was yet far from a settlement. In some respects the situation had improved. Owing to the policy of restriction of imports, and owing also to a remarkable increase in British exports – 11½ millions higher for July 1916 than for the same month in the previous year – our adverse trade balance was being reduced. In July 1916, for example, it was 22½ millions as against 31½ millions for July 1915. But ahead of our statesmen loomed this difficulty: we were paying for American imports for ourselves and our Allies mainly out of "dollar securities" – those American bonds which British owners had lent or sold to the Treasury. At the present rate we should have exhausted this form of

SIR JOHN LAVERY *"Rigids" at Pulham, 1918 – R.23 Type*

currency before midsummer 1917, and we might then be faced with a real crisis. It was urged with great reason that it would be well to adopt at once some drastic method of reducing unnecessary imports, and so lessening foreign payments, if we did not wish to find our military effort crippled at the moment when it should have been gathering power for the *coup de grâce*.

Economy in this respect could only be effected by the Allies jointly, since British credit had to cover all purchases; and it was now made possible by the unification which we have seen effected in the Allied Staff work. The pooling of resources was in theory complete. Frequent conferences, economic, political, and strategic, gave assurance that every atom of strength would be directed to a single end. The whole Allied force now held one great battle front – from Riga to the Bukovina; then, after a gap, from the Gulf of Orfano to west of the Vardar; then from the Isonzo to the Stelvio Pass; and, lastly, from Belfort to the North Sea. The Russians were the right wing, the Salonika army the right centre, the Italians the centre, the French the left centre, and the British the left wing. Staff work had been recognized at its proper value by all the Allies, since the appointment of Sir Archibald Murray and the revival of the British General Staff in October 1915. The military Conference in Paris in May 1916 had for the first time prepared for the whole front one common strategic plan. The Central Powers, who had won what they had won by their superior unity, were now confronted with an Alliance no longer loose and divergent, but disciplined and directed. At last the machinery was adequate to the impulse to strive and the resolution to conquer.

This sense of energy well directed induced in all the Allied peoples a new confidence and peace of mind. France, keyed to a high pitch by her marvellous deeds at Verdun, was in no mind to criticize her colleagues, and still less to find fault with her leaders. In Britain the mist of suspicion grew thinner between the Government and the people. Critics forsook their quest for a man of destiny, and were content to help fallible statesmen to make the best of things. In Russia the popular temper, always staunch and cheerful, was fired to enthusiasm by the great sweep of Brussilov and his armies. It would be wrong to pretend that there were no differences within the Allied unity. In Russia especially the first sun of success seemed to be about to warm into activity some of those parasites which had aforetime preyed on her, and which had been driven to hibernate during the chill winter of the long retreat. But as the months passed it grew clear to each of the Allies that the domestic affairs of their colleagues were for these colleagues themselves, and that the Alliance had no concern with internal politics save in so far as they affected the conduct of the war. It was realized that if the Alliance was to endure, each unit must have complete domestic freedom, and that unity in the great issues did not preclude the widest difference in lesser matters. Provided the weapon was keen and bright, the rest of the accoutrement was the business of the individual soldier. In the wise words of a distinguished Russian publicist, M. Egorov, "We wish to stand on our own feet, even if they be ill-shod."

The position of neutrals had in certain respects changed materially during the past year. Bulgaria had entered the war on the side of the Central Powers.

The British blockade had revolutionized the oversea commerce of those powers which still stood aloof from the contest. No neutral save Portugal had joined the Alliance; but, so far as could be judged, no other neutral was likely to join the enemy. Romania was still waiting with a single eye to her own territorial interests, but every mile that Brussilov advanced in the north increased the chances of her intervention on the Allied side. Greece had attempted to play the same game, but in each move had shown a singular folly. Bulgaria's invasion of her territory had roused a national feeling which the Court and Army chiefs, blinded by the spell of Germany, could neither understand nor in the long run control. M. Venezelos, the leader of Greek nationalism, bided his time, and watched, with shame and melancholy, as did all well-wishers of Hellas, the hucstering and blundering policy of the Athens Government. The *Graeculus esuriens* was not dead. Still, as of old, he tended to be too clever by half, and, from his absorption in petty cunning, to wreck the greater matters of his own self-interest. Spain remained aloof from the struggle, her hierarchy and the bulk of her upper classes leaning in sympathy towards Germany, and the mass of her people favouring the Allies. Holland and the Scandinavian States preserved a strict neutrality, and, as the German star grew dimmer, Sweden found less to admire in her trans-Baltic neighbour. On these states, who were in close proximity to Germany, the restrictions of the British blockade bore very hard. On the whole they faced the difficulties with good temper and good sense, and their collaboration in the "rationing" system was of inestimable advantage to the Allies. Switzerland had, perhaps, the hardest fate of all. The war had greatly impoverished her, and the two widely different strains in her population kept her sympathies divided between the belligerents. To her eternal honour she played a diligent and kindly part in facilitating the exchange of prisoners on both sides, and in giving hospitality in her mountain health resorts to the badly wounded. The country which had originated the Red Cross service was faithful to her high tradition in the works of mercy.

The Unites States' triumph over Germany on the submarine question – real in principle but trivial in results – gave to President Wilson's Government a stock of credit in foreign policy which carried them through the summer. America's interest was presently absorbed by her coming Presidential election, when Mr Wilson was to be opposed from the Republican side by Mr Hughes, assisted by Mr Roosevelt and the Progressives. This meant that foreign affairs would be considered mainly from the electioneering standpoint. Neither side wished to alienate the German electors, both sides wished to appear as the champions of American interests, and at the same time Mr Wilson, whose trump card was that he had kept America out of the war, was unwilling to embroil himself with either the Central Powers or the Allies. The British blockade had made some kind of "Black List" necessary, in order to penalize neutral firms that were found trading with the enemy. This step naturally roused great discontentment in America; much strong language was used, and the President was given drastic powers of retaliation. But, till the elections were over, relations with the United States had a certain unreality. Her statesmen were bound to speak and act with one eye on the facts and the other on the hustings.

One final aspect of the world situation demands a word. Germany, it is probable, had set more store by her gains in the Near East than by any occupation in Poland or in the West. To the devotees of Pan-Germanism and to her high finance the road to the East was the main necessity for Germany's future. In that direction alone could the Central Powers keep clear the highway to the outer world. She had hoped, as we have seen, to produce an anti-British crusade throughout the Moslem lands. In that she signally failed. The revolt of the Sherif of Mecca in June drove a wedge between the essential tradition of Islam and Constantinople. Henceforth the conservatives of that most conservative faith were strongly on the Allied side. Germany could win her end now solely by territorial conquests – by her mastery of the Balkans, and, through Turkey, of Persia and Mesopotamia. She could hope for nothing from the vast, vague forces of sentiment and religion, and must rely only on the sword.

The year had not brought to light any new great figure in politics or war. In Germany this barrenness was conspicuous. "This is a war of small men," Herr Zimmermann had observed early in the struggle, and the phrase was singularly true of his own land. On the whole von Mackensen was probably the best fighting general in the highest command that Germany possessed, and in von Falkenhayn and von Ludendorff she had two conspicuously able staff officers. Von Hindenburg was now pretty generally recognized as one of those favourites of fortune who acquire popular repute beyond their deserts. Since Tannenberg he had shown no special military genius, and he had made many failures. He was a grim and impressive figure, and he was good enough at hammer-blows, but in professional skill he ranked considerably below several of the Allied generals. The German system did not allow of the rise of new men. A proof is that by the summer of 1916 the High Commands in both East and West were more and more falling into the hands of royal personages. Such were, on the Austrian front, the Archdukes Karl and Eugene, and on the German fronts, Prince Leopold, the Imperial Crown Prince, the Crown Prince of Bavaria, and the Duke of Wurtemberg. It was as if Germany, having given up in despair the quest for supreme talent, had fallen back upon the glamour which in her eyes still surrounded her inconsiderable princes.

On the Allied side one great reputation had been made. Alexeiev, the Russian Chief of Staff, had revealed in the retreat a military genius which it is hard to overpraise. No less remarkable was his judgement during the long winter stagnation, and his power to seize the psychological moment when the hour for the offensive struck. Of the other Russian generals, Yudenitch in Transcaucasia and Brussilov in Galicia had greatly increased their fame. In the West de Castelnau had proved himself another Alexeiev, and a new fighting man had arisen in Pétain, whose discretion was as great as his resolution and fiery energy. The British armies had had little chance during the year to throw up new men, but in Sir Douglas Haig and Sir William Robertson they had soldiers who possessed the complete confidence of their troops and their Allies, and there were many army, corps, and divisional commanders who waited only for a great movement to prove their quality. At sea Sir John Jellicoe and Sir David Beatty had revealed beyond doubt the gifts of great sailors; and Admiral Kannin had handled the Russian Baltic Fleet with remarkable judgement and skill.

In civil statesmanship the French Premier, M. Briand, had shown qualities which made him an admirable leader of his nation in such a crisis. His assiduity and passion, his power of conciliation, his personal magnetism, and his great gift of speech enabled him to interpret France to the world and to herself. In Britain the death of Lord Kitchener had removed the supreme popular figure of the war – the man who played for the British Empire the part of General Joffre among the French people. He was succeeded by Mr Lloyd George, the only British statesman who possessed anything like the same power of impressing the popular imagination. The year had brought one notable discovery. Lord Robert Cecil, the Minister of Blockade, had perhaps the most difficult department in the Government, and in it he revealed much of the patience and coolness, the soundness of judgement, and the capacity for the larger view which had characterized his distinguished father. He now ranked among the foremost of those ministers whose reputation was not measured by parliamentary dialectic or adroitness in party management, but by administrative efficiency and the essentials of statesmanship.

But it should not be forgotten that in looking only at prominent figures we are apt to misread the picture. This was a war of peoples, and the peoples were everywhere greater than their leaders. The battles were largely soldiers' battles, and the civilian effort depended mainly upon the individual work of ordinary folk whose names were unknown to the Press. Everywhere in Britain, France, Russia, and Italy there was a vast amount of honest efficiency, and on this hung the fortunes of the Allies. Many of the ablest business and professional men were now enlisted in the service of the State. It was the work of the middle-class German in production and administration, far more than that of von Falkenhayn or von Helfferich or von Batocki, that kept Germany going, and it was the labour of the same classes among the Allies that enabled them in time to excel the German machine.

By the end of June 1916 the German outlook had appreciably darkened. The great Allied offensive had begun, and its end could not be foreseen. Germany was strategically and tactically on the defensive, and the wiser heads among her people were compelled to envisage a war of sheer endurance. In such a war there must be some sacrifice of previous gains, and the admission of unpalatable facts. It is probable that from this time dates the inclination to limit, if possible, her commitments – a policy to which the succeeding months were to add a special urgency. Von Falkenhayn ceased to be Chief of the General Staff. He was succeeded by von Hindenburg, and von Hindenburg's Chief of Staff, von Ludendorff, became First Quartermaster-General. Many reasons were given for this change. It was alleged that von Falkenhayn suffered the penalty of his failure at Verdun, and this, which was true in part, was the view taken by the German people. It was alleged, on the other hand, that the whole thing was a plot between von Falkenhayn and the Kaiser to discredit von Hindenburg, whose popularity had become dangerous; that the old field-marshal was to be given his head, in the certainty that he would run it against a wall. But the probable explanation was simpler. When a ministry is compelled to follow an unpopular course, it entrusts the work to that man among its members who has the greatest popular prestige, in the hope that he may gild the pill. The victor of Tannenberg had become a demigod for the German people. If losses had to be met, if territory had to be relinquished, if the truth had at last to be told, he alone could perform the task and carry the nation with him.

There were signs, too, at this time that in certain quarters in Germany some were beginning to look forward not merely to a defensive war of endurance, but to an ultimate débâcle. No hint of it appeared in the Press, and men scarcely dared to admit it to each other, but the suspicion was there. It was a prospect too dark for human fortitude. If a nation makes war for a noble cause and is defeated, there is ample consolation. If a nation makes war for self-interest and loses, but has conducted itself with a certain decency, it may rise in time from its failure. But if a nation forces on a war for the grossest self-interest, behaves in advance as if the world lay at its feet, and throughout violates every canon of law and honour and humanity, then there are no rags to be found in the wide earth to cover its nakedness. Compared with such shame the bitterness of death is sweet.

(Vol. XV pp. 35-49, 52-67)

THE BATTLE OF THE SOMME

The first Battle of the Somme – in reality a series of related battles over a twenty-five-mile front – lasted from 1 July to 18 November 1916. Buchan devoted an entire volume of some 263 pages to it.

Originally it was intended that the French should mount this offensive, but their losses at Verdun led the British to play the dominant role with a smaller French presence on the right of the line. The object was quite simply to break through the German positions and end the stalemate of trench warfare. In the event it was not achieved. When the fighting wound down the Allied line had inched forward, at great cost and in a few sectors only, at most five or six miles, while elsewhere the gains in ground won from the enemy were far less. On the first day, described in the following pages, the British Army suffered about 60,000 casualties and whole battalions of the "New Armies", in action for the first time, were decimated. These extracts show something of the beginning of the offensive which neither side could claim as a victory.

ALL ALONG the Allied front, a couple of miles behind the line, captive kite balloons, the so-called "sausages", glittered in the sunlight. Every gun on a front of twenty-five miles was speaking, and speaking without pause. In that week's bombardment more light and medium ammunition was expended than the total amount manufactured in Britain during the first eleven months of war, while the heavy stuff produced during the same period would not have kept our guns going for a single day. Great spurts of dust on the slopes showed where a heavy shell had burst, and black and white gouts of smoke dotted the middle distance like the little fires in a French autumn field. Lace-like shrapnel wreaths hung in the sky, melting into the morning haze. The noise was strangely uniform, a steady rumbling, as if the solid earth were muttering in a nightmare, and it was hard to distinguish the deep tones of the heavies, the vicious whip-like crack of the field guns, and the bark of the trench mortars.

About 7.15 the bombardment rose to that hurricane pitch of fury which betokened its close. It was as if titanic machine guns were at work round all the horizon. Then appeared a marvellous sight, the solid spouting of the enemy slopes – as if they were lines of reefs on which a strong tide was breaking. In such a hell it seemed that no human thing could live. Through the thin summer vapour and the thicker smoke which clung to the foreground there were visions of a countryside actually moving – moving bodily in débris into the air. And now there was a fresh sound – a series of abrupt and rapid bursts which came gustily from the first lines. These were the new trench mortars – wonderful little engines of death. There was another sound, too, from the north, as if the cannonading had suddenly come nearer. It looked as if the Germans had begun a counter-bombardment on part of the British front line.

The staff officers glanced at their watches, and at half past seven precisely there came a lull. It lasted for a second or two, and then the guns continued their tale. But the range had been lengthened everywhere, and from a bombardment the fire had become a barrage. For, on a twenty-five mile front, the Allied infantry had gone over the parapets.

✳ ✳ ✳

The British aim in this, the opening stage of the battle, was the German first position. In the section of assault, running from north to south, it covered Gommecourt, passed east of Hébuterne, followed the high ground in front of Serre and Beaumont Hamel, and crossed the Ancre a little to the north-west of Thiepval. It ran in front of Thiepval, which was very strongly fortified, east of Authuille, and just covered the hamlets of Ovillers and La Boisselle. There it ran about a mile and a quarter east of Albert. It then passed south round the woodland village of Fricourt, where it turned at right angles to the east, covering Mametz and Montauban. Half-way between Maricourt and Harde-court it turned south again, covered Curlu, crossed the Somme at the wide marsh near the place called Vaux, covered Frise and Dompierre and Soyecourt, and passed just east of Lihons, where it left the sector with which we are now concerned.

The British front of attack was disposed as follows: from opposite Gomme-court to just south of Beaumont Hamel lay the right wing of Sir Edmund Allenby's Third Army and General Hunter Weston's 8th Corps. From just north of the Ancre to Authuille was General Morland's 10th Corps. East of Albert lay General Pulteney's 3rd Corps, one division being directed against Ovillers, and another against La Boisselle. South, curving round the Fricourt salient to Mametz, lay General Horne's 15th Corps. On the British right flank adjoining the French lay General Congreve's 13th Corps.

It is clear that the Germans expected the attack of the Allies, and had made a fairly accurate guess as to its terrain. They assumed that the area would be from Arras to Albert. In all that area they were ready with a full concentration of men and guns. South of Albert they were less prepared, and south of the Somme they were caught napping. The history of the first day is therefore the story of two separate actions in the north and south, in the first of which the Allies failed and in the second of which they brilliantly succeeded. By the evening the first action had definitely closed, and the weight of the Allies was flung wholly into the second. That is almost inevitable in an attack on a very broad front. Some part will be found tougher than the rest, and that part having been tried will be relinquished; but it is the stubbornness of the knot and the failure to take it which are the price of success elsewhere.

COLIN U. GILL *Observation of Fire*

The divisions in action were three from the New Army, two of the old regulars, which had won fame both in Flanders and Gallipoli, and one Territorial brigade. They had to face a chain of fortified villages – Gommecourt, Serre, Beaumont Hamel, and Thiepval – and enemy positions which were generally on higher and better ground. The Ancre cut the line in two, with steep slopes rising from the valley bottom. Each village had been so fortified as to be almost impregnable, with a maze of catacombs, often two storeys deep, where whole battalions could take refuge, underground passages from the firing line to sheltered places in the rear, and pits into which machine guns could be lowered during a bombardment. On the plateau behind, with excellent direct observation, the Germans had their guns massed.

It was this direct observation and the deep shelters for machine guns which were the undoing of the British attack from Gommecourt to Thiepval. As our bombardment grew more intense on the morning of 1st July, so did the enemy's. Before our men could go over the parapets the Germans had plastered our front trenches with high explosives, and in many places blotted them out. All along our line, fifty yards before and behind the first trench, they dropped 6-inch and 8-inch high-explosive shells. The result was that our men, instead of forming up in the front trench, were compelled to form up in the open ground behind, for the front trench had disappeared. In addition to this there was an intense shrapnel barrage, which must have been directed by observers, for it followed our troops as they moved forward.

At Beaumont Hamel, under the place called Hawthorn Redoubt, we had constructed a mine, the largest yet known in the campaign. At 7.30 acres of land leaped into the air, and our men advanced under the shadow of a pall of dust which turned the morning into twilight. "The exploding chamber", said a sergeant, describing it afterwards, "was as big as a picture palace, and the gallery was an awful length. It took us seven months to build, and we were working under some of the crack Lancashire miners. Every time a fresh fatigue party came up they'd say to the miners, 'Ain't your grotto ever going up?' But, my lord! it went up all right on 1st July. It was the sight of your life. Half the village got a rise. The air was full of stuff – wagons, wheels, horses, tins, boxes, and Germans. It was seven months well spent getting that mine ready. I believe some of the pieces are coming down still."

As our men began to cross No Man's Land, the Germans seemed to man their ruined parapets, and fired rapidly with automatic rifles and machine guns. They had special light *musketon* battalions, armed with machine guns and automatic rifles, who showed marvellous intrepidity, some even pushing their guns forward into No Man's Land to enfilade our advance. Moreover they had machine-gun pits far in front of their parapets, connected with their trenches by deep tunnels secure from shell-fire. The British moved forward in line after line, dressed as if on parade; not a man wavered or broke rank; but minute by minute the ordered lines melted away under the deluge of high-explosive, shrapnel, rifle, and machine-gun fire. There was no question about the German weight of artillery. From dawn till long after noon they maintained this steady drenching fire. Gallant individuals or isolated detachments managed here and there to break into the enemy position, and some even penetrated well behind it; but these were episodes, and the ground they won could not be held. By the evening, from Gommecourt to Thiepval, the attack had been everywhere checked, and our troops – what was left of them – were back again in their old line. They had struck the core of the main German defence.

(*Vol. XVI pp. 30-31, 34-40*)

THE MASTERY OF THE AIR

Aircraft played a considerable role in the battles of Verdun and the Somme. In the autumn of 1916 numbers of German airships attacked targets on the British mainland.

THE SUMMER and autumn of 1916 saw no such spectacular revival in German aeronautics as marked the close of 1915. The Fokker had found its level, and though Germany struggled hard to find new types, she did not again steal a march upon the Allied construction. Moreover, the opening of the Somme offensive saw an immense advance in the tactical use of aeroplanes by the Allies, an advance marked by such boldness and ingenuity that the question of aerial supremacy seemed to be clearly decided. The French and British airmen had beyond doubt won the initiative. This was recognized by the enemy, and captured letters were full of complaints of the inadequacy of the German reply. The Battle of the Somme in its later stages showed, indeed, something of the old see-saw. There came moments when the German airmen recovered their nerve and made a stout defence. But it was always a defence, and the war was never seriously carried into the Allied camp.

The popular phrase, the "mastery of the air", was in those days apt to be misused. There were weeks when the Allies' total of loss seemed to be higher than that of their adversaries, and pessimists complained that our mastery had been lost. Mastery in the absolute sense never existed. The Allied squadrons still ventured much when they crossed the enemy lines, and they paid a price, sometimes a heavy price, for their successes. But they maintained continuously the offensive. Daily they did their work of destruction and reconnaissance far inside the enemy territory, while the few German machines that crossed our lines came at night, and at a great elevation. Hourly throughout the battles they gave to the work of the infantry a tactical support to which the enemy could show no parallel. If the Allied losses had been consistently higher than the Germans' the superiority would still have been ours, for we achieved our purpose. We hampered the enemy's reserves, destroyed his depots, reconnoitred every acre of his hinterland, and shattered his peace of mind. For such results no price could have been too high, for our air work was the foundation of every infantry advance. As a matter of sober fact, the price was not high; it was far less than Germany paid for her inadequate defence.

During the later Verdun battles and the great offensive on the Somme, the four main aerial activities were maintained which were set forth in an earlier chapter. Our aeroplanes did long-distance reconnoitring work, they "spotted" for the guns, they bombed important enemy centres, and they fought and destroyed enemy machines. The daily communiqués recorded the destruction of enemy dumps and depots and railway junctions, and a long series of brilliant conflicts in the air, where often a German squadron was broken up and put to flight by a single Allied plane. To a watcher of these battles the signs of our superiority were manifest. Often at night a great glare behind the lines marked where some German ammunition store had gone up in flames. The orderly file of Allied kite balloons glittered daily in the sun; but the German "sausages" were few, and often a wisp of fire in the heavens showed that another had fallen victim to an Allied airman. A German plane was as rare a sight a mile within our lines as a swallow in November, but the eternal crack of anti-aircraft guns from the German side told of the persistency of the Allied inroads.

The most interesting development brought about by the Somme action was that of "contact patrols". The machines used were of the slowest type, and it was their business to accompany an infantry advance and report progress. In the intricate trench fighting of the modern battle nothing is harder than to locate the position at any one moment of the advancing battalions. Flares may not be observed in the smoke and dust of battle; dispatch runners may fail to get through the barrage; the supply of pigeons may give out or the birds be killed *en route* – and the general behind may be unable in consequence to give orders to the guns. With the system of "creeping barrages" it is vital that the command should be fully informed from time to time of the exact situation of the infantry attack. The airman, flying low over the trenches, can detect the whereabouts of his own troops and report accordingly. Again and again during the Somme, when the mist of battle and ill weather had swallowed up the advance, aeroplanes brought half-hourly accurate and most vital intelligence. A check could in this way be made known, and the guns turned on to break up an obstacle; while an advance swifter than the timetable could be saved from the risk of its own barrage. Curiously enough, except for rifle and machine-gun fire from the German trenches, these flights were not so desperately risky. They were made usually at a height of something under 500 feet, and the German anti-aircraft guns, made to fire straight into the air, and usually mounted on the crests of the ridges, could not be trained on the marauders. These aeroplanes did not content themselves with reconnaissance. They attacked the enemy in the trenches with bombs and machine-gun fire, and on many occasions completely demoralized him. There was one instance of a whole battalion surrendering to an aeroplane. Bouchavesnes was taken largely by French fire from the air, and the last trench at Gueudecourt fell to a British airman.

✳ ✳ ✳

During the greater part of the Somme battle the Allied machines were at least equal to the German in pace and handiness. The little Nieuport scouts, in especial, dealt death to the kite balloons, and the Martinsyde and De Havilland fighting planes were more than a match for the Fokker. In October, however, the enemy produced two new types – the Spad and the Halberstadt – both based on French models and possessing engines of 240 hp. With them his airmen could work at a height of 20,000 feet and swoop down upon British machines moving at a lower altitude. Hence there came a time, at the close of the Somme operations, when the see-saw once again slightly inclined in the Germans' favour. The moment passed, and long before the great Spring offensive began the arrival of new and improved British types had redressed the balance.

The aerial warfare of 1916, as summarized by the French Staff, showed that 900 enemy aeroplanes had been destroyed by the Allies, the French accounting for 450, and the British for 250. Eighty-one kite balloons had been burned, fifty-four by the French, and twenty-seven by the British. Seven hundred and fifty bombardments had taken place, of which the French were responsible for 250 and the British for 180. Apart from tactical bombardments immediately behind the fighting line, the record of the year was least conspicuous in the matter of bomb dropping. Experience had shown that the German public were peculiarly sensible to this mode of attack; but the preoccupation of the Allies with great battles limited the number of machines which could be spared for that purpose. Nevertheless some of the raids undertaken were singularly bold and effective, as a few examples will show. On 12th October a Franco-British squadron of forty machines attacked the Mauser rifle factory at Oberndorf on the Neckar, dropped nearly a thousand pounds weight of projectiles, and fought their way home through a hornet's nest of enemy craft. On 9th October Stuttgart was attacked; on the 22nd the ironworks at Hagondage, north of Metz, and the railway station of Thionville. On 22nd September two French airmen, Captain de Beauchamp and Lieutenant Daucourt, in a Sopwith biplane, visited and bombed the Krupp works at Essen – a *tour de force* rather than a work of military importance, for Essen could not suffer much from the limited number of bombs which could be carried on a 500-mile journey. On 17th November Captain de Beauchamp in the same machine flew over Friedrichshafen to Munich, which he bombed, and then crossed the Alps and descended in Italy. But the most sensational achievement was that of Second Lieutenant Marschal on a special type of Nieuport monoplane, who on the night of 20th June flew over Berlin, dropping leaflets, prefaced with these words: "We might have bombarded the open town of Berlin, and killed women and innocent children, but we content ourselves with this." He was making for Russia; but unfortunately he had trouble with his machine, and came down at Cholm, in Poland, where he was taken prisoner. He was then only sixty-three miles from the Russian trenches, and had travelled 811 miles.

✳ ✳ ✳

Saturday, 2nd September, was a heavy day, with an overcast sky, which cleared up at twilight. The situation on the Somme was getting desperate, and

Germany resolved to send against Britain the largest airship flotilla she had yet dispatched. There were ten Zeppelins, several of the newest and largest type, and three Schütte-Lanz military airships, and their objective was London and the great manufacturing cities of the Midlands. The Zeppelins completely lost their way. They wandered over East Anglia, dropping irrelevant bombs, and received a warm reception from the British guns. At least two seem to have been hit. One lost her observation car, which was picked up in East Anglia, and this may have been the airship which was seen next morning by Dutch fishermen, travelling slowly and in difficulties, jettisoning stuff as she moved.

The military airships made for London. Ample warning of their coming had been given, and the city was in deep darkness, save for the groping search-lights. The streets were full of people, whose curiosity mastered their prudence, and they were rewarded by one of the most marvellous spectacles which the war had yet seen. Two of the marauders were driven off by our gunfire, but one attempted to reach the city from the east. After midnight the sky was clear and star-strewn. The sound of the guns was heard and patches of bright light appeared in the heavens where our shells were bursting. Shortly after two o'clock on the morning of the 3rd, about 10,000 feet up in the air, an airship was seen moving south-westward. She dived and then climbed, as if to escape the shells, and for a moment seemed to be stationary. There came a burst of smoke which formed a screen around her and hid her from view, and then far above appeared little points of light. Suddenly the searchlights were shut off and the guns stopped. The next second the airship was visible like a glowing cigar, turning rapidly to a red and angry flame. She began to fall in a blazing wisp, lighting up the whole sky, so that countryfolk fifty miles off saw the portent. The spectators broke into wild cheering, for from some cause or other the raider had met its doom.

The cause was soon known. Several airmen had gone up to meet the enemy, and one of them, Lieutenant William Leefe Robinson, formerly of the Worcester Regiment, a young man of twenty-one, had come to grips with her. When he found her, he was 2,000 feet below her, but he climbed rapidly and soon won the top position. He closed, and though the machine gun on the top of the airship opened fire on him, he got in his blow in time. No such duel had ever been fought before, 10,000 feet up in the sky, in the view of hundreds of thousands of spectators over an area of a thousand square miles. The airship fell blazing in a field at Cuffley, near Enfield, a few miles north of London, and the bodies of the crew of sixteen were charred beyond recognition. They were given a military funeral according to the fine traditions of the Flying Corps. Lieutenant Robinson received the Victoria Cross, for he was the first man to grapple successfully with an enemy airship by night, and to point the way to the true line of British defence. It was no easy victory. Such a combat against the far stronger armament of the airship, and exposed to constant danger from our own bursting shells, involved risks little short of the most forlorn hope in the battlefield.

On the night of 23rd September the raiders came again. Twelve Zeppelins crossed the eastern shoreline, making for London. Almost at once they were scattered by gunfire, and only two pursued their journey to the capital, where they succeeded in dropping bombs in a suburb of small houses. Of the others one attacked a Midland town. The total British casualties were thirty killed and 110 injured. But they paid dearly for their enterprise. One, L33, was so seriously damaged by our anti-aircraft guns that she fled out to sea, and then, realizing that this meant certain death, returned to land, and came down in an Essex field. Her men, twenty-two in number, set her on fire, and then marched along the road to Colchester till they found a special constable, to whom they surrendered. The destruction was imperfectly done, and the remains gave the British authorities the complete details of the newest type of Zeppelin. A second, L32, was attacked by two airmen, Second Lieutenant F. Sowrey and Second Lieutenant Alfred Brandon of the Royal Flying Corps, who had been waiting for months for such a chance. The end was described by a special constable on duty. "In the searchlight beams she looked like an incandescent bar of white-hot steel. Then she staggered and swung to and fro in the air for just a perceptible moment of time. That, no doubt, was the instant when the damage was done, and the huge craft became unmanageable. Then, without drifting at all from her approximate place in the sky, without any other preliminary, she fell like a stone, first horizontally – that is, in her sailing trim – then in a position which rapidly became perpendicular, she went down, a mass of flames."

Germany had begun to fare badly in the air, but popular clamour and the vast sums sunk in Zeppelin manufacture prevented her from giving up the attempt. On the night of Monday, 25th September, seven Zeppelins crossed the east coast, aiming at the industrial districts of the Midlands and the north. The wide area of the attack and the thick ground mist enabled them to return without loss, after bombing various working-class districts. The Germans claimed to have done damage to the great munition area, and even to have "bombarded the British naval port of Portsmouth". As a matter of fact, no place of any military importance and no munition factory suffered harm. The losses were among humble people living in the flimsy houses of industrial suburbs.

A more formidable attempt was made on 1st October. It was a clear, dark night when ten Zeppelins made landfall on their way to London. But they found that the capital was ringed by defences in the air and on the ground which made approach impossible. The attack became a complete fiasco. About midnight one Zeppelin, L31, approached the north-east environs, and was engaged by an aeroplane piloted by Second Lieutenant Tempest of the Royal Flying Corps. The watching thousands saw the now familiar sight – a glow and then a falling wisp of flame. The airship crashed to earth in a field near Potter's Bar, while the crowds at every viewpoint sang the National Anthem. The crew perished to a man, including the officer in charge, Lieutenant-Commander Mathy, the best-known of all the Zeppelin pilots. He it was who had

NORMAN G. ARNOLD
The Last Fight of Captain Ball, V.C., D.S.O., M.C., 17th May, 1917

commanded the raiding airships in September and October 1915, and had
given to an American correspondent a flamboyant account of his experiences.
He had always ridiculed the value of aeroplanes as an anti-Zeppelin weapon. "I
am not afraid of them", he had said. "I think I could make it interesting for
them, unless there was a regular swarm." By the irony of fate he was to fall to a
single machine, guided by a young officer of twenty-six.

During the wild weather of late October and early November there was a
breathing space. The next attempt, warned by past experiences, steered clear of
London, and aimed at the north-east coast, which, it was assumed, would be
less strongly defended. It came on the night of 27th November, in cold,
windless weather. How many airships were concerned is not certain, but the
likelihood is that there were at least five. One, after dropping a few bombs in
Durham and Yorkshire, was engaged by Lieutenant Pyott of the Royal Flying
Corps off the Durham coast. Once again came the glow and then the wisp of
flame. The airship split in two before reaching the sea. The debris sank, and
when day broke only a scum on the water marked its resting-place. Another
wandered across the Midlands on its work of destruction, and in the morning
steered for home, closely pursued by our aeroplanes and bombarded by our
guns. It left the land going very fast at a height of 8,000 feet, but nine miles
out to sea it was attacked by four machines of the Royal Naval Air Service, as
well as by the guns of an armed trawler. The issue was not long in doubt, and

presently the Zeppelin fell blazing to the water. The credit of this exploit belonged to three young Naval airmen, Flight Lieutenant Pulling, Flight Lieutenant Cadbury, and Flight Sub-Lieutenant Fane.

The year 1916 was disastrous to the Zeppelin legend. The loss of twelve of these great machines, each costing from a quarter to half a million pounds to build, was admitted by the enemy, and beyond doubt there were other losses unreported. The Zeppelin fleet was now sadly reduced in effectives, and it had lost still more in repute. A way had been found to meet the menace, and it was improbable that any future adaptation of the Zeppelin could break down the new defence. But the peril from the air was not over, as some too rashly concluded. Throughout the year there had been a number of attacks by German aeroplanes, which rarely extended beyond the towns in the south-eastern corner of England. Such attacks were not formidable, the raiders being as a rule in a desperate hurry to be gone. But it occurred to many, watching the advent of the new Spad and Halberstadt machines on the Western front, that in that quarter lay a threat to England more formidable than the airship. An aeroplane with a 240-hp. engine, which could fly at a great speed at a height of close on 20,000 feet, could operate in broad daylight, and pass unchallenged to its goal. If we had not the type of machine to climb fast and operate at the same altitude, such a raider would be safe from attack alike by aeroplane and gunfire. On the 28th of November a German machine, flying very high, dropped nine bombs on London. The raider was brought down in France on its way home, and among its furniture was a large scale map of London. The incident was trifling in itself, but in many minds it raised unpleasing reflections. Our aeroplanes had beaten the invading Zeppelin. We might still have to face the invading aeroplane.

(Vol. XVII pp. 149-56, 161-67)

THE THIRD YEAR OF THE WAR

When he came to write his summary of the third year of the war, Buchan had two especially important factors to discuss. The first was the Russian Revolution, the consequences of which were to loom large over the entire field of subsequent world history; the second, and more significant for contemporary observers, was the entry of the United States of America into the war. Their first troops landed in France on 25 June 1917.

AT THE end of June 1916 the Germans in the West had exhausted their capacity for the offensive, and the long Allied battle-line from the North Sea to the Adriatic was about to move forward. While Brussilov was pressing hard in Volhynia and Galicia and the Bukovina, the Battle of the Somme began, and by the close of the year it had effected its main purpose . . . It forced the enemy from positions which he thought impregnable, gravely depleted his manpower, dislocated his staff-work, and disorganized his whole military machine. It compelled him to make superhuman efforts to increase his forces, and to construct a new defensive position to be the bulwark of his French and Belgian occupations. All along the Western front the Allies were successful. At Verdun, before the close of the year, Nivelle, by shattering counterstrokes, had won back what Germany had gained in the spring and summer. Cadorna had taken Gorizia, and had pushed well into the Carso fastnesses. On the Russian front Brussilov, after destroying three Austrian armies, had been stayed before Halicz in September; and during the autumn and early winter von Mackensen and von Falkenhayn had overrun the Dobrudja and Wallachia, taken Bucharest, and driven the Romanians to the line of the Sereth. But this victory, won against a small and ill-equipped nation, was the solitary success of the Central Powers. On all the main battle-grounds they had been unmistakably beaten in the field.

To the most conservative observer at the beginning of 1917 it seemed almost a matter of mathematical certainty that during that year the Teutonic Alliance must suffer the final military defeat which would mean the end of the war. No larger effort would be required from Russia than Brussilov's attack of 1916; let that be repeated, and the Western Allies would do the rest. The Allied plan was a great combined advance as soon as the weather permitted, for an attack in spring would leave the whole summer and autumn in which to reap the fruits. The enemy must be driven back on his Siegfried Line during the first months of the year, and then must come the combined blow on the pivots of his last defences. Russia, now well supplied with munitions, would take the field at the first chance, and Cadorna would press forward against Trieste. In the Balkans Sarrail would engage the two Bulgarian armies, and even if he could not break them, he could pin them down and ease Romania's case. In the East Yudenitch would press south from the Caucasus, and the British armies of Syria and Mesopotamia would press northward, and between them the Turkish forces would be hemmed in and the campaign in that area brought to a decision. On paper the scheme seemed perfect; as far as human intelligence could judge, it was feasible; but in war there may suddenly appear a new and unlooked-for factor which shatters the best-laid plan.

That new factor was the Russian Revolution. In April 1917, when the offensive was due to start, it was still an uncertain quantity, but some consequences were at once apparent. The disorganization of the Russian armies prevented Yudenitch's movement from the Caucasus. It enabled German reinforcements to be sent westward against France and Britain. It gave much-tried Austria a breathing space, and allowed her to strengthen her Isonzo and Carso fronts. Above all, it introduced uncertainty, which to a strategic plan is as grit in the bearings of a machine. A new vague element had appeared, which, like the addition of some ingredient to a chemical combination, altered subtly and radically all the original components. The great spring offensive miscarried, though many local victories were won. The pivots of the Siegfried Line were not broken. The contemplated "drive" of the Turkish armies in the East did not succeed. Partly this was due to elements of weakness in the Allied armies, to the comparative failure of Nivelle on the Aisne, and to the confused methods of Sarrail at Salonika. Partly it was due to weather, which is beyond the authority of any General Staff. But the main cause was the increased strength of the enemy caused by the defection of Russia from the battle-line.

Nevertheless, at the close of June 1917, the position of the Allies was strong and hopeful. During the preceding year France and Britain had captured from the German armies 165,000 rank and file, 3,500 officers, nearly a thousand guns, and some 3,000 lesser pieces. They had won almost all the chief observation posts of the enemy in the West – the Bapaume Ridge, the Chemin des Dames, the Moronvilliers hills, Vimy, and Messines. Since the blow on the Siegfried pivots had failed, Sir Douglas Haig was making ready another plan, and by his victory at Messines on 7th June had cleared his flanks for the new movement. Italy had won substantial victories on the Isonzo heights and on the Carso. Though the Balkan attack had miscarried, Venizelos was now in power in Greece, and the danger to the rear of the Salonika army had gone. Sir Archibald Murray had been checked at Gaza, but Sir Stanley Maude had taken Bagdad, and had pushed his front well to the north and east of the city. America had entered the war, and was preparing with all her might to play an adequate part. Finally, there were rumours that Russia was about to take the offensive; and those who did not realize the complete chaos of that country talked wisely of what might be accomplished by a revolutionary army, where each soldier fought under the inspiration of the new wine of liberty.

PAUL NASH *Ruined Country – Old Battlefield, Vimy*

The situation had, therefore, many hopeful aspects; but to the careful student it seemed that that hope did not rest on reasoned calculations. The harsh fact was that the great plan of 1917, of which the Somme and indeed all the Allied fighting and preparation since 1915 had been the logical preliminaries, had proved impossible. New plans could be made, but they would not be the same. For the elements were no longer calculable. By the failure of one great partner the old military cohesion of the Alliance had gone. Much might still be hoped for from Russia, but nothing could be taken for granted. The beleaguering forces which had sat for three years round the German citadel were wavering and straggling on the East. The war on two fronts, which had been Germany's great handicap, looked as if it might change presently to a war on a single front. Whatever victories might be won during the remainder of 1917, it was now clear that the decisive blow could not be delivered. The Teutonic Alliance, just when it was beginning to crumble, had been given a new tenure of life.

The year had been fruitful in tactical developments, mainly on the Allied side. The Somme saw the principle of limited objectives first put methodically into practice – a principle which led to brilliant success at the winter battles of Verdun, at Arras, and most notably at Messines, and in regard to which

Nivelle's attack at the Aisne was the exception that proved the rule. It saw, too, the most valuable advance in artillery tactics during the war – the Allied device of the "creeping barrage". On the enemy side the chief novelty was the use of "shock troops" for the counter-attack. In the main battle area he had been continuously on the defensive, and his method had been to hold his front line lightly, and rely on a massed counter-attack before the offensive had secured its ground. This was for the normal sector, but on the Siegfried Line he trusted to the immense strength of his positions and his endless well-placed machine guns to prevent any loss of ground. Neither mode of defence wholly succeeded. By the end of June he had already lost seven miles of the Siegfried Line; and in the rest of the battlefield he had, with the solitary exception of Fresnoy, failed to win back any ground by his counter-attacks. But this is not to say that his tactics were not the best possible in the circumstances. He was playing for time, husbanding his manpower, and dragging out the contest till his submarine campaign should bring Britain to her knees. He was successful in so far that he was able to stave off a decisive blow, and he was busy perfecting other devices which were to give us serious food for thought later in the year. The defensive of the German High Command was no supine or unintelligent thing.

On one side the enemy showed remarkable energy. Before the close of the Somme he had realized his weakness in the air, and had appointed General von Höppner, the Chief of Staff of Otto von Below's Sixth Army, to control all his flying service. The result was a striking advance in effectiveness. Before Arras, indeed, he was beaten from the field, but only at the cost of a heavy Allied sacrifice. Von Höppner perfected new types of battle-planes, notably the two Albatrosses; he was the chief promoter of the Gotha bomb-carrier, which was soon to become a familiar name in England; he vastly improved the personnel of the service; he concentrated on the production of high-powered engines; and he greatly increased the output of the standardized factories. The command of the air, as has often been pointed out in these pages, could never be an absolute thing. On the whole, the Allies had the superiority; but there were long spells when the battle was drawn, and at moments the honours seemed to be on the other side. It was a ceaseless struggle both for the airmen at the front and for the factories at home, and a single error in foresight or a single strike of workmen might incline the wavering balance against the side responsible for it.

But developments in tactics and *matériel* were of secondary importance compared with the great question of manpower. We have seen the difficulties of the Central Powers up to the spring of 1917, when the Russian Revolution gave them a new lease of life. All the combatants were suffering from the depletion of their ranks. France had reached her maximum at an earlier stage, and was naturally anxious to conserve her remaining resources. She was holding roughly two-thirds of the Western front; but as the main operations were in the British section, the enemy's strength per mile against the latter was more than double his strength per mile against the French. Generally speaking, in the West the two Allied forces were of about equal strength, and it was clear that a further increase could only come from Britain, whose exhaustion was conspicuously less than that of her neighbour.

But for Britain the problem of reserves was far from easy, for she could not give undivided attention to the question of men for the front, since she was the chief munitioner of all the Allies. She had some two and a quarter million men engaged in shipbuilding, munitions, and kindred work; she had well over five millions under arms, of whom nearly three and a quarter millions were in expeditionary forces, and of these nearly two and a quarter millions in France and Flanders. Her losses had not been on the French scale, but her non-combatant commitments were far greater. Hence for her the balance must be most delicately hung. More men must be got to face the German divisions released from the East, for each month of the war had made it clearer that no decision could be won without a crushing numerical superiority. Moreover, these men must be ready in time, so that they could be fully trained before entering the line; for every dispatch of Sir Douglas Haig insisted upon the folly of flinging raw troops into a modern battle. But the reinforcements came slowly. In the spring of 1917 Sir William Robertson, in a public speech, asked for half a million new levies by July. He did not get them, for the conflicting claims could not be balanced. The country passed through acute phases of opinion, in which the building of new tonnage, the production of food supplies at home, the construction of a vast aeroplane programme, seemed successively the major needs. But vital as these were, the great permanent demand was men for the fighting line. As Sir William Robertson said truly, it was idle to put a limit to the number of men needed for the army. Everybody was needed who could conceivably be spared from vital industries. For without a great preponderance of numbers on the front the most ample munitionment carried by the most impregnable mercantile navy could not give us victory.

It was to this problem especially that America's entry into the war seemed to provide an answer. We have not yet reached the stage when it is necessary to describe in detail the war measures of the great Western Republic. They were instant and comprehensive. From the day of the declaration of war America flung herself whole-heartedly into the work of preparation. Her resources were enormous, for within a few years it was calculated that she could put fifteen millions of men into the fighting line and provide some hundreds of thousand millions sterling of money. But she had to do the things which her Allies had done two years earlier, and at this stage of the contest, if her assistance was to be effective, it must be furiously speeded up. America's effort must be made against time. Her first step was to introduce compulsory service under a system of selective conscription. The measure was passed by Congress on 28th April, and in five months a million and a half soldiers were in training. The regular army was brought up to its full strength of 400,000 by voluntary enlistment; the National Guard was brought up to half a million; the ballot for conscripts gave some 700,000. Vast camps sprang up throughout the country like mushrooms in a night.

The mobilization of America for war was hurried on in all other branches of national effort. More than 20,000 million dollars was voted, of which 7,000 millions were loans to America's Allies. The immense sum of £128,000,000 was set aside for aeroplane contracts. A huge programme of merchant ship-building was entered upon. The President was given power to assist the Allied blockade by putting an embargo on certain exports to neutral countries, and he did not let the weapon rust. Controllers of food and the other chief commodities were appointed, as in Britain. Treason and espionage were put down with that high hand which can only be used by a democracy sure of itself.

Monday 25th June was an eventful day, for it saw the landing of the first units of American troops in France. They were only forerunners, to prepare the way for those who should follow; for there were few troops as yet available for the field, and the small regular army had to be distributed as stiffening among the new divisions. The American Commander-in-Chief was Major-General Pershing, who had been a conspicuous figure in the Spanish and Mexican Wars – a man still in early middle life, with many years of practical campaigning behind him. The old American army had been small, but its officers had followed the life for the love of it, and were to a high degree professional experts. For its size, the staff was probably equal to any in the world. Those who watched the first American soldiers on the continent of Europe – grave young men, with lean, shaven faces, a quick, springy walk, and a superb bodily fitness – found their memories returning to Gettysburg and the Wilderness, where the same stock had shown an endurance and heroism not surpassed in human history. And they were disposed to agree with the observer who remarked that it had taken a long time to get America into the war, but that it would take much longer to get her out.

The year in naval warfare had been inconspicuous so far as above-water actions were concerned. The essay of Jutland was not repeated. The battle-ships and the battle cruisers lay idle in harbour, or patrolled seas where there was no sign of the enemy. There was, indeed, much sporadic raiding. During the first months of 1917 the *Seeadler* repeated in the South Atlantic the exploits of the *Moewe* the previous year. All through the first months of 1917 the German flotillas from Zeebrugge and Ostend were busy about the British shores. On 22nd January Commander Tyrwhitt's forces met an enemy destroyer division off the Dutch coast – sank one vessel and scattered the rest. Then followed a series of German raids on the Kent and Suffolk coasts, and the bombardment of the much-tried little seaport towns. In April the British counter-attacked with some success, and in a brilliant action off Dover, on the night of 20th April, the *Broke*, commanded by Commander Evans, the Antarctic explorer, and the *Swift*, Commander Peck, engaged five or six vessels, and sank at least two of them. The fight of the *Broke* was memorable because she rammed a German destroyer, and repelled boarders in the old style with fist and bayonet. On 5th June the Dover patrol bombarded Ostend so effectually as to destroy most of the

THOMAS DERRICK *American Troops at Southampton Embarking for France*

workshops and make the harbour untenable; while Commander Tyrwhitt's Harwich flotilla engaged six destroyers — sank one and severely damaged another.

It was very clear that these Belgian bases were a perpetual menace to our shores and to the safety of the Allied trade. Not only did they serve as the home of the aircraft which were beginning to make bold assaults upon England, but they were the source of the raiding flotillas and the harbour of all the smaller submarines. The mind of the High Command in the field was more and more turning towards the smoking out of this nest of mischief by a land attack, as at once the best offensive and defensive possible. Some words of Sir John Jellicoe's at this time foreshadowed a policy which was soon to result in the Third Battle of Ypres. "The Germans", he said, "have applied to this length of sand-fringed coast the same principle of intensive fortifications adopted higher up on the North Sea and the island of Heligoland. The coastline is studded with heavy guns, which in themselves constitute infinitesimal targets at a range of over 20,000 yards on which any bombardment could be carried out. Moreover, the enemy has not been slow to make the fullest use of aircraft and smoke screens by way of protection. Ostend offers the best target; but it can only be attacked at rare intervals, when a favourable combination of wind, weather, and sea conditions can be attained. Zeebrugge, in the wide sense of the word, is not a naval base, but merely an exit from the inland port of Bruges, with which it is connected by a wide deep-water canal. There is little to hit at Zeebrugge. Still, I hope that the problem which the Belgian coast presents is not insoluble."

But if the year was barren of fleet actions, it was none the less destined to form an epoch in naval history, for the early weeks of 1917 saw the submarine become the most potent single weapon of the war. During the summer and autumn of 1916, the range of the German underwater craft had been extended and their numbers largely increased. On February 1, 1917, Germany's campaign of unlimited submarine warfare began. Hitherto, she had been restrained, not by considerations of decency or of international law, but solely by the fear of bringing America into the contest. Now, largely as a result of the Somme, she had made up her mind that at all costs she must deal a final blow to her main enemy if she were to avoid a general defeat. She believed that the economic condition of Britain was very grave, and that by a mighty effort she might force starvation upon that people, cripple their military effort, and bring them to their senses. She had reasoned out the matter carefully, and was confident of her conclusions. She ran a desperate risk, but the stakes were worth it. America might declare war; but that price would not be too high to pay for the destruction of Britain as a fighting force, and perhaps as a coherent state. Beyond doubt, when the German Government yielded to the policy of von Tirpitz and von Reventlow, it was because they believed that they were gambling on a certainty.

On 31st January Germany announced the danger zone to the world. All the waters in a wide radius round Britain, France, and Italy, as well as in the Eastern Mediterranean, were declared to be blockaded areas. A narrow lane was left for shipping to Greece. The ensuing campaign was waged in deadly earnest. The weekly tables which the British Admiralty issued as from 25th February showed a heavy and growing loss of British and Allied tonnage. During the month of April we lost some 550,000 tons gross of shipping, and there were those who, looking at the brilliant Arras offensive, declared that the problem for Germany was to defeat Britain at sea before the British army could win on land. After April the wastage slowly declined, so that in July the gross tonnage lost was only 320,000. On 21st February Admiral von Capelle told the Reichstag that the expectations attached to the U-boat campaign by the German people had been fully justified by results. The end of April was popularly fixed as the limit of British endurance under this new attack; then it was postponed to August; but May passed and August came, and there was no sign of yielding. To that extent Germany's gamble failed. It brought in America against her, but it was very far from forcing Britain to sue for peace. The military stores carried overseas to the fighting fronts were in September, 1917, more than twice what they had been in January.

Nevertheless, the situation was sufficiently grave. From the beginning of the war till February 1, 1917, we had lost some four and a half million tons to the enemy; we lost approximately that amount in the first seven months of the new submarine warfare. At that rate the Allied tonnage would presently be reduced to a point which would forbid not only the decent provisioning of the civilian peoples at home, but the full maintenance of the armies at the fighting fronts. To meet the menace, five lines of policy must be pursued concurrently. All unnecessary imports from overseas must be firmly checked. Home production, both of food and raw materials such as ores and timber, must be immensely increased. New tonnage must be built, or borrowed where it could be had. Existing merchant shipping must be protected as far as possible by escorts and by the organization of convoys. Finally, a truceless war must be waged against the U-boats, in the hope that the point would be reached when we could sink them faster than Germany could build them.

British statesmen made earnest appeals to their countrymen, and met with a willing response. By the early summer of 1917 Great Britain had grown into one vast market garden, and every type of citizen had become an amateur food-producer. There were periodic shortages of certain articles of diet, and the supply of certain imported materials, such as pulp for paper-making, steadily declined. But on the whole the British people showed an adaptability in the crisis with which their best friends had scarcely credited them. The shipbuild-ing programmes were enlarged and speeded up. During peace time Britain had produced some two millions of new tonnage a year. In 1915 this figure fell to 688,000; in 1916 to 538,000. During the first six months of 1917 the tonnage built was 484,000, and in his speech of 16th August the Prime Minister told the House of Commons that the total new tonnage built at home and acquired from abroad during the year would be 1,900,000. When we consider that this was almost the amount of peace construction, and reflect on the depletion and diversion of British manpower, the achievement must seem highly creditable. The convoy system was successful, and in the Atlantic presently gave good results. As for our offensive against the submarine, it proceeded slowly but surely, by a multitude of devices the tale of which cannot yet be told. Our system of naval intelligence was perfected, and our aircraft became deadly weapons both for the detection and destruction of the German craft. The enemy losses increased slightly during the first quarter of the year; during the second quarter they rose more sharply; and after June the curve mounted steeply. It must be realized that our problem both of defence and offence was far more difficult than when submarine attacks were confined to the Narrow Seas. It was possible to defend our channels and estuaries by a dozen methods which could not be used against craft operating in the wide ocean.

The main problem for the Allies during the first year of the war was men for the field; it was munitions during the second, and tonnage in the third. The only enemy offensive was now on the sea. This problem affected all the Allies; but it bore most heavily on Britain, partly because of her large necessary import

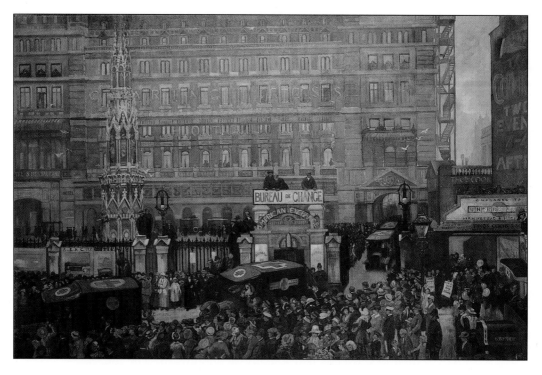

J. HODGSON LOBLEY *Outside Charing Cross Station, July, 1916*

trade, partly because of her position as universal provider. It was beyond her power to solve it by the immediate creation of new tonnage to replace losses, since, in building up her armies and munition factories, she had drawn too largely on her strength for any large effort in a new direction. The solution lay with America, and in a special degree it was America's contribution to the campaign. It was Germany's submarine policy which had brought the United States into the struggle, and the daily record of cold-blooded barbarities was the most potent appeal to her citizens to wage war in earnest. Germany conducted her campaign without pity, and the torpedoing of hospital ships like the *Gloucester Castle*, the *Dover Castle*, the *Lanfranc*, and the *Donegal* did more, perhaps, to rouse American feeling than the not less barbarous treatment of humble merchantmen. From the beginning America realized her responsibility in this matter, but she had a long way to go before she could carry policy into deeds. There was much fumbling over the question at the start, and some needless delay in the first stages of preparation. If she could produce six million tons of new shipping a year the problem was solved, even if there was no decline in the scale of German successes. The task was well within her power, for it required only a tenth of her annual output of steel and a mere fraction of her great labour reserves. It was in a peculiar degree her own problem, for unless she provided the ships her armies could never make war in Europe. Without the new tonnage her admirable military activity was merely beating the air.

Meantime the Navy was the first part of America's fighting force to take the field beside her Allies. In May a flotilla of American destroyers under Vice-Admiral W. G. Sims arrived in British waters, and assisted in the protection of the Atlantic trade. The vessels were admirable in construction, and their officers and crews were true seamen, who earned at once the respect of their British colleagues. In June, when Admiral Bayly, commanding on the Irish coast, went on leave, Admiral Sims took his place, and the Stars and Stripes floated for the first time in history from a British headquarters.

It was not to be expected that the new and startling developments of naval war should leave the administration of the British Admiralty unchanged. By the close of 1916 Sir Edward Carson had become First Lord, and Sir John Jellicoe First Sea Lord. Presently Sir Eric Geddes, the Director-General of Military Transportation, was brought in as Controller of the Navy – the revival of an historic office which gave him the supervision of new construction. In June there was a further readjustment, and in July Sir Edward Carson entered the War Cabinet as Minister without portfolio, and Sir Eric Geddes succeeded him as First Lord. The functions of the Board of Admiralty were divided into "operations" and "maintenance", and the members were grouped into two committees accordingly. The operations committee was made up of the First Sea Lord and those officers responsible for the details of strategy; the maintenance committee consisted of the officers responsible for personnel, *matériel*, supplies, construction, and finance. The effect of the change was threefold. It brought into Admiralty administration men from the fleets who had recent fighting experience and were still young. It separated the two functions of Command and Supply, which required different talents and training. Above all, it made possible a real Naval Staff, a thinking department which had laid upon it the duty of deducing the logical lessons from the new facts of sea warfare, and working out future plans on a basis of accurate knowledge. All naval theory had gone into the melting pot, and the creeds of 1914 had to be drastically revised. It stood to reason that the younger men, who had themselves been forced to grapple in bitter earnest with the new imperious needs, should be largely used to frame the tactics and strategy of reply.

The most significant events of the year had been in the sphere of politics. France and Italy had not changed conspicuously the personnel of their civil Governments, save that in March M. Ribot succeeded M. Briand in France as Prime Minister. In Germany, in June 1917 von Bethmann-Hollweg still held the reins of power. But in Britain a radically new Government had appeared, and in Russia a new world. Everywhere the atmosphere had become different. The half-forgotten general purposes and the immediate strategical aims, which had filled men's minds in the early years of war, were giving place to a craving for first principles, and, on Germany's part, to a tortuous diplomacy based on this new instinct. The movement had begun with the Emperor's offer of peace terms in December 1916; for though the offer had been summarily rejected by the Allies, it had set a ferment working in the mind of all the world. The tremendous events of the spring in Petrograd and the entry of America into the struggle changed the outlook of every belligerent people. Henceforth not the methods but the aims of the war became the common subject of speculation and controversy. Offensives ceased to be military only, and became political, and the idealist and the idealogue emerged from their closets.

The development was a salutary one, and, as we shall see, it had an immense and immediate effect upon every phase of the campaign. It both cleared and narrowed the issues between the combatants. The Allies had entered on the campaign with a very simple and honourable conception of the goal they strove for, but by the spring of 1917 all had grown a little hazy as to their precise objective. Each of them had one primary aim – to crush finally, not the German people or the German state, but that evil thing which had become dominant there, and that made the world unsafe for peace or liberty. Once that thing was crushed, there was little need for talk about guarantees, for the main peril would have gone. Until it was crushed no guarantee which the wit of man could devise would safeguard civilization. But there were a number of secondary purposes which each of the Allies held, and which they were apt to talk of as conditions of peace. In such purposes were not included the relinquishment by Germany of the territories occupied, and the restitution of Belgium and Serbia. These were not terms of peace, but the necessary pre-conditions without which no discussion of peace was possible. By secondary purposes were meant the various territorial adjustments spoken of in connection with France and Italy, and such matters as the much-canvassed economic restrictions on the Central Powers. These were not primary aims; they were matters of machinery which were of value only in so far as they gave effect to the primary aim. It was possible to be convinced on the main issue, and yet to be doubtful about the merit of more than one of the secondary aims. The latter were for the most part safeguards and guarantees, and if the primary aim were forgotten and negotiations were attempted on their basis, then the most rigid and excessive guarantees must be sought to give security. But if the primary aim was accomplished, all the secondary aims took a new complexion.

There was some perception of this truth in two phrases which were variously interpreted – the demand of the Russian Revolutionaries for "no indemnities and no annexations", and President Wilson's famous phrase, "Peace without victory". The Allies' object in the war was to make a world where law, not force, should rule, and where the smallest people should be secure in peace and freedom. It was not to redistribute territory, except in so far as that was necessary to the main end. Every secondary aim must therefore be tested by the main purpose. "Peace without victory" was a true formula, if by it was meant that the Allies did not want a victory which would leave a lasting sense of bitterness and injustice, and so defeat their chief aim. "No annexations or indemnities" was also a just formula, if annexations were considered as a spoil of conquest and not as contributing to the main purpose. But in another sense no peace could come without victory – final victory over a perverted Prussianism; and annexations and indemnities might be essential if they were a logical part of the general purpose of pacification.

Now, America had entered into the war without any interest in secondary aims. From her detached position she saw the struggle only in its broadest lines. She did not miss the wood behind the trees. She knew that the question was not whether this or that territorial change should be made, but that the mischief should be rooted out of Germany and the world. To say that France fought for Alsace-Lorraine and Italy for Trieste and the Trentino, or Britain for the safety of India, was to adopt a formula too narrow for the facts. America's appearance compelled all the Allies to revise their notions and return to the first things. It helped them to distinguish between method and purpose, between machinery and design. To concentrate upon secondary aims could lead only to disputes. It was the duty of the whole Alliance to test everything by a single question: Would it help towards that lasting peace and that cleaner and better world which they fought to create?

Moreover, America emphasized and brought into the foreground the greatest of all the methods for the realization of the Allied purpose. There were many at the time who were inclined to dismiss all questions of a League of Nations and an international peace-making authority as academic and irrelevant. This was not the view of President Wilson and the American people, nor was it the view of the Allied leaders. If there was any horizon beyond the battle smoke, the question of international right and an adequate machinery to enforce it was the most fundamental which the Allies could consider. It was far more practical than discussions about where certain new borderlines should run – questions which at this stage of the war no one had the data to settle. To belittle the importance of what was coming to be called "internationalism" was to obscure one of the most vital aspects of the common purpose. No speech of the year so moved the British nation as that delivered by General Smuts in May at the dinner given in his honour by both Houses of Parliament, when he expounded the doctrine of the British Empire as historically the first instalment of a greater League – "the only system in history in which a large number of nations has been living in unity."

But with the true internationalism came the false – the fanatical creed which would have destroyed all the loyalties and sanctions of patriotism, and put in their place a materialistic absorption in class interests. War, which with most men intensifies local affection and national devotion, has with those of a certain type the effect of dissipating the homely intimacies of race and country and substituting for them a creed of class selfishness and dogmatic abstractions. Such men are the intellectual outlaws of society. They may be honest, able, and brave, but they are inhuman; and though they can destroy they can never build, for enduring institutions must be founded on human nature. Nevertheless in the long strain of war there come moments when such dogmas have a fatal appeal, and in the first half of 1917 they gained ground among the *déracinés* of all countries. They spread like wildfire in Russia, where they found conditions naturally favourable; they were preached by the remnants of the old *Internationale* in Switzerland, Holland, and Scandinavia; they were welcomed by the left wing of French Socialism, and by the same group in Italy; while in Britain they found adherents in the Independent Labour Party, as well as among the handful of professional wreckers who are always found in any great industrial society. The true internationalism includes nationalism, and provides a safeguard for nationalities. These men were the foes of all national units; and since the war was fought largely for the sake of nationalism, they were, consciously or unconsciously, the opponents of the war. They tended always to become apologists for Germany, and spiritually they had more kinship with the unfeatured universalism of German autocracy than with the rich and varied liberties of Western civilization.

It was necessary for all the belligerents to take account of this new attitude of mind. The Allies were gradually compelled to emphasize the true internationalism of their aims, though their statesmen were slow in recognizing the necessity. Germany after her fashion turned the movement to her own purpose. Meantime, in his Glasgow speech of 29th June, the British Prime Minister, following President Wilson, put the issue in a new form. The menace of Prussianism could be got rid of in two ways – either by a crushing field victory, or by the revolt of the German people themselves against the false gods which they had worshipped. In both cases the result would be the same – the degradation of a heresy in the eyes of those who had pinned their faith to it. "We shall enter", said Mr Lloyd George, "into negotiations with a free Government in Germany with a different attitude of mind, a different temper, a different spirit, with less suspicion, with more confidence, than we should with a sort which we knew to be dominated by the aggressive and arrogant spirit of Prussian militarism. The Allied Governments would, in my judgement, be acting wisely if they drew that distinction in their general attitude towards the discussion of the terms of peace." Such an appeal was clearly on delicate ground. If unwisely phrased, it might appear to be an interference with the domestic concerns of Germany, which would rally her people to a more vigorous resistance. But beyond doubt, as delivered, it met with a response from certain powerful elements among the Central Powers; their political tactics were directed towards a democratization of their government which should have the maximum of show and the minimum of substance, and the preaching of a version of internationalism which came easy to men who had no regard for any nationalism but their own.

In June 1917, at the end of the third year of war, the attitude of the Central Powers – or, more correctly, that of Germany, their master – towards war aims showed little of the unanimity which had marked it during the earlier stages of the campaign. So far Germany had made no explicit statement of her demands. In his speech to the Reichstag on 15th May the Imperial Chancellor declined to disclose his peace terms. In the absence of official evidence, Germany's war aims

BERNARD MENINSKY *Victoria Station, District Railway*

could only be gathered from the utterances of her press and public men, and they tended to wide divergency among themselves. But on one point it may be said that all were unanimous. Any settlement must recognize that the Central Powers had not been defeated. There must be no net loss in territory or revenues as compared with the position in August 1914. On this matter the issue with the Allies was abundantly clear.

The great majority of the German people would have put it otherwise. They claimed that Germany had been victorious, and that peace must bring to her a net gain. Only the Minority Socialists and a small section of the Majority were prepared as yet to accept a peace on the status quo ante basis. There was great difference of opinion as to what the gains should be, and the difference was determined by the various views held of Germany's true interests. We may distinguish five main war aims. In the first two years of war most Germans had held all the five, but after Verdun and the Somme had taught moderation the various schools were inclined to concentrate on one of the batch. The first, which was the creed of the Pan-Germans and the extreme annexationists, included the "freedom of the seas" – by which they meant the increase of German sea-power to a level with Britain's; the annexation of the Belgian coast as well as of sundry French Channel ports; the annexation of the Briey mining district and frontier fortresses like Longwy. The second was the Mittel-Europa school of Naumann, which sought the creation of a Central European bloc of states, militarily, politically, and economically united. The third, led chiefly by Paul Rohrbach, had for its chief aim the control of the Ottoman Empire and the extension of Germany's sphere of influence to the Persian Gulf. The fourth, inspired by Delbrück and Solf, preached a German colonial empire, especially in Africa. The fifth demanded large annexations of Russian soil in Courland and Lithuania, so that by agricultural settlement there should be an expansion not only of German power but of the German people.

Few now held all five aims, though many combined several in their creeds. The Pan-German was critical of Mittel-Europa, and men like Delbrück were strongly opposed to annexation in the West. But all, even the most modest, sought some solid net gain for Germany, and were thus in hopeless conflict with the views of the Allies. All, too – even the most extravagant – were encouraged by the German Government with a view to a margin for future bargaining. Nevertheless there was serious disquiet even among those who planned out most generously the scheme of Germany's gains. To the military chiefs, von Hindenburg and von Ludendorff, the débâcle of Russia had come as a godsend to help them to resist the deadly pressure in the West. It enabled them to think once again in terms of the offensive, and they still looked to the submarine campaign to weaken Britain's effort and to strangle America's at birth. But the ferment in the East was not without its perils. The disease of revolution might spread into their own decorous sheepfold, and against the wild intangible forces let loose in Russia no military science could strive. The "shining sword" could not do battle with phantoms. Hence they were compelled to admit new factors into their problem, and grapple with data abhorrent to their orderly minds.

Two main schools of thought remained distinct among the rulers of Germany. The military chiefs and the fanatics of Pan-Germanism still believed that a little more endurance, a little more sacrifice, would bring the Allies to their knees, and enable Germany to secure gains which would make all her losses worth while, and ensure her future on the grandiose lines which they had planned. The other, the *politiques*, urged that a stalemate had come, and that the balance should now be struck. For against the German war map they saw the solid economic advantages which the Allies possessed, both for the present and for the future. The spectre of post-bellum conditions haunted their minds. Unless she could barter her territorial occupations for economic assistance, Germany might have her hands far over Europe and Asia, and yet be dying at the heart.

The economic position of all the belligerents had become grave by the end of the third year of war. By July 1917 Britain had spent well over 5,000 millions, of which more than one-third was raised by taxes, and two-thirds by the proceeds of loans. It was a colossal indebtedness which faced her, and it had been incurred not wholly on her own account, for over a thousand millions were loans to her Allies, and about 160 millions loans to her own Dominions. She carried on her back the financial burden of her European confederates, and with it all her credit was unweakened, and the elasticity of her revenue-producing power undiminished. New taxes habitually produced far more than their budget estimates, and alone among the European belligerents she remained on a gold basis. She was spending now at a rate of close upon seven millions a day; but as the figure included her advances to Allies, the daily cost of the war was rather less than the four and a half millions spent by Germany. In one respect Britain differed from her colleagues and opponents. Germany financed the war almost wholly by loans; France, till the end of 1916, had practically imposed no new taxes; while Britain had trebled her taxation, so that on an average every man, woman, and child within her borders contributed three shillings a day towards the cost of the campaigns. The immediate difficulty of foreign purchases had been solved by America's appearance as an ally, and it might fairly be claimed that, for a country approaching the fourth year of a worldwide war, Britain was in a state of reasonable financial health. France was in a similar state; Italy was being "carried" by her neighbours; and the resources of America were good for another decade.

The Central Powers were in a simpler though far less sound position. Germany, who "carried" the others, had a huge debt, already above 6,000 millions, and increasing at the rate of two billions a year. To pay interest upon it in full would consume the entire surplus production of her people in peace. At present she was paying it out of further borrowings. She had merged the two structures of private and public credit, and peace without indemnities would lead inevitably to the utter downfall of both, and the reduction of her Government bonds to the position of the paper of a defaulting South American republic. Before the war her citizens groaned under a budget of 160 millions; peace without indemnities would compel them to raise 400 millions for the payment of interest alone. To find a solution would be a giant's task, but for the present it did not trouble her. Victory would solve the problem, and defeat in any case would spell bankruptcy. She had staked everything on the war, and awaited the issue with a gambler's fortitude.

For the actual conduct of operations the financial position of a country is the less important, provided money can be obtained by one device or another. But the economic position, which may be influenced, indeed, by unsound finance in the direction of inflated prices, is a matter of the most urgent gravity. The submarine campaign was a serious blow to the economic strength of all the Allies. It was serious, but not crushing; it complicated every question of supply, but it did not make them insoluble. The pressure was most severe on Italy, who was a heavy importer of grain and coal, and found herself crippled in her war industries, and faced with an awkward problem for the coming winter. Among the Central Powers the situation was far worse. Turkey had long been suffering from naked famine. Bulgaria was on very short commons. In Austria there was starvation in Istria, Bosnia, and German Bohemia, and all-night queues in the cities for the bare necessaries of life. The milk supply of Vienna had dropped to a sixth, and the output of beer to one-sixteenth. In Germany the food supply was better than it had been the year before, for the stocks were far better administered; but its quality was poor, and there was an immense amount of gastric disease everywhere throughout the country. The clothing of the people had gone to pieces, and the footgear had become anything from sabots to dancing pumps. But the most serious fact was the lack of machinery. Every scrap available was used for war purposes, and the little left in private hands could not be renewed, or even kept in order, because of the lack of lubricants. For the same reason transportation was in an evil case. The rolling stock was falling into disrepair, and the permanent ways could not be properly cared for owing to the scarcity of labour and material. The result was that even military traffic suffered. At one time it had taken six days to move a division from East to West; it now took nearer a fortnight.

All this made for intense discomfort, and a consequent lowering of spirits. But the main inducement to depression was the doubt as to what would be Germany's fate after the war, whatever the issue. Nothing short of an overwhelming victory would give salvation; and this was clearly impossible, except in the minds of a few dreamers. She had a vast paper issue; but she could do nothing with it, for it was not accepted beyond her borders. She was very much in the position of the ancient Greek city state which could play any pranks it liked with its currency at home but had nothing valid for foreign exchange. But she had considerable stocks of manufactured goods, and she had a fair gold reserve. With these she hoped to pay for the imports necessary to restart her industrial life. They might suffice, or they might not, for her requirements in the way of imports would be stupendous. Moreover, the Allies controlled all the world's producing grounds of raw material, without which she must be speedily bankrupt. She could not force them to share; and they might well refuse to share, for they had their own stocks to build up. Economically she was at their mercy; and, to those in Germany who faced this fact squarely, all talk of the "war map" and shining swords must have seemed foolish bluster. Her deeds had made her a blackleg in the trade union of nations, since she had defied the law of the common interest. She had arrayed against her a world which could in the long run starve her to death.

To those of Germany's citizens who were preoccupied with such perplexed forecasts the resuts of her unrestricted submarine campaign must have foreboded ill. For more than one neutral followed the example of the United States, and declared war or broke off relations. Every month brought news of some new recruit to the ranks of her enemies. In March it was China; in April it was Cuba and Panama; and by the autumn of 1917, of the South American states only the Argentine and Chile had not declared against her. Eighteen countries had proclaimed war, and nine more had severed diplomatic connections. It was the verdict of the civilized world on the wrongdoer, and — more important for Germany — it was the verdict of those countries which between them possessed the monopoly of the raw materials without which she could not live.

COLIN U. GILL *The Captive*

The European neutrals were in a position of growing embarrassment and discomfort. Scandinavia lost heavily in ships from the German submarines, and its trade was grievously crippled. Food conditions were worse, perhaps, in Sweden, Holland, and Switzerland, than among any of the belligerent Allies. Spain for a moment seemed about to break with the Central Powers; but the strong Germanophil elements among her people compelled her Government to pocket its pride. The Allied blockade, owing to America's action, was enormously tightened, for President Wilson's decree of 9th June prohibited the export without special Government licence of any article or commodity which could conceivably be of use to the enemy. The main difficulty which had always confronted the British blockade policy was the necessity of considering American interests, and that handicap was now removed. The Chancelleries of Europe, during the summer of 1917, were filled with the complaints of helpless neutrals; and history may well pity the fate of those small nations thus ground between the upper and the nether millstones.

The outlook for the Allies at the close of June 1917 had not the hope of the previous midsummer, or the apparent assurance of the beginning of the year. The sky had suddenly become mysteriously clouded. Wherever the Allies in the West had attacked the enemy they had beaten him soundly; but the final victory in the field, which was theirs by right, seemed to be slipping from their grasp owing to the defection of Russia. Britain's mastery of the sea, too, seemed in danger of failing her at the most vital moment owing to the new campaign under water – a campaign with which by June she had got on terms, but which she had not succeeded in checking. In that obviously lay the crisis of the war. Unless it could be reduced within limits, everything – the military efficiency of the Allied armies, the potentialities of America, the industrial pre-eminence of Britain, even the life and security of the British people – was in dire jeopardy. By June the solution had not been found, and the future was therefore still misty. Moreover, the essential problems of the war were becoming blurred. Up till then the campaign had been fought on data which were familiar and calculable. The material and human strength of each belligerent was known, and the morale of each was confidently assessed. But suddenly new factors had appeared out of the void, and what had seemed solid ground became sand and quagmire. It was the old Europe which waged war up till the first months of 1917, but a new Europe had come into being by midsummer, in which nothing could be taken for granted. Everywhere in the world there was the sound of things breaking.

But to those who drew from these facts a pessimistic conclusion there was one answer. The business of the Allies was to destroy Germany's power for evil, by defeating and discrediting those elements in her Government which had been responsible for her outrage on civilization. The break-up of Germany's military machine in the field would have achieved this end; but the same purpose might be gained if her existing regime were so discredited by failure that the break-up came from within her own borders. That might follow if the Allies succeeded in wrecking Germany's hope for the future. It was too often forgotten what was the decisive weapon in war. Now, as ever, it was economic pressure. When countries were small and self-supporting, this was exercised by the defeat of their armies and the invasion and occupation of their territories, so that their life was paralysed. But in modern war, when the defensive has become all-powerful, another method must be found. Had the Allies been able to break through Germany's trench system and drive her to the Rhine and beyond, that success would have been only a preliminary to the determining and final pressure caused by the dislocation of her whole economic life. But while Haig and Nivelle were battering on the Western gate, that final pressure was already being exercised. The Allies controlled all the oversea trade routes and all the world's chief supply grounds of raw material. Compared with such assets and gains the war map of von Bethmann-Hollweg was a child's toy. Without any final field victory the Allies already had secured the results of the greatest field victory: they were choking Germany, and ruining her future as much as if they had forced von Hindenburg back to the Elbe.

Such an answer to pessimism was in its essence sound, but it needed qualification. To rid the world of Prussianism something more was wanted. The thing must be made a sport and contempt to Germany herself, and, while an overwhelming military débâcle would have ensured this, the slow and indirect forces of economic pressure could not produce the same moral effect on the German temperament. Before victory was won there must be a recognition of failure in every German mind, and that was still postponed. Prussianism sat still enthroned, for it had persuaded its votaries that this was a defensive struggle, and that it alone stood between the people and the malice of their enemies. Not till it was revealed to the humblest eye as the sole begetter of the war, the parent of all the ills which had descended upon the nation, the wanton devilry which had shattered the edifice their fathers had builded, would civilization have won the victory it needed. Again, the Allied siege, stringent as it was, had its weak points. The submarine counter-attack was not yet under control, and the condition of Russia might still permit the enemy so to add to his material resources as to obtain a new lease of endurance long enough to defeat the Allied strategy. These crucial matters in midsummer of 1917 were still in the balance. While, therefore, there was no cause for despondency among the Allies at the close of the third year, there was no cause for confident dogmatism. They had won greatly, but the end was not yet. On the knees of the gods yet lay the major issues of the campaign.

It was still a war of the rank and file. Neither in civilian statesmanship nor in the high military commands had any leader appeared who greatly exceeded the common stature of mankind. There were many able men in every country, but the ship seemed too vast and the currents too infinite for any single hand to control the helm. A hundred clung to it; but often it mastered them, and the vessel swung rudderless to wind and tide. A new star had blazed up in the East in Kerenski, but already it seemed that his fires were paling. The two most conspicuous statesmen at the close of the year were beyond doubt the British Prime Minister and the American President. They had scarcely one quality in common. The one was imaginative, reckless, homely, volcanic, essentially human; the other measured, discreet, impersonal, oracular, and aloof. The monarchy produced the democrat; the republic the autocrat. But both had courage and resolution to inspire their people; both spoke *urbi et orbi*; both stood out from the many transient shadows as clear-cut and dominant personalities.

Among the soldiers of the Central Powers the reputation of von Ludendorff had so grown that it was in danger of eclipsing the legendary fame of von Hindenburg himself. Here was a man of first rate executive power, who knew with complete precision what he sought. Von Mackensen still stood highest among the German generals in the field; though von Armin, the new head of the Fourth Army was swiftly rising into fame. Among the Allies, Pétain and Cadorna had increased their reputations; and two British commanders, Sir Herbert Plumer and Sir Stanley Maude, had revealed the traditional British merits of stamina, forethought, and common sense. It was no insular prejudice, too, which saw in the British Commander-in-Chief one who had some claim to rank as the most indispensable soldier of the campaign. Fortune favoured him as little as she had favoured Sir John Moore; but he met her buffets with an inflexible patience and an unfailing courage, and on the Somme, at Arras, and at Messines he showed himself the most brilliant exponent of the new methods of war.

(Vol. XX pp. 11-50)

SIR WILLIAM ORPEN *The Household Brigade Passing to the Ypres Salient, Cassel*

THE BATTLE OF CAMBRAI

The Third Battles of Ypres, which began in the summer of 1917 and went on until the early days of November, had begun with the capture of Messines Ridge, and ended when the village of Passchendaele fell to the Canadian Corps on 6 November. The name of this village, still full of

resonance and emotion, became synonymous with one of the bloodiest struggles on the Western Front. The battlefield, with shelling and constant rain, became a quagmire in which trenches disappeared and men drowned . . . Because the British Commander-in-Chief, Sir Douglas Haig, persisted in attacking, casualties in what became a battle of attrition were higher than they might have been. This fact – although Buchan does not say so – was to a great extent responsible for British failure to exploit the action by tanks at Cambrai, where the German line was pierced.

Tanks had been used, in small numbers, without great success during the Battle of the Somme. At Cambrai they were for the first time deployed in larger numbers, on suitable terrain, and broke through the German line with few casualties. The plan was for this success to be supported by infantry who would consolidate the work of the tanks; but it came to nothing because so many men who might have made this engagement a decisive blow against the German army had perished earlier in the fruitless battle of "Third Ypres".

ON 6TH NOVEMBER with the taking of Passchendaele the Third Battle of Ypres drew to a close. It had been a protracted and costly operation. On 29th October, in both Houses of Parliament, the leaders of all parties had paid grateful tribute to the exploits of the British Army. "When I read of the conditions under which they fought," said the Prime Minister, "I marvel that the delicate and sensitive instrument of the human nerve and the human mind can endure them without derangement. The campaigns of Stonewall Jackson fill us with admiration and with wonder, as we read how that man of iron led his troops through the mire and swamps of Virginia; but his troops were never called upon to live for days and nights in morasses under ceaseless thunderbolts from a powerful artillery, and then march into battle through an engulfing quagmire under a hailstorm of machine-gun fire." But splendid as the record had been, the British High Command could not contemplate the situation with much comfort. Many German divisions had been broken at Ypres, but the stagnation of the winter war would give them time to rest and refit. Already large enemy forces had been brought from Russia, more were on their way, and there were many more to come. If the enemy were left in peace, he had it in his power to create a dangerous situation for the spring. Moreover, Italy, fighting desperately on the Piave, deserved by all the laws of war some relief in the shape of an Allied diversion. Weary as his troops might be, Sir Douglas Haig was not able to grant them the rest which they had earned and most urgently required.

If another blow was to be struck, it must not be delayed. The operations at Passchendaele had compelled the Germans to concentrate heavily on the threatened front and reduce their strength in other sectors. These dispositions still continued; but presently, when it was clear that the pressure had been relaxed, their troops would be more evenly distributed. If the British could strike at once in an unexpected quarter, they might have the benefit of a real surprise, and at the moment the thoughts of the Allied Command, like that of the German General Staff, were running on some means of breaking the rigidity of trench warfare and restoring the element of the unexpected. Should such a blow succeed, it would have a real effect upon the morale of the enemy, for after Third Ypres he would not anticipate a fresh Allied effort yet awhile. It would give him an uneasy winter, for it would not permit him to reduce the strength of any part of his front, as had been his former practice, and so would cripple that heavy local concentration which might be looked for in the spring. In deciding the question a final consideration affected Sir Douglas Haig. The British tanks had greatly increased in number and efficiency. At Third Ypres ground and weather had prevented their effective use, and decreased their reputation in the enemy's eyes. But a terrain might be found where they could work freely, and if so, they might form a further element of surprise. The mind of Sir Douglas, like that of Ludendorff, was working towards the discovery of a new tactic.

Having decided on his policy, the British Commander-in-Chief looked around for a suitable area for its application. He found it in that sector of the old Siegfried Line which lay in front of Havrincourt Wood, between the Bapaume-Cambrai road and the Scheldt Canal. It was a country of rolling downs, grey with the withered grasses of November, and patched with the rank and blackened growths of thistle and dock and ragwort which spring up on land once closely tilled and now derelict. From any ridge east of Bapaume the observer could grasp the terrain at a glance. Eight miles from our front rose the spires and factory chimneys of the town of Cambrai. Half-way the deep cutting of the Scheldt Canal zigzagged across the landscape, for the most part empty of water, but forming a better barrier than any running stream. On the west side of the canal the long Flesquières ridge ran north and south, rising on the left to the dominating point of Bourlon Wood between the Arras and Bapaume roads – a wood of oak and ash, with a dense undergrowth, and still untouched by shellfire. East of the canal the ground fell away to the flat plains of the Scheldt, but the village of Rumilly offered a flank position on the last incline of the uplands.

The merits of this area for a surprise attack were many. In the first place, it was dry, open country, where tanks could operate. In the second place, behind the British lines, notably in the big wood of Havrincourt, there were places where they might be concealed without the knowledge of the Germans. In the third place, the sector was very thinly held by the enemy. Finally, any considerable British advance would endanger a vital part of the enemy's front, and seriously hamper his communications. Cambrai, a main centre, would be brought under our guns, as would the great lateral railway which ran through it. If Bourlon could be won, the canal crossed, and a defensive flank established towards Rumilly, we should command the main Arras-Cambrai road, and take in rear the enemy positions in the southern part of the Drocourt-Quéant line and the Sensée valley.

The British tactical plan was conceived on novel lines. There was to be no preliminary bombardment. Tanks were relied upon to break through the enemy's wire, and the six infantry divisions were to advance on a six-mile front, supported as far as possible by our guns shooting at unregistered targets. The German defences were complicated and very strong. First came certain forward positions in the nature of outposts at the ridge of La Vacquerie and at the north-eastern corner of Havrincourt Wood – a method borrowed from von Armin's system in the Ypres salient. Behind lay the Siegfried Line proper, running north-west to Havrincourt from the Scheldt Canal at Banteux – a line with specially wide trenches which, it was hoped, would prevent the passage of tanks. A mile or so behind that lay the famous Siegfried Reserve Line, tunnelled to a great depth and heavily wired. Between three and four miles to the east ran the final German position, covering Cambrai, from Beaurevoir by Masnières to Marquion.

Sir Douglas Haig's object was not the capture of Cambrai; that might happen, but his advance in the direction of the town was rather to secure his right flank. His main objective was towards the north-east, Bourlon, and the Arras-Cambrai road. He hoped to break through all the enemy's lines of defence on the first day; and, since he believed that no serious German reinforcements could appear before forty-eight hours, he considered that he would have time to exploit and secure any success. The cavalry were to be kept ready to go through and disorganize the enemy communications, and he arranged with General Pétain to have a strong French force of infantry and cavalry within call in the event of fortune providing one of those happy chances which he had hitherto been denied. The possibilities which he had in mind are best described in the words of his dispatch:

> In view of the strength of the German forces on the front of my attack, and the success with which secrecy was maintained during our preparations, I had calculated that the enemy's prepared defences would be captured in the first rush. I had good hope that his resisting power behind those defences would then be so enfeebled for a period that we should be able on the same day to establish ourselves quickly and completely on the dominating Bourlon Ridge from Fontaine-notre-Dame to Moeuvres, and to secure our right flank along a line including the Bonavis Ridge, Crèvecoeur, and Rumilly to Fontaine-notre-Dame. Even if this did not prove possible within the first twenty-four hours, a second day would be at our disposal before the enemy's reserves could begin to arrive in any formidable numbers. Meanwhile, with no wire and no prepared defences to hamper them, it was reasonable to hope that masses of cavalry would find it possible to pass through, whose task would be thoroughly to disorganize the enemy's system of command

JOHN SINGER SARGENT *Two Soldiers at Arras*

and inter-communication in the whole area between the Canal de l'Escaut, the river Sensée and the Canal du Nord, as well as to the east and north-east of Cambrai. My intentions as regards subsequent exploitation were to push westward and north-westward, taking the Hindenburg Line in reverse from Moeuvres to the river Scarpe, and capturing all the enemy's defences, and probably most of his garrisons, lying westward of a line from Cambrai northwards to the Sensée, and south of that river and the Scarpe. Time would have been required to enable us to develop and complete the operation; but the prospects of gaining the necessary time, by the use of cavalry in the manner outlined above, were, in my opinion, good enough to justify the attempt to execute the plan.

There will be few to deny that this plan was both bold and feasible. As a scheme for a substantive operation it was at least as skilful and prudent as any which the British High Command had yet adopted. But at this point arises a difficulty. Was the battle which followed to be considered a substantive operation? Sir Douglas Haig has described how weary were his troops after the close of Third Ypres; how inadequately his losses had been replaced; and explained that many of the new drafts included in the ranks of his armies were not yet fully trained. In such circumstances a substantive operation – that is, one designed to occupy and hold a considerable extent of new ground – must be hazardous in the extreme; for even if only a small force was required in the first instance, and if this force could be supplied from comparatively fresh divisions, it was certain that, as the battle developed, reserves must be found, and that these could only be got from tired and depleted troops who had already borne the brunt of Third Ypres. It has been the fashion in many quarters to describe Cambrai as no more than a raid on a generous scale. Now, it is the essence of a raid that it does not occupy ground. The men engaged in it harass and weaken the enemy, and then return to their old line. But Sir Douglas Haig contemplated an advance on the first day of between five and six miles, and thereafter elaborate operations on the north and north-west. Such successes would in any case demand large reinforcements. Again, the essence of a raid is that, if the enemy proves unexpectedly strong, it is given up. But since this attempt was on so large a scale, would it be possible to withdraw the troops after their initial advance, should the situation change? Was it not more probable that they would become so deeply committed that they must continue the battle? It may fairly be said in criticism of the Cambrai plan that it contemplated a limited and local operation, which in the nature of things could not be limited and localized, much less easily broken off. It designed a raid with a few divisions; but such a raid must inevitably develop into a battle and demand supports, and these supports could only come from troops who *ex hypothese* were in no condition for a new and desperate conflict.

The Cambrai sector from Bullecourt to the Oise was held by the German Second Army, under von der Marwitz, which at the moment had only eleven divisions in line. In the threatened area it had only three – from left to right, the 5th, the 2nd, and the 20th, with three more in reserve. The British force was the Third Army, which had not been seriously engaged since the Battle of Arras in the spring. When Sir Edmund Allenby was transferred to Palestine in June it was placed under Sir Julian Byng, who had commanded the Canadian Corps at the taking of Vimy Heights. On the six-mile front of the main attack he had in line six divisions – from left to right, the 36th, 62nd, 51st, 6th, 20th, and 12th. On the left, in the Bullecourt area, two divisions, the 16th and the 3rd, were detailed for a subsidiary attack. In immediate support in the main area was the 29th Division. The mounted force at his disposal contained the 1st, 2nd, 4th, and 5th Cavalry Divisions.

Secrecy was vital in the matter, and Sir Julian Byng directed the preparations with consummate skill. The flotillas of tanks were assembled in every possible place which offered cover, notably in Havrincourt Wood. The tank is not a noiseless machine, and it says much for the ingenuity of the Third Army that the enemy had no inkling of our designs. It was anxious work, for a single enemy aeroplane over Havrincourt or a single indiscreet prisoner taken would have wrecked the plan. Before the attack an enemy raid took prisoners, but he seems to have learned little from them, though it would appear that he suspected tanks in the neighbourhood and served out special ammunition. Had he been really forewarned, he might have so honeycombed his front with contact mines that our advance would have been completely frustrated. The weather favoured Sir Julian Byng. The days before the assault saw the low grey skies and the clinging mist of late November.

Tuesday, 20th November, dawned with heavy clouds that promised rain before evening. At twenty minutes past six a solitary gun broke the silence. It was the signal, and from just north of the Bapaume road to the hamlet of Gonnelieu in the south a long line of tanks crept forward into the fog, their commander, General Hugh Elles, leading them in his "flagship". Gas and smoke were released everywhere from the Scarpe to St Quentin, and in front of the tanks a dense smoke barrage blinded the enemy's guns. The British artillery broke loose and deluged the German rear with shells, while, behind the tanks, quietly and leisurely moved the six divisions of assault. At Epehy on the south and at Bullecourt on the north the subsidiary attacks were launched at the same moment.

The enemy was taken utterly unawares. The tanks cut great lanes in his wire, broke up his machine-gun nests, and enfiladed his trenches, while the British infantry followed to complete the work. At once the outposts went, the main Siegfried Line followed soon, and presently the fighting was among the tunnels of the Reserve Line. By half-past ten that also had vanished, and the British troops, with cavalry close behind, were advancing to their final objectives in open country.

Let us glance at the progress of the several divisions. On the left, west of the Canal du Nord, the 36th (Ulster) Division drove the enemy from the canal bank, pushed up the Siegfried Line, and carried the whole German trench system west of the canal as far as the Bapaume road. On their right the 62nd Division of West Riding Territorials began that brilliant advance which was to give them the honours of the day. They took Havrincourt village, turned northward, carried the Siegfried Reserve Line, and occupied Graincourt, where their accompanying tanks had the satisfaction of themselves destroying two anti-tank guns. Before evening they were in Anneux, an advance of four and a half miles from their original front – the longest advance that so far in the war any single British division had made in one day. South of the Yorkshiremen the 51st (Highland Territorials) were adding to their many laurels. They breasted the slopes of the Flesquières ridge, and carried the formidable defences of the château grounds by noon. They were held up, however, in front of the village, which remained uncaptured during the day, the apex of a sharp salient. Here our tanks suffered from direct hits from the German field guns beyond the crest of the ridge, many of them obtained by a German artillery officer who served a gun single-handed till he died at his post. "The great bravery of this officer", says the official dispatch, "aroused the admiration of all ranks."

South of Flesquières the 6th Division took Ribecourt, while the 20th Division, after disposing of La Vacquerie, stormed the defences of the hill which we called Welsh Ridge towards Marcoing. The 12th Division, on the extreme right, moved along the Bonavis ridge, and, after a fierce struggle, took

Lateau Wood, which sheltered many German batteries. Meantime the 29th Division had been pushed through between the 6th and 20th as a spearhead. Accompanied by tanks, it took Marcoing and Neuf Wood and the passage at that point of the Scheldt Canal; while the 6th Division, advancing from Ribecourt in the afternoon, moved north and seized Noyelles-sur-l'Escaut. The 29th then turned south and entered Masnières, but not before the enemy had managed so to weaken the bridge over the canal that the first tank which tried to cross fell through. They had trouble in the north end of the village, with the result that the Germans had the chance to occupy Rumilly and the sector of their final line of defence south of it.

All this time the cavalry were fighting in close alliance with the infantry – the 1st Cavalry Division in the northern part of the battleground, and the 5th Cavalry Division in the south. They were moving on Cantaing and Anneux; but the vital point was the bridge at Masnières, and unfortunately that was half destroyed. This delayed what might have otherwise been the final blow to the enemy defence, for had the cavalry been able to cross the canal in force there was little between them and Cambrai. A temporary bridge was, indeed, constructed south of Masnières, and one squadron of the Fort Garry Horse, belonging to General Seely's Canadian Brigade of the 5th Cavalry Division, crossed, broke through the Beaurevoir-Masnières line, charged and captured a German battery, cut up a body of 300 German infantry, and only retired when most of its horses had been killed or wounded.

The day closed with a remarkable record of success. The subsidiary attacks had done well, the 16th (Irish) and the 3rd Division having captured the remainder of the Siegfried Reserve Line at Bullecourt, with 700 prisoners. On the whole front already over 5,000 prisoners had been brought in. Sir Julian Byng had carried the outposts, the Siegfried Line, and the Siegfried Reserve Line on most of his front, and had broken into the final line at Masnières. He had won nearly all his objectives; but at three points, and vital points, he had not succeeded. He had not got Rumilly and Crèvecoeur, and so had not yet obtained that defensive flank which he needed for his swing to the north. Nor had he won the crossings of the Scheldt Canal, and breached the final line widely enough to let the cavalry through. For this the destruction of the bridge at Masnières was to blame, and more especially, perhaps, the check of the 51st Division at Flesquières village. This last also prevented the attainment of the most important objective of all, the Bourlon ridge, the garrison of which had by now been reinforced. Only twenty-four hours remained to complete the work before the enemy would have received reinforcements. In that time Bourlon might be won, and perhaps Rumilly and Crèvecoeur; but, now that the first shock of surprise had passed, the chance for the cavalry was gone.

The rain began to fall after midday on the 20th, and continued into the morning of the 21st. By 8 a.m. Flesquières village had fallen, turned from the north-west, and by eleven the final German line had been breached to the north of Masnières. The enemy counter-attacked from Rumilly and was beaten off,

COLIN U. GILL *Evening, after a Push*

and at Noyelles part of the 29th Division and dismounted regiments of the 1st and 5th Cavalry Divisions were hotly engaged during the day. On our right we captured the hamlet of Les Rues des Vignes, between Bonavis and Crèvecoeur, but lost it again; and our attack towards Crèvecoeur itself was hung up by machine-gun fire at the canal crossings. On our extreme left the 36th Division, pushing north of the Bapaume road, got into the skirts of Moeuvres, where they found a strong resistance. But the vital point was on the left centre, where the 51st and 62nd Divisions, assisted by tanks and squadrons of the 1st Cavalry Division, were struggling desperately towards Bourlon. The advance began at 10.30 a.m., as soon as possible after the clearing of Flesquières. The West Riding troops completed the capture of Anneux, and early in the afternoon the 6th and 51st Divisions took Cantaing, close upon the Scheldt Canal. The Highlanders pressed on to the edge of Bourlon Wood, and late in the evening took the village of Fontaine-notre-Dame, on the Bapaume road between Bourlon and Cambrai. Bourlon Wood itself was a nest of machine guns, which barred the infantry advance, though a few tanks penetrated some way into its recesses.

With dawn on the 22nd the forty-eight hours of grace ended, the period during which the enemy must fight without his reserves. His reinforcements were hurrying up; the night before the 1st Guards Reserve had arrived from Lens, and other divisions were on their way from Flanders. Our new line left the old front at a point half-way between Bourcies and Pronville, ran east through the skirts of Moeuvres to the Canal du Nord; then along the southern face of Bourlon Wood to Fontaine-notre-Dame, where it turned south-east, covering Cantaing, Noyelles, and Masnières to a point east of the Scheldt Canal half-way between the last named village and Crèvecoeur. Thence it passed along the eastern and southern slopes of the Bonavis ridge to our old front near Gonnelieu. We had failed to win certain vital positions for a defensive flank, such as Rumilly and Crèvecoeur; above all, we did not hold the dominating ground of Bourlon Wood and village. Clearly we could not remain where we were. Either we must go on till Bourlon was taken, or fall back to the Flesquières ridge and secure our gains. Sir Douglas Haig had now to decide whether to treat the action as a lucky raid, and hold himself fortunate for what he had already achieved, without risking more; or to regard it as a substantive battle, and press for a decision.

Inevitably he leaned to the second alternative. To make the *gran rifiuto* when much has been won and still more seems within reach, is possible for few commanders, even when they have less weighty reasons for their conclusion than were now present to the mind of the British general. The choice which he now made had been really implied in his original plan. He was impressed by the acute significance of the Bourlon ridge. If he could only gain and hold it, the German front south of the Scarpe and Sensée would be turned, and the enemy must be compelled to abandon all the elaborate defences of that sector. It was such a nerve centre as we had rarely before had the chance of striking at. It was true that German reinforcements were arriving, and that our troops were so exhausted that we too must delay a little for reliefs. But he considered that any German reserves that could appear for several days would be only sufficient to replace the enemy losses in the past fighting, and that there was some evidence of a wholesale German withdrawal. In any case he believed that he had sufficient forces to strike at Bourlon before that position could be strengthened. Two divisions, under orders for Italy, had been placed at his disposal, and with this accession of strength he hoped to win the ridge forthwith. Lastly, there were ever present to his mind the needs of the Italian situation. Any pressure on the Cambrai front, even if unsuccessful in its main object, would do something to relieve the strain on the Piave. He accordingly decided to continue the action till Bourlon was won. In the light of subsequent events it is clear that the decision was unwise. Sir Douglas Haig had too small a force to achieve his purpose and to defend his gains against the attack which the enemy could develop. But to foresee the future with precision is not in the power of the most sagacious commander, and to take risks is of the essence of war.

The 22nd November was spent in relieving some of the divisions which had suffered most in the battle, and organizing the ground won on our right and right centre. A little after midday the enemy regained Fontaine-notre-Dame, which was commanded not only by the height of Bourlon, but by the positions at La Folie Wood and on the canal towards Cambrai. That night the 36th (Ulster) and the 56th Division of London Territorials were engaged in the Moeuvres area, and a battalion of the Queen's Westminsters from the latter carried Tadpole Copse, a point in the Siegfried line west of Moeuvres, which was of value as a flanking position for the attack on Bourlon Wood.

On the morning of the 23rd came the serious assault on the Bourlon heights. The 51st Division attacked Fontaine-notre-Dame, but were repulsed; in the afternoon they tried again, but could not clear the village, though our tanks entered it and remained there till dusk, to the inconvenience of the enemy. Meantime on their left the 40th Division attacked the wood, captured the whole of it, including the highest point of the ridge, and entered Bourlon village.

The battle was now concentrated in the Bourlon area, and for some days in that ragged wood, and around the shells of the two villages, a fierce and bloody strife continued. On the morning of the 24th a counter-attack drove us out of the north-east corner of the wood, but the 14th Argyll and Sutherland Highlanders of the 51st Division, the dismounted 15th Hussars, and what was left of the 119th Brigade of the 40th Division, re-established our front. Assaults from the west were also repulsed by dismounted cavalry. That afternoon the 40th Division attacked Bourlon village, and captured the whole of it. All along the line from Tadpole Copse to Fontaine it was clear that the enemy was gaining in strength, and next evening, 25th November, Bourlon village was retaken by the Germans, though part of the 13th East Surreys held out in the south-east corner till they were relieved two days later. The 40th

Division, which had had most of the fighting here, was now replaced by the 62nd Division, and the enemy continued to press so hard that on the 26th he had entered the northern skirts of Bourlon Wood.

Our position was now too awkward to be long maintained, and on the 27th we made an effort to secure the whole Bourlon ridge as well as Fontaine-notre-Dame. Two divisions, supported by tanks, were designed for the task – the Guards against Fontaine, and the 62nd on their left against Bourlon. Once more we succeeded in gaining both villages; once again counter-attacks later in the day drove us out of them. We held a strong position on the Bourlon ridge, but we had not yet established it. Accordingly we relieved the divisions which had borne the brunt of the fighting, and set to work to design a final attack which should give us what we sought. Meantime on other parts of the line we had improved our situation. The 12th Division on our right had pushed out towards Banteux, on the Scheldt Canal, and on our left the 16th Division had won ground in the Siegfried Line north-west of Bullecourt. In the week's fighting we had taken over 10,500 prisoners and 142 guns; we had carried 14,000 yards of the main Siegfried Line and 10,000 yards of the Reserve Line; we had wrested more than sixty square miles from the enemy, and retaken ten villages. We now held a salient formed like a rough rectangle, some ten miles wide and six miles deep. It was a salient awkwardly placed, for we had not won either on north or east the positions which would have made it secure, and during that week the enemy, by means of his admirable communications, was hurrying up troops for a counterstroke.

Cambrai had beyond doubt startled the German High Command. They had not dreamed of such an event, and they realized that only by the narrowest margin had they escaped catastrophe. The joy bells which rang prematurely in England woke uneasy thoughts in Germany, and the people for a moment were gravely depressed. It was Ludendorff's business to cheer his countrymen by a dramatic counterstroke; for, knowing the immense sacrifice he was to demand from the nation in the coming spring, he could not afford to permit any check to their confidence. Accordingly, during the last week of November, sixteen fresh divisions were brought to the battlefield, and on the 29th von der Marwitz issued an order to the Second Army:

> The English, by throwing into the fight countless tanks on 20th November, gained a victory near Cambrai. Their intention was to break through; but they did not succeed, thanks to the brilliant resistance of our troops. We are now going to turn their embryonic victory into a defeat by an encircling counter-attack. The Fatherland is watching you, and expects every man to do his duty.

The British High Command were aware of this activity; they were even aware that its area extended outside the battleground as far south as Vendhuille; and they took measures to prepare for the worst. In the area between Moeuvres and Cantaing they had two fresh divisions – the 47th London Territorials and

PAUL NASH *The Mule Track*

the 2nd, and one – the 56th – which had been only partially engaged. On the ten miles between Cantaing and the ravine at Banteux lay five divisions – the 62nd, 6th, 29th, 20th, and 12th – all of which had been previously in action, and were more or less weary. South of Banteux our line was very weak; but there the 55th Division held a front which had been in our possession for months, and consequently its defence was well organized. Moreover, our hold on the Bonavis ridge increased the security of the line between Banteux and Vendhuille. In immediate reserve were the Guards and the 2nd Cavalry Division, and in general support the 48th (South Midland) Division, and the 4th and 5th Cavalry Divisions. It seemed certain that, since our hold on Bourlon ridge was so insecure, and the place meant so much to the enemy, the chief weight of any counterstroke would fall there, and in that area, as events showed, we were well prepared. Everywhere on our front the warning was given, and especial precautions were taken on that bit of our old line between Villers Guislain and Vendhuille. "Troops were warned to expect an attack, additional machine guns were placed to secure supporting points, and divisional reserves were closed up. Special patrols were also sent out to watch for signs of any hostile advance."

Nevertheless, the enemy secured a tactical surprise. His plan – it was framed by Ludendorff himself – was to strike hard on our two flanks, and then to press in the centre. On his right he hoped to win the line Flesquières-Havrincourt, and on his left the line Ribecourt-Trescault-Beaucamp-Gouzeaucourt, and so nip off all the British troops in the front of the salient. Twenty-four divisions, the bulk of them fresh, were used for the attempt. He used also his new tactics, designed on the Eastern front and first practised at Caporetto; and these tactics meant surprise.

At 7.30 a.m. on the morning of Friday, 30th November, a storm of gas shells broke out on the ten miles between Masnières and Vendhuille. There was no steadily advancing barrage to warn us of the approach of the enemy's infantry, and the thick morning mist enabled him to reach our trenches when our men were still under cover. The result was that from the north end of the Bonavis ridge to Gonnelieu, and from Gonnelieu to Vendhuille, our line was overwhelmed. At once the enemy was on the edge of La Vacquerie, and pressing up the deep ravine between Villers Guislain and Gonnelieu. Isolated British detachments in advantageous positions offered a gallant resistance. Such were the parties at Lateau Wood and south-east of La Vacquerie: such were the 92nd Field Artillery Brigade north-east of La Vacquerie; the troops on the high ground east of Villers Guislain: and south of that village the garrison of Royal Lancasters and Liverpools at Limerick Post. But the advance could not be stayed. The batteries at La Vacquerie were taken – the first British guns to be lost since Second Ypres – and at 9 a.m. the enemy was in Gouzeaucourt.

The situation was grave indeed, for our position in the front of the salient was turned in flank and rear. It was saved by the 29th Division at Masnières. That gallant body – made up of English, Scottish, Welsh, Irish, Guernsey, and Newfoundland battalions – had by its exploits at Gallipoli and on the Somme won a reputation second to none in the British Army. This day it gained still higher renown. Though the enemy, covering it on flank and rear, overran its divisional and brigade headquarters, and took its batteries in reverse, it did not yield its ground. Swinging back its right to form a defensive flank, it clung to Masnières and beat off all attacks. Its heroic resistance defeated the German plan of a frontal assault, and gave Sir Julian Byng time to attend to his broken right wing.

At midday the Guards came into action west of Gouzeaucourt, with the 5th Cavalry Division filling the gap on their right towards Villers Guislain. Gouzeaucourt was retaken, and for the rest of the day there was a fierce struggle on the St Quentin ridge and at Gauche Wood, east of the village. There every kind of unit was engaged – three battalions of tanks, a field artillery brigade of the 47th Division, a detachment of the 29th Division, and a company of North Midland sappers. By the evening they had found touch with the garrison of La Vacquerie, who in turn were linked up with the defenders of Masnières, and our line was reconstituted.

Meantime, the greater part of the enemy force had hurled itself against the front between Moeuvres and the Scheldt Canal, held by the 56th, 2nd, and 47th Divisions. These three divisions, one of old Regulars and two of London Territorials, were forewarned of the attack by a severe preliminary bombardment followed by a barrage. A little after 9 a.m. the German infantry came on in wave after wave, so that as many as eleven waves advanced in one area during the day. The fiercest thrust was west of Bourlon Wood. There a company of the 17th Royal Fusiliers of the 2nd Division was in course of being withdrawn from an exposed position when the storm burst on it. Captain Stone "sent three of his platoons back, and with a rearguard, composed of the remainder of his company, held off the enemy's infantry until the main position had been organized. Having faithfully accomplished their task, this rearguard died fighting to the end with their faces to the enemy." The day was starred with heroic deeds. Between Moeuvres and the Canal du Nord a company of the 13th Essex of the 2nd Division found itself isolated. "After maintaining a splendid and successful resistance throughout the day, whereby the pressure upon our main line was greatly relieved, at 4 p.m. this company held a council of war, at which the two remaining company officers (Lieutenant J. D. Robinson and Second-Lieutenant E. L. Corps), the company sergeant-major, and the platoon sergeants were present, and unanimously determined to fight to the last, and have 'no surrender.' Two runners who were sent to notify this decision to battalion headquarters succeeded in getting through to our lines, and delivered their message. During the remainder of the afternoon and far into the following night this gallant company were heard fighting, and there is little room for doubt that they carried out to a man their heroic resolution." So, too, when three posts held by the 1st Royal Berkshires of the 2nd Division were overwhelmed. "When, two days later, the three posts were regained, such a heap of German dead lay in and around them that the bodies of our own men were hidden." So, too, when on the right of the 47th Division a gap was found between the 1/5 and 1/15 battalions of the London Regiment, the two battalion commanders counter-attacked with every man they could lay their hands on – cooks, orderlies, runners, and signallers – and restored the position. Before such soldierly resolution the German waves broke and ebbed, leaving immense numbers of dead, and by the evening the assault had most signally failed.

But the battle was not over. On 1st December the Guards advanced, captured the St Quentin ridge and entered Gonnelieu, taking several hundred prisoners and many machine guns. Farther south, with the help of tanks and the dismounted Ambala brigade of Indian cavalry, they took Gauche Wood, but failed to enter Villers Guislain. There was heavy fighting also at Bourlon and Marcoing, and the 29th Division at Masnières beat off no less than nine attacks. But the Masnières position, with the Bonavis ridge in the enemy's hands, was now precarious, and that night the 29th Division withdrew to a line west of the village. Next day there was a further withdrawal. The enemy pressed up Welsh Ridge, north-east of La Vacquerie, and won ground north and west of Gonnelieu. On the 3rd he took La Vacquerie, and since our position beyond the Scheldt Canal near Marcoing was now becoming an acute salient, our troops were brought to the west bank of the canal.

Little happened for the next two days but local fighting; but it was clear to

Sir Douglas Haig that, although the enemy's impetus seemed to be exhausted, the British front was in a highly unsatisfactory state. Either we must regain the Bonavis ridge, which meant a new and severe engagement for which we had not the troops, or we must draw in our line to the Flesquières ridge. He had no other course before him but to give up the Bourlon position for which his troops had so gallantly fought. The shortening of the line was begun on the night of the 4th and completed by the morning of the 7th. The operation was achieved no less skilfully than the similar drawing in of the Ypres front in May 1915. The new front, which in its northern part corresponded roughly to the old Siegfried Reserve Line, ran from the Canal du Nord one and a half miles north of Havrincourt, north of Flesquières, and Ribecourt, and along Welsh Ridge to a point one and a half miles north by east of La Vacquerie. South of that it ran west of Gonnelieu and Villers Guislain, rejoining our old front at Vendhuille. For some days there was local fighting at Bullecourt, but the battle was over, and by the end of the year the Cambrai front had returned to the normal winter inactivity.

The main criticism on this singular action has already been alluded to – that it should never have been undertaken, since it would inevitably involve an extension of operations for which we had not adequate strength. A secondary criticism is that it should have been broken off on 22nd November, when the forty-eight hours of grace had passed and we had not secured our most vital objectives. Viewed in the light of the central strategy of the war, Cambrai effected nothing. It was a brilliant feat of arms, which reflected great credit on the British troops and their commanders, but it had no real bearing upon the fortunes of either combatant. It did not weaken the enemy in his positions, for we had to surrender Bourlon; it did not weaken him in personnel, for the losses were probably about the same on both sides; nor in morale, for he retrieved his first disaster. Looked at solely as a feat of arms, the honours were, perhaps, with Sir Julian Byng, for on a balance the British retained sixteen square miles of enemy territory, while the Germans on 30th November won only seven miles of British, and our sixteen included a seven-mile stretch of the Siegfried Line. It is difficult to see that the British Commander-in-Chief could have acted otherwise than he did. He took a legitimate risk. Had he succeeded, his bold strategy would have been lauded to the skies, and he cannot be blamed because he just fell short of the purpose he had set himself. One good result was indisputable. Enemy divisions destined for the Italian front were diverted to Cambrai, and at a most critical period in the stand on the Piave the German concentration against Italy was suspended for at least a fortnight.

Had Sir Douglas Haig succeeded to the full, it is not likely that his success would have had any lasting influence on the campaign, for he had not the strength to follow it up. But there was that in the German counterstroke the full understanding of which, had it been possible for our General Staff, might have had a potent influence on the future. The attack of the enemy right on Bourlon was in the traditional German manner, reminding those who had

C.R.W. NEVINSON *Reliefs at Dawn*

served in the autumn of 1914 of the methods of First Ypres. There was the heavy initial bombardment, and then wave after wave of massed infantry. But it was different on his left between Masnières and Vendhuille. It was believed in Britain at the time that there had been some defect in our intelligence system which should have prevented a surprise, but it is clear from Sir Douglas Haig's account that there was no such defect. We had all the knowledge of the enemy attack which any intelligence corps could give. Nor were we deficient in artillery, nor greatly outnumbered, for the enemy superiority was not more than four to three. Nevertheless it was a surprise, for a system was being tested which had not yet been tried upon a British force.

(Vol. XXI pp. 93-122)

THE FOURTH YEAR OF THE WAR

In the summer months of 1918 the war was coming to a close. On the Western Front the great German push which had brought them within an ace of taking Paris had been decisively beaten. This chapter describes the situation on every battle front in the fourth year of the war.

IF WE make the anniversary of the outbreak of war the day of the Sarajevo murder, we have to look back upon a year of nearly continuous Allied misfortunes. If we take it as 4th August, the date of the actual start of hostilities, we can discern the first flush of the dawn of victory. It had been a twelvemonth of supreme tension and grave searching of heart. The Allies had seen Eastern Europe fall wholly into the grasp of the Central Powers. They had seen a German domination established over a nerveless Russia which it might well take a century to unloose. They had found their whole scheme of battle ineffective in the West. Costly partial victories had succeeded each other until the pendulum swung backwards, and in a week those partial successes had been turned into something not far from disaster. There was a time in April when those who were honest with themselves were compelled to admit that what seemed a little before to be the last stage of the war, had been but the prelude to an indefinable campaign which stretched darkly into the future – unless, indeed, the Allies were to acknowledge defeat.

The crisis called out the noblest qualities of the civilized Powers, and that in itself was a guarantee of victory. But the foundations of popular thought had been shaken, and till the turn of the tide in July there were few willing to prophesy and none to dogmatize. An air of expectation was abroad, for though reason seemed to point to a protracted campaign, the instinct of mankind argued otherwise. This was true of all the belligerents alike. The German people spoke of peace in the autumn – peace on their own terms; the Allied peoples, while preparing for years of further campaigning, had a sense that these preparations would not be called for. All wars are fought under a time limit determined by human endurance, and there was an instinct abroad that that limit was not far off. There was a feeling in the air of a climax approaching. The skies were dim and tenebrous, but behind the clouds men felt that there was light – either apocalyptic lightnings or the glow of a beneficent dawn.

Our object in the present chapter is first to assess the mood in which the nations, while the end seemed yet afar off, yet waited instinctively for its speedy event. Only after some understanding of this can we realize the atmosphere of the last phase. In the second place, we must pick up the tangled threads in the

East. Towards the end of a long struggle destiny seems to select one area in which the ultimate battle is waged. This in truth had always been the West. From 21st March onward the wildest of military dreamers, whose fancies had hitherto ranged throughout the globe, admitted that here the final lists had been set. But the confusion in the East could not be without its effect on the Western campaign, for it must attract to itself not only the troops and guns of the Allies, but much of the time and thought of the Allied leaders. Again, Germany had so mortgaged her assets in the East that what did not help her to victory there would beyond doubt hasten her progress to defeat. If Russia proved a handicap instead of an aid, if Bulgaria and Turkey fell out of the contest, it would go far worse with her than if she never sent a man beyond the Vistula and the Danube. Finally, there could be no universal peace until the Eastern tangle was unravelled, and on the situation left there at the close of war depended the ease or the difficulty of the reconstructive task laid upon the civilized world.

In analysing the popular mood it will be well to select two types of belligerents – Britain and Germany. France and Italy were invaded, and were, so to speak, in the battle-line. Their intimate peril subordinated all other questions to the urgent one of defence, and though they had their malcontents and doctrinaires, the strong discipline of self-protection held them quiescent. America was like a young man girding on his armour for battle. Her spirit was that of Europe in 1914; she had not yet felt the sad satiety of war; she was absorbed in earnest preparation; and President Wilson, after the crisis of March, had abandoned his exploration of the fundamentals of policy for the more urgent task of stimulating and directing the effort of his countrymen. Among the Central Powers, Bulgaria was tired and apathetic; Turkey broken by suffering out of the semblance of a nation; and Austria flaccid with hunger and internal dissolution. Germany had always been the centre of the ill-assorted confederacy, and now she was more than ever its sole support. If we understand her mood we shall understand the policy of the Central Powers. Britain, too, was a mirror for the Allies. Her freedom from invasion gave her a certain detachment; yet she was not less deeply concerned in the war than Italy or France, for her safety, nay, her existence, depended upon victory. We can see in the free expression of her popular opinion the exact reflection not only of the Allies' moods, but of their many and varied ideals and policies.

The catastrophe of March [the Second Battle of the Somme] had roused to a high pitch the courage and resolution of every class of the British people. It was like the case of a runner who, when far advanced in a race, gets his "second wind". But a second wind does not mean that fatigue has gone, or that the limbs are as vigorous as at the start. Below the splendid renascence of the early spring in Britain there lay a great weariness. Behind her stout front there were strained nerves and tired minds. Effort had ceased to be joy, and had become a grim duty – a dangerous phase for the enemy, had he understood it, for Britain has never been so formidable as when she has been heart-sick of a business. She wore down Philip of Spain and Louis XIV and Napoleon because she continued to fight when she would have given anything for peace – except her soul. The strain was shown in gusty minor strifes which blew up like sandstorms in the desert. An instance was the Maurice affair in May. Sir Frederick Maurice, the Director of Military Operations at the War Office, published on 7th May a letter in the newspapers, in which he flatly contradicted certain statements made by the Prime Minister as to the strength of the British front before the attack of 21st March. The letter was intended to provoke a parliamentary inquiry; but Mr Lloyd George had no difficulty in providing in the House of Commons a kind of answer to its statements, and, after a somewhat clumsy defence of General Maurice by Mr Asquith, made the matter a question of confidence in the Government, and secured a large majority. The vote given in the Maurice debate became a test of loyalty to the Prime Minister. The whole controversy was a jumble of half-truths. Many soldiers were justifiably irritated with the Government; the Government, on the other hand, had a right to claim a tolerant judgement in their supreme difficulties; but the affair showed how thin had worn the sheathing on the nerves of large classes in Britain.

It was the same with Labour. The unselfish co-operation of March and April began to show rifts so soon as the worst danger was past. It would have been a miracle if it had not, for the working-man was as weary as other people. In July things came to a head in a serious dispute among munition workers and a threat of a general strike, which was averted by the prompt action of the Government. More serious still was the strike of the London police at the beginning of August, when men serving under discipline extorted from the Government concessions which, whether right or wrong on the merits, should never have been granted to what was in effect a mutiny. British Labour has one enduring characteristic: it is patriotically united in the face of grave peril, as happened in March; it is united, as after August, when victory is dawning; but in periods of stagnation it grows restless and self-conscious – a pathological state and not a reasoned policy, and a condition which it shared with classes who had not its excuse.

Of pacifism in the common sense of the word there was little. Britain does not talk of peace when things are going badly with her. A certain type of shallow intellectual hankered after negotiation with the enemy; read miracles of moderation into every evasive sentence of Czernin or Kuhlmann; and denied the possibility of a decision in the field. But he found only a scanty audience. The ordinary man, with a truer wisdom, saw that the Allies must win decisively in battle or acknowledge an unqualified defeat. He was not distracted by the enthusiasts who preached a League of Nations while they refused to lay its foundations, or dreamed of an *Internationale* when the foes of internationalism were still at large, or who in their folly conceived that the canker of civilization could be cured by laying the axe of Bolshevism to the tree.

On one matter during the spring and summer the mind of the British people

SIR JOHN LAVERY *A Convoy, North Sea, 1918*

was becoming assured. The submarine had been Germany's most trusted weapon, and it was directed mainly against Britain – not only against her belligerent effort, but against the very foundations of her life. While its violence continued a profound uneasiness filled the land, which no success of our armies could allay. It was fortunate that the darkest hour in France should synchronize with a real mitigation of the submarine pest. In the early months of 1918 there were many naval losses. The liner *Tuscania*, carrying American troops, was torpedoed off the Irish coast on the night of 5th February; the hospital ship *Glenart Castle* was sunk in the Bristol Channel on the morning of 26th February; in June U-boats were raiding small craft off the New Jersey and Delaware coasts; on 20th July the large White Star liner *Justicia* was lost after a stout fight in Irish waters. It was clear, too, that British shipbuilding was not keeping pace with our losses. On 20th March the First Lord of the Admiralty told the House of Commons that the first twelve months of unrestricted submarine warfare had cost the world six million tons of shipping, and that the output of British yards must be nearly doubled before the monthly rate of loss was made good. From January 1, 1918, to the end of May enemy submarines sank 1,146,325 tons of British shipping, and in the same period we completed only 629,087 tons – an adverse balance of more than half a million tons. Yet our output during these months was steadily growing and our losses were steadily shrinking, while the progress of the United States in production was advancing by leaps and bounds. It was almost our most urgent problem, for on its solution depended the effectiveness of the great American levies in the field. Meantime, by a thousand devices, we were hunting down the German submarines – by the new Channel barrage, by "mystery" ships and "dazzle" ships, by destroyers and patrol boats and seaplanes. The British Navy by devious ways was at length coming to its own. On 7th August the Prime Minister told the House of Commons that our Navy was, at the outbreak of the war, the largest in the world, with a tonnage of two and a half million, that now it was eight millions, and that, as a proof of its activity, in June it had steamed eight million miles. He added that 150 German submarines had already been destroyed, more than half in the course of the past year, and on 6th September the Admiralty, in proof, published the names of their commanding officers.

Another element should be noted as making for optimism in the British temper. This was the growing understanding with America. The contact with her soldiers in France, the contact with the many thousand Americans who came to these islands on war duties, the appreciation of America's superb activity, and, among thoughtful people, the gratitude to President Wilson for clarifying the issues of the war, combined to create a real warmth of feeling towards the other great branch of the English-speaking people. The Fourth of July, America's Independence Day, was celebrated this year throughout Britain as a popular festival; for it is our illogical and generous fashion, after a deserved defeat, to join with the victors in acclaiming the justice of their triumph.

Yet, when all has been said, the months between March and August 1918 were for Britain the most critical in the war, and made extreme demands on her fortitude and stability. That she emerged from them with credit, and was able to summon all her strength for the final effort, and envisage with clearness and justice the new world of victory and peace, was due in large measure to the Prime Minister. He was the most fallible of mortals, without precision and continuity in his mental processes, too prone to trust to finesse when candour was required, ill-judging often in his methods and his manner, and apt to sow broadcast a needless distrust. Yet beyond doubt he was the foremost political figure of the campaign, and beyond doubt he was as great a War Minister as Britain had ever known. His fierce vitality, his amazing power of inspiration, his unfailing instinct for the heart of a situation, his robustness of soul, which was more than personal courage, and was like a strong wind which fanned the embers of fortitude in every heart – if these do not spell genius, then the word is without meaning.

Before we turn to Germany it is desirable to review the situation in the East during the spring and summer of 1918. It is, indeed, obligatory, for thither Germany looked for the material gains of which her victory in the West would give her quiet possession; and as difficulties thickened in that quarter the loss of this hope was to play a major part in that breakdown of her "home front" which attended her breakdown in the field.

By the end of March the Eastern front, which a year before had been continuous from the Baltic to the Persian Gulf, had largely disappeared. In such a history as this it is impossible to record in detail the mutations of each section – from the Baltic to the Bukovina, from the Bukovina to the Danube mouths, from the Black Sea to the Tigris. Suffice it to say that the Russian wing had been destroyed, the Romanian left centre put out of action, the Caucasian right centre reduced to chaos, and General Marshall in Mesopotamia left to fight his battles without the support of allies, and no longer a partner in a continuous front. The result was that Finland had become an independent state and an ally of Germany's; Germany was advancing between the Baltic and the Black Sea exactly as she pleased; the Caucasus was torn with internal dissensions, and the Turks were pushing eastward towards the Caspian and southward into Persia; while throughout Transcaspia and Siberia combinations of Bolsheviks and Austro-German prisoners were following their own sweet will; and the British in Mesopotamia had not only the enemy to the north of them, but had on their right flank a distracted Persia, which at any moment might become an enemy Power under Turkish and German officers. It was a situation which none of the Allies, least of all Britain, could afford to neglect. A German Finland would give the Central Powers control of the bridge between the Baltic and the Arctic seas. Unless help came, Russian nationalism would be crushed under the twin weights of Bolshevism and Teutonism. The gap of the Caspian offered the enemy a highway into Central Asia, where already he had his outposts. The turning of the Persian flank not only placed Marshall in a position of great danger, but threatened to put a spark to the inflammable stuff around the Indian border.

To be sure, there were encouraging elements in the problem. The Murman coast and Archangel were open to our ships, and there we might form a bridgehead on which the Russian nationalist forces in the north could be based. The Czechoslovaks lay along the line of the Middle Volga, though cut off from the north by a solid wedge of Bolshevism. In the Don and Kuban provinces east of the Sea of Azov the Cossacks and the Nationalists were strong. In the Caucasus the Allies had many potential friends who might, with a little help from outside, prevent the Turks from making their way to the Caspian. The Czechoslovaks were at Vladivostok and also in Western Siberia, though the country between was in Bolshevik hands. In Mesopotamia Marshall had little to fear from an attack down the Tigris, and might be able to detach troops to keep Persia quiet, hold the south shore of the Caspian, and even defend Baku from the Turks. Allenby in Palestine was secure, and at any moment might begin to exercise a pressure which would distract the Turk from his Caucasian adventure.

The plain task of the Allies was to reconstitute the Eastern front. To do this it was necessary to occupy the Murman coast to keep guard on Finland; to land troops at Archangel and push south from that bridgehead to join hands with the Czechoslovaks on the Volga; to assist by some means or other Alexeiev and Denikin to continue the Czechoslovak left wing to the Caspian; to intervene in East Siberia, so as to control with the help of the Czechoslovaks the whole Trans-Siberian railway, and provide communications for supplying the front on the Volga; to send troops to Transcaspia to hold the enemy there in check; to assist the Armenians and Georgians to resist the Turk in the Caucasus; and to continue the line of defence from the Caspian through North Persia till it met Marshall's front in Mesopotamia. Such was the ideal towards which the Allied Staffs laboured. All of it was common sense and sound policy; much of it was impracticable, considering the limited numbers at their command and their intense preoccupation in the West. A more difficult problem, perhaps, never confronted an Alliance, and it was not made simpler by a certain divergence of political views among the Allied Governments. To build up the Eastern front with the few divisions spared with difficulty from other battlefields might well have seemed as hopeless as to stem the Atlantic with a broom. Yet the attempt was gallantly made; and if it failed to achieve complete success, it yet served to check the enemy's main ambition, and to strip him of his most confident hope. Let us take the long front from north to south, and consider in turn the position in European Russia, Siberia, the Caucasus, Persia and Mesopotamia.

The story of the doings of the Bolsheviks after the Treaty of Brest-Litovsk is partly tragedy and partly *opéra bouffe*. It is tragic because of the hideous sufferings of Russia, and comic from the failure alike of the Bolshevik tyranny and its German exploiters. During April and May Trotsky sulked and raved in his tent, threatened vengeance against Germany, half-persuaded the Allies that he and his friends represented an undying hostility to German aims, and made abortive efforts to raise a Red Army to defy the invaders. But presently came the menace of the Czechoslovaks, which Germany was forced to treat with respect. She made a bargain with Lenin, undertaking not to advance farther east than a certain line from the Gulf of Finland to the Black Sea, so that the Red Forces would be able to give undivided attention to the danger on the Volga.

But she found that she had stumbled on a hornet's nest. In no part of her new sphere of activity did things go well during the summer. In Finland, which she regarded as now her own preserve, and proposed to endow with a German kinglet, Red Guards and White Guards continued their struggle; and when the former were beaten, there came the threat of the British from Murman. In Russia itself there seemed no substance hard enough for her steel to bite upon. Trotsky was now sufficiently tame; but his writ ran in narrow bounds, and he was faced everywhere with hatred, conspiracy, and anarchy. The honest elements in Russia were struggling to draw together, struggling for the most part in vain, for they were widely scattered, and had no leaders; but their efforts gravely impeded the German machine. For the stiff German soldiers and the supple German diplomats it was like building on sand; the foundations were sucked in before the first stones could be laid of the superstructure. A Bolshevik ambassador was sent to Berlin; a German ambassador, Count Mirbach, was dispatched to Moscow; but on 7th July Count Mirbach was assassinated, and his successor, Helfferich, paid a hurried visit and then departed from so insalubrious a habitation. The most that Germany could do was to lend troops to stiffen the Red Army now disputing with the Czechoslovaks on the Volga.

In the Ukraine she made a disastrous blunder. She showed too openly her hand, and methodically set about plundering the place of supplies. She got little, for the peasants rose in revolt, and everywhere there were murders and guerilla war, culminating in the assassination of Field-Marshal von Eichhorn, formerly of the X Army, on 30th July, in the streets of Kiev. The Ukraine had become a German province under an ataman, General Skoropadski, who was nominated by Berlin; conscription had been decreed; the peasants had been forced to return property taken from the landlords the previous autumn, and compelled to cultivate their land for the benefit of Germany. The result was a *jacquerie* and universal resistance, and the effect was felt over the whole of Russia. Had Germany handled the matter with discretion she might have won a great triumph. Russia had lost most of her ideals, and sought only peace; even men like Miliukov inclined to favour the German faction because it promised a relief from anarchy. But Germany's treatment of the Ukraine had been too barefaced to leave any doubt as to her policy. She had entered Russia to bring not peace but fetters, and the spectacle convinced the bulk of the people that the German cure for Bolshevism was no better than the disease.

As for Lenin and Trotsky, they had now sold themselves to their masters, and provided proof of what Kerensky in June told the British Labour Conference, that "the actions of the Bolsheviks made them the vanguard of triumphant German militarism." About this time Trotsky seems to have lost his nerve, and the actual leadership passed wholly into the hands of Lenin. He had far greater nerve and courage than the other, and knew precisely what he wanted. He cared nothing for the dismemberment of Russia; he did not want peace; he welcomed anarchy, for only by the road of universal anarchy could the world reach the communism of which he dreamed. The advent of the Czechoslovaks and the imminence of Allied intervention brought the wildest spirits to the front, and what had formerly been a class tyranny now became a class vendetta and an orgy of brigandage and murder. On 16th July the ex-Tsar was shot at Ekaterinburg, in the Urals, after a mock trial; and somewhere in that region, about the same time, the other members of the Imperial household perished miserably. The tragedy of the Romanovs had not even the dignity of the fall of the Bourbons. Secretly, squalidly, they were murdered in the wilds by madmen, and the world heard only by accident of their fate.

The story of Transcaucasia at this period is one of the most confused in the war, and it cannot be dissociated from the obscure happenings in Transcaspia and Central Asia, for it was to the Caucasus that Germany looked for an alley to a new Asian dominion. The Russian Revolution of March 1917 had produced a national self-consciousness throughout the country, and, under the influence of Georgia, politically the most mature of the peoples, the independence of Transcaucasia was proclaimed in November, and a general Transcaucasian Government was formed in a republic to include Georgians, Armenians, and Tatars. Meantime there was anarchy among the Russian troops of the Caucasus, and Prjevalsky, who had succeeded Yudenitch, was compelled to ask Turkey for an armistice. The advance of the Turks began to weaken the allegiance of the Tatars to the new Government, and in March 1918 came the Brest-Litovsk treaty, making over Batum, Kars, and Ardahan to Turkey. These cessions were a serious blow to the Georgians, but they had no alternative except to submit. Presently Turkey increased her demands beyond the Brest clauses, and at a conference held in Batum in May the Georgian delegates refused to accept them. The Transcaucasian Government had now ceased to exist; an independent Armenian republic of Erivan was proclaimed under Turkish protection; a Tatar republic on the same terms, which included Baku, was established in Azerbaijan; and Georgia was compelled to appeal to Germany.

Turkey, it was clear, intended to deal high-handedly with Transcaucasia, and this Germany had no mind to permit. She cared little what happened to the Armenians, but she was determined to control Baku and its oilfields, and she had selected the Georgians to be her special allies and to play the part she had cast for the Finns in the north and the Bulgarians in the Balkans. General Kress von Kressenstein was recalled from Syria – where he was soon to be sorely needed – and sent to the Caucasus; and German troops were marched into Georgia, while German trading houses endeavoured to secure every possible contract for the development of the region. An attempt was made in July to settle affairs with Turkey by a Conference at Constantinople, and the Turks were categorically informed that they must abide by the Brest treaty. They paid no attention, continued their intrigues throughout the whole Caucasus, and advanced steadily to Baku. Their aim was to control the region by means of the Moslem inhabitants, and all Germany could effect was to withdraw Georgia from their influence, and to make a contract for oil with the Armenians and Bolsheviks of Baku, which would be worthless when the Turks took the town. The rift between Germany and her Moslem ally was widening.

Such is a rough sketch of the main events of six months of plot and counterplot. It was a matter in which Britain was acutely interested, for not only did it directly affect her Mesopotamian campaign, but it prejudiced the whole future of Persia and the immediate hinterland of India. Events east of the Caspian were equally disquieting. After nearly a year of contest, the Soviet of Tashkent had beaten the Provincial Government at Kokand, and overpowered all resistance between Baku and Ferghana. In May Russian Turkestan had been

declared a Soviet republic. These events thrust the moderates into the background, and inclined the Central Asian Moslems towards Germany and Turkey
as possible deliverers from this thralldom, while Pan-Islamic and Pan-Turanian
propaganda took on a new lease of life.

The nearest British troops were the small contingents in Persia and Marshall's army in Mesopotamia, and their problem was sufficiently complex. In
the first place, the road from Bagdad to the Caspian must be kept open against
the Turkish assaults from the west. In the second place, the advance of the
Transcaspian Bolsheviks must be checked. They had taken Merv, and if they
had further successes, they might be joined by the Turcomans, and the whole
region be set ablaze. Again, if the Eastern front was to be restored, the Caspian
and its shipping must be mastered, and this meant that Baku must be held
against the Turk. A British force was sent to Transcaspia, and after many
vicissitudes succeeded in beating the Bolsheviks so soundly that they
exchanged military operations for local atrocities. This remote sideshow had in
reality immense political importance for Britain, since the line from Merv to
Kushk ended within two days' ride of Herat, the key of Afghanistan.

The defence of the Bagdad-Caspian route was maintained, in spite of the
forays of Turkish cavalry from Tabriz and the ceaseless raids of the hill tribes,
notably the Jangalis around Resht. But the main interest centred in Baku,
where, on the night of 25th July, the Bolsheviks were overthrown and a new
Government set up, which at once begged for British assistance. They had
control at the moment of the shipping on the Caspian, and sent transports to
Enzeli to fetch the small British force under Major-General Dunsterville, which
was now more than 1,000 miles from its base. The main difficulty was the
shipping, for the Caspian Fleet was not to be relied on. The second was the
quality of the local levies – 7,500 Armenians and 3,000 Russians – who proved
wholly useless in action. On 17th August the former refused to fight, and
presently went home; and a strong Turkish assault on the 26th August was
repulsed only by two British battalions, the North Staffords and the Worcesters. At the close of the month Dunsterville was in serious straits. The Turks
were round the town, and on the 31st the local troops failed once again, and the
Warwicks had to cover their retirement.

Help came suddenly out of the void. The Russian partisan leader, Bichar-
akov, who had done good work with Marshall in Mesopotamia, took Petrovsk,
on the Caspian, 200 miles to the north, and sent reinforcements to Baku. These
arrived on 9th September; and after further trouble with the Russian Fleet, and
a serious rearguard action on the 14th, the British evacuated Baku and reached
Enzeli in safety – a result which must be considered fortunate in view of the
immense risks run by the expedition. It had never been our intention to
garrison Baku ourselves, but merely to assist the local Government to establish
their hold on the oilfields, and to secure the Caspian shipping. Since the local
Government proved incompetent to organize resistance, there was nothing for
Dunsterville to do but to leave the place to the Turks. It was a possession which

they were not destined to enjoy for long.

The situation around the Caspian condemned General Marshall to inactivity on his main battle ground. He found himself involved in adventures many hundred miles from his front, and while this duty continued, he must remain inactive on the Tigris, though much could be done to restore order and prosperity to the ancient land which his predecessor had redeemed. Sir Stanley Maude died on November 18, 1917. In December an attack was delivered against the Turkish 13th Corps, holding the Diala and the Jebel Hamrin passes, and on the 5th it was driven towards Kifri with heavy casualties. On the 9th Khanikin was occupied. Early in the New Year General Marshall resolved to advance his front on the Euphrates, and to break up the new Turkish concentration two miles north of Hit. On 8th March it was discovered that the enemy had retired fifteen miles upstream to Salahiya, and next day Hit was occupied. The Turks were still retiring, and on the 10th Marshall was in Salahiya. It was resolved to try an encircling operation against the position at Khan Baghdad, where the enemy proposed to stand. By 11.30 on the night of 26th March our cavalry had got round his flanks and cut off his retreat; and our infantry, attacking next morning at dawn, completed his discomfiture. Major-General Sir H. T. Brooking occupied Haditha without trouble, and pursued the Turks for seventy-three miles along the Aleppo road, taking over 5,000 prisoners. In April the centre of interest moved to the Tigris, where we advanced along the Mosul road, taking Kifri on the 27th and over 1,000 prisoners, and entering Kirkuk on 7th May without opposition. Thereafter, as we have seen, came the distractions on the Caspian, and the arduous task of relief work on the Persian border; and General Marshall was forced to retire his right wing. It was not till October that he struck again on the Tigris, and then he had before him a breaking enemy.

In reviewing these strange months we may say on the whole that for the Allies the balance leant to the credit side. They had failed, indeed, to recreate the Eastern front. At the most they had established it in patches, which left the strategical position precarious. Poole was still far from the Czechoslovaks on the Volga. The latter had both their flanks turned, and, though communications were now open behind them, they had as yet received no supports or supplies; Kornilov was dead, Alexeiev was dying, and Denikin could make little way north of the Caspian; the Turks were in Baku; Persia was still disruptive and wavering, and Marshall could not carry out his proper task for attending to her vagaries.

Yet if we compare the situation in September with that after the signature of the Brest-Litovsk treaty in March, we shall see how far astray had gone Germany's forecast. She had by her conduct in the Ukraine involved herself in a mesh of troubles; hopelessly antagonized the orderly elements in Russia; and got little in the way of supplies for herself. She had lost Siberia, and seen the Czechoslovaks spring up like a new seed of Cadmus, to dispute with her the way to the East. She was at variance with Turkey over the Caucasus, as she was at

STUART REID *A Handley Page Aeroplane Bombing Nablus by Night*

variance with Bulgaria over the Dobrudja. She was rapidly losing Finland, the northern pillar of her Eastern ambitions. Above all, the two Prussianisms – one of which was called Bolshevism – had proved incompatible, in spite of their formal alliance. A belief in force and the tyranny of a class is insufficient as a bond of union, if the two parties differ as to the class; and a common ruthlessness is more likely to lead to quarrels than to co-operation.

Germany had played with fire, and it was about to scorch her hands. To her statesmen it was plain long before September that the policy which seemed so hopeful at Brest-Litovsk had utterly failed. There was no make-weight to be found in the East against a draw in the West; and if disaster befell in the West, from the East assuredly could come no succour. Nay, her oriental acquisitions would be like a millstone round the neck of a sinking man. When Prince Leopold of Bavaria and his glittering staff crossed the Vistula by the Warsaw bridge on that July day in 1915, they saw the sky reddened with the fires of great burnings, which marked the retreat of Russia into her wild spaces. It was the sight which Napoleon had seen, and it carried the same omen. Russia had retired into the wastes both of the earth and of the spirit, and the invader had followed to his destruction.

These things, as we have said, were beginning to be perceived by Germany's rulers. Their people had followed them blindly, and taken from them a confidence ready-made, for they had little reasoned assurance of their own. If the nerve of the leaders failed, there would be no popular endurance. We pass now to consider the mutations of German opinion between March and September.

In April Burian, who in December 1916 had been displaced by Czernin, succeeded him as Foreign Minister of the Dual Monarchy. It was one of those aimless changes of personnel which proved nothing except the rudderless character of Austrian statecraft. She was drifting now in an archipelago of reefs – the nationalism of her subject peoples, the truculence of Hungary, a cracking army, a starving population. Without affection or hope she continued to follow the will of her stronger partner, and, though passionately desirous of peace, she had not the energy left to initiate any independent policy. It was very clear that Austria could not secede from the war of her own will, for she had no strength in her limbs; but it was clear, too, that some day soon her limbs might collapse beneath her.

In Germany the people had been moved to a sudden hope by the promises of February and the achievements of March and April. After that the hope waned, but a conviction endured – that there must be peace before the winter. The confidence of most of her statesmen had a longer life – till well into September. There were exceptions, and the most notable was the Foreign Minister, von Kuhlmann. He had never favoured the spring offensive, and by May he had convinced himself of its futility. Accordingly, on 24th June, in the Budget debate in the Reichstag, he warned his hearers that it was idle to look for a decision in the field. It was a remarkable speech, which revealed the perturbation of German civilian statesmen. He admitted the failure of the Eastern policy by granting that the Brest-Litovsk treaty needed revising, and by candidly stating the difficulties with Turkey. He repeated the old tale of Germany's innocence of any thought of world dominion. She sought, he said, only the boundaries drawn for her by history, sufficient overseas possessions to correspond to her greatness, and freedom of trade with all continents over a free ocean. She was willing to listen to any honest offer of peace, and trusted that her opponents would approach her with a proposal; but she would make no statement about Belgium which would bind her without binding her enemies. If one looked only to the battlefield no decision could be said to be in sight, and he quoted Moltke very much to the purpose. Germany could not be conquered, but "in view of the enormous magnitude of this coalition war, in view of the number of Powers, including those from overseas, involved in it, an absolute end can hardly be expected through military decisions alone."

The speech was the swan-song of Kuhlmann's diplomacy, of the whole policy of the German *politiques*. It was an attempt to break to the German people the news that the promises of February could not be met, and that the boasting of the early summer had been idle. Did Kuhlmann speak for himself alone? It is highly improbable. Ludendorff's own confidence was waning, and it is likely that he used Kuhlmann to prepare the popular mind for worse tidings; for the great stroke on the Aisne had not brought victory, and he was far too good a soldier not to see the dangers ahead of him. The result proved that both he and Kuhlmann had miscalculated the popular mood. The drop was too sudden, and the outcry was violent. The Pan-Germans assailed the Foreign Minister as a partisan of Britain; he was made to explain away his speech by an admission of the necessity of victory in the field, and the Imperial Chancellor made a further and most unflattering apology for the "accidental" indiscretions of his colleague. He found he had no supporters, for truculence had become the fashion again, and even Scheidemann bowed to it. He was made the scapegoat, too, of all the blunders of the Government, for, as von Holstein once observed to Prince Bülow: "When the sun shines the Chancellor suns himself; when it rains, it is the Foreign Secretary who gets wet."

On 10th July he resigned, and was succeeded by Admiral von Hintze. He had been the exponent of the practicable, or what seemed to him the practicable, as against the megalomaniacs, and there was no place for him in a world where calculations were becoming as futile as dreams. Two days later Hertling, with the support of the Majority Socialists, declared the policy of Germany on confident lines, announcing, among other things, that she held Belgium as "a pawn for future negotiations", and thereby refusing what the Allies had always maintained to be a pre-condition of any discussion of peace terms. The last German offensive was due in three days, and it was necessary to stiffen the spirit of the country.

July came to a close, and with it any confidence that remained to the High Command. During August there were signs that it was the leaders in the field rather than the *politiques* who wished to mitigate the arrogance which they had aforetime fostered. Hindenburg, now somewhat a lay figure, found himself compelled early in September to issue a manifesto against the growing movement towards compromise. He chose to explain it by the success of Allied propaganda inside Germany – propaganda which it was the fashion to decry in the countries of origin, but which the Germans had come to regard with uneasy respect. On 12th September the Vice-Chancellor, von Payer, made a curious speech in which, while declaring that he did not believe in a peace of conquest, he expounded Germany's terms in the fashion of a conqueror. There could be no handing back of Poland or Finland or the Baltic states to Russia, or any paring down of Germany's acquisitions in the East. "We can never permit any one to meddle with us in this matter from the standpoint of the present European balance of power, or rather British predominance. Just as little will we submit to the Entente, for its gracious approval or alteration, our peace treaties with the Ukraine, Russia, or Romania. In the East we have peace, and it remains for us peace, whether it pleases our Western neighbours or not."

These were brave words, but they were inopportune. The unhappy Govern-

JOHN SINGER SARGENT *The Interior of a Hospital Tent*

ment at Berlin might speak boldly one day, but the compulsion of events compelled it to change its tone on the morrow. On 14th September Germany made an offer of a separate peace to Belgium, who at once rejected it. She offered also to refrain from attacking Eastern Karelia if the Allied troops would withdraw from the Murman coast, having found it impossible to induce Finland to make any effort to fight for the territory she had claimed. More significant still, Austro-Hungary addressed a Note to all belligerents and neutral states proposing a conference for a "non-binding confidential discussion" as to the possibility of peace. This offer, though Germany officially denied any connection with it, was undoubtedly made with her knowledge. The truth is, that Austria was desperate, and was approaching that condition when she must sue for peace on any terms. Germany was willing to permit the Note as a *ballon d'essai*. If it failed, she could save her dignity by repudiating any part in it; if it succeeded, it would give her the conference for which she had always intrigued.

The reply of the Allies was instant and unequivocal; and it was that of Lucio's comrade in *Measure for Measure* – "Heaven grant us its peace, but not the King of Hungary's!" Mr Balfour, on 16th September, asked pertinently what use would such a conference be, if the policy of the Central Powers was the policy of von Payer's speech of 12th September. That same day came America's answer: "The Government of the United States feels that there is only one reply which it

DOROTHY J. COKE *Wounded Men on Duppas Hill, Croydon*

can make to the suggestion of the Imperial Austro-Hungarian Government. It has repeatedly and with entire candour stated the terms on which the United States would consider peace, and can and will entertain no proposal for a conference upon a matter concerning which it has made its position and purpose so plain."

This, then, was the position in the third week of September. The German people were in a mood of deep depression, careless of the arguments booming above their heads, but clinging blindly to the certainty of a peace of some kind before the winter. Their rulers were not less disconsolate. They saw their front in the West cracking, and the whole fabric of their power in the East beginning to crumble about their ears. They knew the terms upon which alone the Allies would think of peace, and these terms meant the downfall of all they had builded, and the reversal of Germany's policy since the days of Bismarck. They could not bring themselves as yet to bow to them, and they hoped against hope for some diversion, some gift from the gods at the eleventh hour. On 24th September both the Imperial Chancellor and the Vice-Chancellor spoke in the Reichstag, clinging to their old dogmas, but striving so to phrase them that, while maintaining their substance, they might fall more soothingly on Allied ears. It was clear that Germany would not admit defeat till her armies were decisively beaten in the field.

(Vol. XXIII pp. 23-39, 49-63)

THE SURRENDER OF GERMANY

The stage was set for what Buchan calls "the last act of the play". Its action was to be short. The allied advance on the Western Front was swift and decisive: by November 1918 the German army and its allies had been defeated. The only battle front where fighting continued was East Africa where, because of communication difficulties, news of the German surrender did not reach their commander, General Paul von Lettow Vorbeck, until 23 November. The Great War had ended and, as Buchan put it, "The old world had passed away."

LUDENDORFF HAD gone, and the Supreme Command was in commission. His nominal successor was von Groener, the Würtemberg general; but von Groener was an administrator rather than a strategist, and such strategical direction as was still possible seems to have been in the hands of von Lossberg, formerly Chief of Staff to von Armin's IV Army in Flanders. Hindenburg contented himself with appeals for German unity; and the Emperor, who on 29th October sought refuge with Army Headquarters at Spa from the troubles of the capital, was in no position to interfere. He was occupied with adapting democratic tunes to the damaged trumpets of absolutism.

Foch was now on the eve of his last step in the West. He had to get Gouraud and Pershing forward so as to cut the Metz-Montmédy-Mezières line, and limit the avenues of retreat for the army groups of the Bavarian and Imperial Crown Princes to the gap of Liége, and at the same time to push his British centre down the Sambre towards Namur, so as to make the retirement of the latter impossible. Then would come the final operation – the swinging of his American right north-eastward between Metz and Longuyon so as to cut the Metz-Arlon-Namur railway, and shepherd into captivity the whole of the southern German armies. In such an event only a few beaten divisions would escape by the pass between Dutch Limburg and the Ardennes, and the most complete catastrophe in all history would have overtaken the German command.

Haig, having crossed the little streams between the Forest of Mormal and the Scheldt, was ready for his final movement. He was in the position of Wellington on the evening of Waterloo, when he raised his hat as a signal for "everything to go in". For three months the British armies had been locked in a continuous battle; for nearly ten months they had been in the forefront of the struggle. From 21st March to 27th October no United Kingdom division had been on an average more than sixty-nine days out of the line, while the

Australian average was seventy-nine days, and the Canadian one hundred and two days. During the same period the percentage of casualties to strength in the British divisions was one hundred and eighteen for officers and one hundred and twenty-one for men. The strain had been colossal, but the reward was very near, and however great the weariness of the Allied troops, it was a small thing compared to the exhaustion of the enemy. The boys of the 1921 class, who had been called up for "national auxiliary service" in occupied territory, were being transferred to the fighting line, so that the ranks of Germany were becoming like the levies of France when in 1814 they fell back before Blücher and Schwarzenberg. But in this case the defeated armies had no Napoleon.

As a preliminary to the British advance, Valenciennes must fall. At 5.15 on the morning of 1st November, the Canadians and the 22nd Corps of Horne's First Army and the 17th Corps of Byng's Third Army attacked on a six-mile front south of the town. The struggle was sharp, and the enemy resisted strongly on the flooded banks of the river; but his defences had been constructed to meet an attack coming from the west, and the Canadians struck upward from the south. That afternoon four companies of Canadians entered Valenciennes from the west, and the 49th and 4th Divisions of the 22nd Corps crossed the Rhonelle. Next day, 2nd November, the 4th Canadians completed the capture of the city of Sir John Froissart, and the 22nd Corps were well beyond the Rhonelle, taking Maresches and Préseau, and the high ground two miles to the east. On the 3rd the Germans fell back on the front south of Valenciennes, and also north of Tournai; and there were signs of a more extensive withdrawal, since our drive south of the Scheldt had turned the line of the river, and was threatening the southern enemy front towards Avesnes. The moment was ripe for the last great British effort.

Meantime there was good news from the Allied right. On Friday, 1st November, Gouraud and Pershing went into action, and the French attacking north and east of Vouziers, and the Americans advancing between Olizy and the Meuse. Gouraud thus took in flank the German divisions opposed to Pershing, and enabled the First United States Army to get clear of the desperate country of woods and pockets in which for weeks it had been fighting. The whole line swung forward. On Saturday, in wild weather, Gouraud reached the south bank of the Ardennes Canal, and Pershing took Halles, and advanced more than six miles. Next day the Americans, at a range of some 20,000 yards, were looking north by Stenay to the Metz railway. At last the shell of this stubborn defence had been cracked. In three days, on an eighteeen-mile front, Pershing had advanced twelve miles. By the morning of Monday, the 4th, he held positions which enabled him to bring the railway at Montmédy and Longuyon under his fire.

On the morning of 4th November Haig delivered his great attack on the thirty miles between Valenciennes and Oisy on the Sambre. He was moving against formidable defences – the canalized channel of the Sambre in the south; the great Mormal Forest in the centre; and on his left the fortifications of the town of Le Quesnoy, and the broken woody country intersected by many streams which lay northward towards the Condé Canal. But his troops knew they were on the eve of victory, and were not to be checked by any defences.

The battle opened at dawn, and presently all the German first position had fallen. It was the task of Rawlinson on the right to cross the Sambre south of the Mormal Forest, of Byng in the centre to clear the Forest itself, and of Horne to cross the marshes north of Valenciennes and advance east of the little river Aunelle. Meantime, Débeney, with the First French Army on Haig's right, was to advance to conform into the Forest of Nouvion and along the Upper Oise. The whole plan moved like clockwork. Sir W. P. Braithwaite's 9th Corps, on Rawlinson's right, took Catillon, in two hours were across the Sambre, and by the afternoon were well to the east of Fesmy in the south and La Folie in the north. Sir T. L. N. Morland's 13th Corps, attacking a little later with the 25th, 50th, and 18th Divisions, had a stiff fight with the 1st Guard Reserve Division at the Sambre crossings near Landrecies. But ere nightfall the 25th Division had occupied the little town, where in the August dusk in the first month of war Haig's 1st Corps had faced and checked the great sweep of the enemy from the Belgian frontier. In the Third Army area the 5th Corps, under Lieutenant-General Shute, fought their way into the pathless thickets of the Mormal Forest, and by dawn on the 5th had reached its eastern edge, taken the woodland village of Locquignol, and advanced a mile to the east of it. On their left the 37th and New Zealand Divisions of the 4th Corps swept through the northern part of the Forest, taking Jolimetz and Herbignies; and at four in the afternoon the garrison of Le Quesnoy, now hopelessly cut off, made its surrender. On their left, the 62nd Division took Orsinval and, advancing along with the Guards, carried Frasnoy and Preux-au-Sart, and reached the edge of Gommegnies. The left corps of the Third Army, the 17th, met with less opposition, and by the evening were east of Bry and Eth and the two Wargnies, and so beyond the upper streams of the Aunelle. That day Horne, moving forward to conform, had his right well east of the Aunelle at Sebourg, while his Canadians were in the streets of Rombies.

It was a day of almost bewildering success. Twenty British divisions had scattered thirty-two German divisions, taking 19,000 prisoners and more than 450 guns. Nor was the success only in the central area. Débeney crossed the Sambre Canal on his whole front, and on the 5th was in Guise. The Belgians had driven von Armin behind the Ghent-Terneuzen Canal and were closing in on Ghent. Plumer and Humbert were fording the Scheldt. Mangin and Guillaumat had breached the Hunding Line between Sissonne and Condé-lès-Herpy, Gouraud had crossed the Ardennes Canal between Montgon and Le Chesne, and the Aisne farther west towards Rethel. Pershing was continuing his brilliant advance, and his Second Army under Liggett was now moving forward on the right bank of the Meuse with a view to thrusting the enemy off the last of the heights into the plain. His van was at Pouilly, where he was only six miles from the bend north of Montmédy on the Metz railway.

ALFRED HAYWARD *The Soldiers' Buffet, Charing Cross Station, 1918*

On Tuesday, 5th November, the enemy's resistance was finally broken. Henceforth he was not in retreat but in flight. The two wings of his armies were separated for ever. The Hunding and Brynhild zones had gone the way of the Siegfried. The opening of the pocket was now the fifty miles between Avesnes and Mezières, and through this gut the whole remaining German forces in the south must squeeze if they would make good their escape. But that gut was hourly narrowing. Gouraud and Pershing were approaching Mezières; Mangin and Guillaumat were pressing towards Hirson, with nothing to bar the road; while Haig, now east of the Mormal Forest, had the Sambre valley as an avenue to Namur. Moreover, Foch had still his trump card to play, the encircling swing of his right, north of Metz, to close the last bolt hole. If a negotiated armistice did not come within a week there would be a *de facto* armistice of complete collapse and universal surrender.

During that week in Germany the mutterings of the storm of revolution were growing louder. Some issued heated appeals for a patriotic closing up of ranks in a last stand against the coming disaster; others attempted to make a scapegoat of the unhappy Ludendorff; but everywhere was apparent a rising anger against the Emperor and the Imperial House. He had fled to the army, but the army was in no case to protect him. The Social Democrats in the

Government, led by Scheidemann, were clamouring for his instant abdication, and they had the support of the great mass of the people. Everywhere there reigned a frantic fear of invasion, especially in Bavaria, where the collapse of Austria made the populace expect to see at any moment the victorious Italians in their streets; and invasion was no cheerful prospect to Germany when she remembered her own method of conducting it, and reflected that for four years she had been devastating the lands and torturing the peoples of the Powers now marching to her borders.

Strange things, too, were happening within her own confines. In the first days of November the stage had been set for a great sea battle. Her High Seas Fleet was ordered out, but it would not move. The dry rot, which had been growing during the four years' inaction, had crumbled all its discipline. "Der Tag" had come, but not that joyous day which her naval officers had toasted. She had broken the unwritten laws of the deep sea, and she was now to have her reward. On 4th November the red flag was hoisted on the battleship *Kaiser*. The mutiny spread to the Kiel shipyards and workshops, where there had always been a strong socialist element; a Council of soldiers, sailors, and workmen was formed; and the mutineers captured the barracks, and took possession of the town. The trouble spread like wildfire to Hamburg, Bremen, Lübeck, and adjacent ports, and it was significant that in every case the soldiers and sailors took the lead. Deputations of Social Democrats were sent down post-haste by the Government, and succeeded in temporarily restoring order, but the terms on which peace was made were the ruin of the old regime. In Cologne, in Essen, and in other industrial centres there were grave disturbances, and everywhere the chief outcry was against the Emperor and the Hohenzollerns. He who had been worshipped as a god, because he was the embodiment of a greater Germany, was now reviled by a nation disillusioned of dreams of greatness. At the same time the Empire was dissolving in its periphery. The Polish deputies from Posen and Silesia seceded from the Reichstag, and Schleswig demanded liberation.

It was hard to tell where in Germany the seat of power now lay. On the 5th the Army Command invited to Headquarters representatives of the majority parties in the Reichstag to discuss the next step, and search was made for military officers who might be least inacceptable to the Allies. On that day the Government in Washington transmitted to Germany, through Switzerland, the last word on the matter of negotiations. This Note gave the reply of America's Allies to the correspondence which had been formally submitted to them. They had accepted the President's Fourteen Points as a basis of peace with two provisos: first, they reserved their own liberty of action on the question of the freedom of the seas, since that phrase was open to so many interpretations; second, by the word "restoration" in the case of invaded territories, they declared they understood "compensation by Germany for all damage done to the civilian population of the Allies, and to their property by the aggression of Germany by land, by sea, and from the air." President

Wilson signified his assent to these provisos, and announced that Marshal Foch had been authorized by all the Allies to receive properly accredited representatives of the German Government, and to communicate to them the terms of an armistice.

Germany made haste to choose her delegates. They were Erzberger, now a Secretary of State; General von Gündell, an old associate of Marshal von Bieberstein, and the German military delegate to the Hague Conference of 1907; Count Oberndorff, sometime German Minister in Sofia; and General von Winterfeld, who had once been military attaché in Paris, and had recently acted as von Falkenhausen's Chief of Staff at Brussels. The Allied plenipotentiary was Foch, who had associated with him Sir Rosslyn Wemyss, the British First Sea Lord, to represent the British Navy. On the afternoon of Wednesday, the 6th, the German delegates left Berlin, Foch having directed them by wireless to approach the French outposts by the Chimay-Fourmies-La Capelle-Guise road. That day Prince Max of Baden, as Imperial Chancellor, issued an appeal to his people that negotiations might not be endangered by indiscipline. "For more than four years the German nation, united and calm, has endured the severest sufferings and sacrifices of war. If at the decisive hour, when only absolute unity can avert from the whole German people the greatest dangers for its future, our internal strength gives way, then the consequences cannot be foreseen. The indispensable demand which must be made in this crisis by any people's Government is the maintenance of the calm which has hitherto prevailed under voluntary discipline."

We leave the delegates on their embarrassed journey, while we review the last days of the Allied advance.

Let us look first at the British centre. Before Haig, if anywhere, the Germans must attempt a stand, for he was marching straight for Namur and the one narrow door still open to their frontiers. No soldier will withhold his tribute of admiration to the gallantry of his foe, and during these desperate days the German armies still made forlorn attempts at resistance to gain for other parts of the line a little respite. But it was like the efforts of a mop to stay the advance of the ocean. The great victory of 4th-5th November had opened the roads of the Condé Canal and the Sambre valley. On the 5th Rawlinson advanced four miles beyond Prisches and Maroilles, while that evening Byng was approaching Bavai, which had been French's headquarters at the start of the Battle of Mons. Horne had a harder day. His 22nd Corps crossed the Belgian frontier, but was held up for some time in front of the village of Angre and the line of the Honnelle stream. Next day, Wednesday, 6th November, Horne broke down the resistance, took Angre and crossed the Honnelle, while the Canadians captured Quievrechain. That night came another enemy landslide, and early on the morning of the 7th the Guards Division of Byng's army entered Bavai. On the 8th Rawlinson occupied Avesnes, and Byng took Hautmont, and reached the outskirts of Maubeuge.

In these days the weather was wet and chilly, very different from the bright

August when British troops had last fought in that region. The old regular forces which had then taken the shock of Germany's first fury had mostly disappeared. Many were dead or prisoners or crippled for life, and the rest had been dispersed through the whole British Army. The famous first five divisions of the Retreat from Mons were in the main new men. But some were there who had fought steadily from the Sambre to the Marne, and back again to the Aisne, and then for four years in bitter trench battles, and who now returned after our patient fashion to their old campaigning ground. Even the slow imagination of the British soldier must have been stirred by that strange revisiting. He was approaching places which in 1914 had been no more than names to him, half-understood names heard dimly in the confusion of the great retreat. But some stood out in his memory – the fortress of Maubeuge, on which France had set such store; above all, the smoky coal pits of Mons, which had become linked for ever in the world's mind with the old "Contemptibles". Then he had been marching south in stout-hearted bewilderment, with the German cavalry pricking at his flanks. Now he was sweeping to the north-east on the road to Germany, and far ahead his own cavalry and cyclists were harassing the enemy rout, while on all the packed roads his airmen were scattering death.

On the night of the 7th the thrust of the Fourth, Third, and First Armies bore fruit in the north. The line of the Scheldt broke. Horne's left corps, the 8th, and Birdwood's right corps, the 1st, crossed the river south of Antoing on the 8th, and took Condé. This was the end of the Tournai bridgehead, and that evening Birdwood occupied the western part of the ancient city. On the 9th the Guards entered Maubeuge, while the Canadians with Horne were sweeping along the Condé Canal towards Mons. Birdwood cleared Tournai and took Peruwelz, and Plumer crossed the Scheldt on his whole front and reached Renaix. Next day the Belgians had Ghent.

In the south the advance of the Allies was still more rapid, for Débeney and Mangin, Guillaumat and Gouraud had little before them, and Pershing's gallant Americans were at last reaping the fruits of their fierce October struggle. On the 6th Débeney advanced six miles, passed the Forest of Nouvion, and entered Vervins, while Gouraud took Rethel, and Pershing's two armies crept down both sides of the Meuse nearer to the Metz railway. It was a race for the three points of Hirson, Mezières, and Sedan. On the afternoon of the 7th the vanguard of the First United States Army took that part of the town of Sedan which lies in the meadows on the west bank of the Meuse. On the 8th Gouraud reached Mezières, and held the Meuse shore as far east as Bazeilles; the Second United States Army completed its conquest of the Heights of the Meuse; and Débeney entered Hirson. But indeed the record of places captured was now meaningless; over much of the battlefield the advance was limited only by the weariness of marching infantry. On the 10th – from north to south – Plumer was far beyond the Scheldt, and approaching the Dendre Canal; Birdwood was across that canal, and had taken Ath; Horne was on the Condé Canal west and north-west of Mons; Byng and Rawlinson were far down the

JOHN SINGER SARGENT *"Thou Shalt Not Steal"*

Sambre and close on the Belgian frontier; Débeney was on the edge of Chimay; Rocroi had been occupied, as had Mezières and Charleville (the old seat of the German High Command in the West); while Pershing had reached Stenay, and his Second Army was well through the Woëvre Forest. This was on Sunday, the 10th; for Thursday, the 14th, Foch had fixed the great sweep of the Americans north-eastward between the Meuse and the Moselle.

These were feverish days both for the victors and the vanquished. Surrender hung in the air, and there was a generous rivalry among the Allies to get as far forward as possible before it came. This was specially noted among the British troops, who wished to finish the war on the ground where they had started. Take as an instance the 8th Division in Horne's First Army. It had spent the winter in the Ypres salient; it had done gloriously in the retreat from St Quentin; it had fought in the Third Battle of the Aisne; and from the early days of August it had been hotly engaged in the British advance. Yet now it had the vigour of the first month of war. On the 10th of November one of its battalions, the 2nd Middlesex, travelled for seven hours in buses, and then marched twenty-seven miles, pushing the enemy before them. They wanted to reach the spot near Mons where some of them (then in the 4th Middlesex) fired almost the first British shots in the war, and it is pleasant to record that they succeeded.

Meantime in Germany the discipline which for generations had held her civilian people was dissolving like snow in thaw. There were few mutinies like that of the northern ports. The old authorities simply disappeared, quietly, unobtrusively, and the official machine went on working without them. Kings and courts tumbled down, and the various brands of Socialists met together, gave themselves new names, and assumed office. There was as yet nothing which approached a true revolution, nothing which involved a change of spirit. Deep down in the ranks of the people there was a dull anger and disquiet, but for the moment it did not show itself in action. They stood looking on while the new men shuffled the old cards. It was everything to these new men that they should establish a stable Government with which the Allies would be disposed to deal, and to preserve stability they must carry on the existing machine. Germany with her lack of training in responsible popular government could not improvise a new order in a night. Throughout the land there was a sporadic formation of Workmen's and Soldiers' Councils, but as yet these meant little, and were well under control.

But it was essential for Germany to get rid of the signposts of the old regime. Bavaria took the lead, and on Friday, the 8th, a meeting of the Workmen's and Soldiers' Council, under the leadership of a Polish Jew, Kurt Eisner, decreed the abolition of the Wittelsbach dynasty. In Frankfurt, Cologne, Leipzig, Bremen, Hanover, Augsburg, and elsewhere, similar councils were formed, who took upon themselves the preservation of order, and declared that they held their power in trust for the coming German Socialist Republic. So far there had been few signs of despotic class demands on the Russian model; in most places the change was made decently and smoothly. Saturday, the 9th, saw the crowning act in the capital. Bands of soldiers and enormous assemblies of workmen patrolled the streets, singing republican songs. There was a little shooting, and a certain number of windows were broken. Troops flung away their badges and iron crosses. Everywhere the royal arms were torn down, and the Red Flag fluttered from the balcony of the Imperial Palace, where, in the first week of August 1914, the Emperor had addressed his loyal people. The day before most of the civil Ministers like Solf and Delbrück had gone to Army Headquarters. Berlin was in the hands of the Workmen's and Soldiers' Council; but, contrary to expectation, there was no friction with the soldiers. The latter had been brought into the city in great numbers with many machine guns; but by early afternoon they were fraternizing with the workmen's processions, and Liebknecht was making an oration from the Castle balcony. General von Linsingen, the officer commanding in the Mark of Brandenburg, resigned, and Prince Max issued a decree announcing the appointment as Chancellor of Fritz Ebert, the Majority Socialist, who, like Cleon, was in private life a merchant of leather.

The two Socialist groups had come together, and a Council of National Plenipotentiaries was formed, consisting of three from the Majority and three from the Minority. For the moment the extremists of the Spartacus group, led by Liebknecht and Rosa Luxemburg, were quiet and biding their time. The revolution had been largely made by reservists, the older men in the home garrisons, who were imbued with the wilder doctrine of Socialism. Some kind of "soviets" had been necessary to give impetus to the change, but the new "People's Government" hoped to absorb them in an orderly democracy. They appealed to all the stable elements in the people to safeguard the transition, and announced to the world that Bolshevism had no partisans in their nation. At the moment it looked as if they might succeed. Berlin took the revolution with complete placidity. Before nightfall on the Saturday the normal life of the city had been resumed, and on the Sunday crowds as usual visited the Karlshorst racecourse.

Yet, orderly as was the first stage in Germany's revolution, and strenuous as were the efforts made to provide administrative continuity, on one side the revulsion was complete. The old absolutism was gone, and monarchy within the confines of Germany had become a farce – hated in some regions, in all despised as an empty survival. For centuries the pretensions of German kinglets had made sport for Europe. Now these kinglets disappeared, leaving no trace behind them. In Bavaria, Saxony, Würtemberg, the Mecklenburgs, Hesse, Brunswick, Baden, the dynasties fell with scarcely a protesting voice. And with them fell the men who had been the pillars of the thrones, the great nobles and the industrial magnates who had risen to power by courtiership. On the Sunday morning came the news of the death of Ballin, the advocate of unrestricted submarine warfare, and one of the main abettors of German megalomania. He chose not to outlive the fabric which he had given his life to build.

With the lesser fell the greater. In Prince Max's decree of Saturday, the 9th, it was announced that the Emperor had decided to abdicate, and that the Imperial Crown Prince renounced the succession. With a revolution behind him and his conquerors before him, there was no place left for him in the world. He did not stay upon the order of his going. On Sunday, the 10th, he left Main Headquarters at Spa, crossed the Dutch frontier, and sought refuge in the house of Count Bentinck at Amerongen. Prince Rupprecht retired to Brussels to await the victors, and the Imperial Crown Prince fled from his armies, and, like his father, found sanctuary in Holland.

History has not often recorded a more ignominious end to a vain-glorious career. The man who had claimed to be the vicegerent of God on earth, and had arrogated to himself a power little short of the divine, now showed less hardihood than the humblest of his soldiers. Other kings and leaders who have failed have been content to go down in the ruin they made, but this actor of many parts had not the nerve for a dramatic exit. His light, emotional mind and his perverse vanity had plagued the world for a generation, and had now undone the patient work of the builders of Germany. Tragic, indeed, was the cataclysm of German hopes, but there was no tragedy in the fall of William the Second, King of Prussia, Margrave of Brandenburg, and Count of Hohenzollern. He who had sought to rule the world stole from the stage like a discredited player, leaving his dupes to pay the penalty. Like Lucian's Peregrinus, his life had been dominated by a passion for notoriety; but, unlike that ancient charlatan, he lacked the heart to round off his antics on a public pyre. His hubris had received the most terrible of retributions, for its end was squalor.

The German delegates, who left Berlin on the afternoon of Wednesday, the 6th, arrived in the French lines at ten o'clock on the Thursday night, and were given quarters in the château of the Marquis de Laigle at Francport, near Choisy-au-Bac. On Friday morning they presented themselves at the train in the Forest of Compiègne which contained Marshal Foch and Sir Rosslyn Wemyss. The French Marshal asked, "Qu'est-ce que vous désirez, Messieurs?" and they replied that they had come to receive the Allied proposals for an armistice. To this Foch answered that the Allies were not seeking any armistice, but were content to finish the war in the field. The Germans looked non-plussed, and stammered something about the the urgent need for the cessation of hostilities. "Ah," said Foch, "I understand – you have come to *beg for an armistice*." Von Gündell and his colleague admitted the correction, and explicitly begged for an armistice. They were then presented with the Allied terms, and withdrew to consider them, after being informed that they must be accepted or refused within seventy-two hours – that is to say, before eleven o'clock on the morning of Monday, the 11th. They asked for a provisional suspension of hostilities, a request which Foch curtly refused.

The delegates declared that they were astonished at the severity of the terms, and sought permission to communicate with Berlin. A courier bearing the text of the armistice was dispatched to Main Headquarters at Spa, and the German

Command was informed by wireless of his coming. He was to cross the French lines that night between six and eight o'clock. The French fire ceased according to arrangement, but the unfortunate messenger had to wait long before the German barrage stopped. It was not till the afternoon of the following day that he could enter the German zone. Once there, he found everything in chaos. The retreating armies had made such havoc of roads and bridges that his car could not proceed, and he did not reach Spa till ten o'clock on the Sunday morning.

The terms were immediately telephoned to Berlin, and a conference of the new Government was held that morning. The hours of grace were fast slipping away, and Foch was adamant about the time limit. The delegates were instructed to accept, and after a protest they submitted to the inevitable. At five o'clock on the morning of Monday, 11th November, this armistice was signed, and Foch telegraphed to his generals: "Hostilities will cease on the whole front as from 11th November, at eleven o'clock. The Allied troops will not, until a further order, go beyond the line reached on that date and at that hour."

The terms were so framed as to give full effect to the victory on land and sea which the Allies had won. All invaded territory, including Alsace-Lorraine, was to be immediately evacuated, and the inhabitants repatriated. Germany was to surrender a large amount of war material, specified under different classes. The Allies were to take control of the left bank of the Rhine and of three bridgeheads on the right bank in the Cologne, Coblenz, and Mainz districts, and a neutral zone was to be established all along that bank between Switzerland and the Dutch frontier. A great number of locomotives and other forms of transport were to be immediately delivered to the Allies. All Allied prisoners of war were to be repatriated forthwith, but not so German prisoners in Allied hands. German troops in Russia, Romania, and Turkey were to withdraw within the frontiers of Germany as these existed before the war. The treaties of Brest-Litovsk and Bucharest were cancelled. German troops operating in East Africa were to evacuate the country within one month. All submarines were to repair to certain specified ports and be surrendered; certain units of the German Fleet were to be handed over to the charge of the Allies, and the rest to be concentrated in specified German ports, disarmed, and placed under Allied surveillance, the Allies reserving the right to occupy Heligoland to enforce these terms. The existing blockade was to be maintained . . . Such were the main provisions, and the duration of the armistice was fixed at thirty-six days, with an option to extend. If Germany failed to carry out any of the clauses, the agreement could be annulled on forty-eight hours' notice.

The acceptance of such terms meant the surrender of Germany to the will of the Allies, for they stripped from her the power of continuing or of renewing the war.

The morning of Monday, 11th November, was cold and foggy, such weather as a year before had been seen at Cambrai. The front was for the most part quiet, only cavalry patrols moving eastwards in touch with the retreat. But at two points there was some activity. The Americans on the Meuse were advancing, and the day opened for them with all the accompaniments of a field action. At Mons, on the Sunday night, the Canadians of Horne's First Army were in position round the place. Fighting continued during the night, and at dawn the 3rd Canadian Division entered the streets and established a line east of the town, while the carillons of the belfries played "Tipperary". For Britain the circle was now complete. In three months her armies had gained seven victories, each greater than any in her old wars; they had taken some 190,000 prisoners and 3,000 guns; and they had broken the heart of their enemy. To their great sweep from Amiens to Mons was due especially the triumph which Foch had won, and on that grey November morning their worn ranks could await the final hour with thankfulness and pride.

The minutes passed slowly along the front. An occasional shell, an occasional burst of firing, told that peace was not yet, but there were long spells of quiet, save in the American area. Officers had their watches in their hands, and the troops waited with the same grave composure with which they had fought. Men were too weary and deadened for their imaginations to rise to the great moment, for it is not at the time, but long afterwards, that the human mind grasps the drama of a crisis. Suddenly, as the watch-hands touched eleven, there came a second of expectant silence, and then a curious rippling sound which observers far behind the front likened to the noise of a great wind. It was the sound of men cheering from the Vosges to the sea.

After that peace descended on the long battlefield. A new era had dawned and the old world had passed away.

(Vol. XXIV pp. 56-82)